CRIMINALS AND VICTIMS

CRIMINALS AND VICTIMS

W. David Allen

STANFORD ECONOMICS AND FINANCE
An Imprint of Stanford University Press
Stanford, California

Stanford University Press
Stanford, California

Special discounts for bulk quantities of Stanford Economics and Finance
titles are available to corporations, professional associations, and other
organizations. For details and discount information, contact the special
sales department of Stanford University Press. Tel: (650) 736-1782,
Fax: (650) 736-1784

Printed in the United States of America on acid-free,
archival-quality paper

Library of Congress Cataloging-in-Publication Data

Allen, W. David, author.
Criminals and victims / W. David Allen.
       pages cm
Includes bibliographical references and index.
ISBN 978-0-8047-6252-6 (cloth : alk. paper)
1. Crime—Economic aspects—United States. 2. Criminal behavior—
Economic aspects—United States. 3. Criminals—United States.
4. Victims of crimes—United States. I. Title.
HV6791.A585 2011
364.973—dc22   2010048410

Typeset by Westchester Book Composition in 10/15 Sabon

For Maria Ragland Davis, Adriel Johnson, and Gopi Podila—
scholars and victims remembered

Contents

Preface

CRIME REPRESENTS one of society's most worrisome and persistent problems. People who commit crime impose harm on victims in a number of significant ways: violent injury, psychological trauma, reductions of personal freedom, or losses of property. Crime also creates inherent external costs: one crime, one person's victimization, inevitably gives pause to *others* in society, often engendering greater fear of crime and motivating behaviors designed to prevent crime or lessen its consequences. The creation of these spillovers makes crime as much a problem for government as for individuals. But, by the same token, our efforts at combating crime often create external *benefits* in their own right; for example, if one person installs a security light at his residence, it might deter someone from burglarizing that house as well as a neighbor's house, even if the neighbor did nothing similar to protect himself. The presence of external benefits suggests that if we figure out effective ways to deter individuals from committing crime and effective ways to make people less vulnerable to crime or its consequences, we will have a chance to lessen the problems of crime and crime victimization.

Our individual and collective efforts at crime prevention may actually be working. In June 2009, on the occasion of a new release of U.S. crime statistics, FBI Director Robert Mueller pointed out several notable declines in the number of serious crimes from 2007 to 2008, including a 2.5% decline in violent crimes like murder and rape and a 1.6% decline in property crimes like burglary and larceny. These figures, in fact, reflect a recent trend, charted and discussed pointedly by Zimring (2007), toward lesser criminality in the United States. Is this pattern here to stay, or will it ultimately prove fleeting? Are governmental efforts at deterrence responsible for this? Or are victims, or at least potential victims, living their lives differently than in the past to make themselves less vulnerable? At what cost? Scholarly research on crime and victimization represents an essential step toward answering questions like these. The central purpose of this book is to illustrate how analytical tools from applied microeconomics can help us more fully understand the commission of crime, the behaviors and motivations of criminals, and the experiences and decisions of victims—analysis that serves as core material for ongoing scholarly research on these issues.

This book, arranged in two parts, presents a unified investigation of economic behaviors and phenomena relating to criminals and victims at the individual level. Part One focuses on offender behavior, Part Two focuses on victim behavior, and each part houses five chapters containing original scholarly studies of topics relevant to our overarching theme, that criminals and victims make important decisions in economically rational ways. Much of the time, both criminals and victims know exactly what they are doing, even if they are acting under serious uncertainty or even physical stress. The micro scope of this book, as the book unfolds over its ten chapters, departs from other scholarly books on this topic that have mostly taken a broader, macro, trend-oriented view of crime and victimization. But, as we shall see, this more micro focus is more in keeping with the seminal economic analysis of crime by Gary S. Becker and other economists.

After providing an overview of how crime economic research has evolved (Chapter 1), Part One features chapters on the planning of crime, violence and damages that occur in the aftermath of crime, criminal evidence destruction, and finally the potential recommission of crime (recidivism). Part Two presents a similar overview of economic research related to victims of crime (Chapter 6), followed by chapters on the individual decision to self-protect against crime, the decision to resist offenders, the decision to report crime, and finally how crime affects the subsequent labor-force participation of victims, one of the often-overlooked consequences of victimization. The two sets of five chapters on offender behavior and victim behavior thus mirror each other in the sense that each set chronicles a logical sequence, or "life cycle," of criminality and victimization. By examining individual criminal and victim behavior—concentrating on how they make decisions and coming to terms with the unique objectives and constraints that shape those decisions—we can gain clarity on how public policy or procedure might ultimately affect outcomes that bear on society as a whole.

By design, the analytical chapters of this book generally contain a blend of theoretical and empirical analysis. One exception, Chapter 4 on the criminal destruction of evidence, presents a purely theoretical discussion of that phenomenon, but the analysis is accompanied by an extensive discussion of empirical implications and possibilities for future empirical research. The theoretical analysis that appears throughout this book demonstrates how we might use applied microeconomic tools to conceptualize the particular issue or phenomenon at hand and aids us in formulating concrete, empirically testable hypotheses. The empirical analysis appearing in the book primarily serves as a means of testing those hypotheses and secondarily illustrates how one might use particular econometric methodologies to address specific research questions that become interesting within the field of crime economics.

In presenting theoretical material, I have endeavored to lay out concepts with a level of mathematical detail commensurate with how scholars in crime economics make theoretical points within the confines of academic journals, where the bulk of the crime economic literature appears. At the same time, however, I always accompany mathematical presentation with a parallel discussion of the economic meaning or intuition that lies behind a particular mathematical assumption, functional property, or derivative. Similarly, in discussing empirical techniques and methodologies, I have sought to show enough econometric detail to make clear exactly what procedure I am undertaking and why, with an eye toward helping the reader understand how scholars currently conduct empirical crime economic research and how you might approach your own empirical studies in the future. Readers interested in econometric detail beyond what appears in the book may find it in the articles and books cited in specific chapters. In general, readers familiar with mathematical economics at the level of Chiang (1984) or Silberberg (1990) should have little trouble with the mathematical exposition appearing in this book. Readers comfortable with statistical and econometric analysis at the level of Greene (2008) will be able to follow the book's empirical discussion.

Although I emphasize an economic approach to the topics covered in this book, my analysis, and that of many economists whose work is highlighted in these pages, frequently takes inspiration from other social-science disciplines. The analysis of the planning of crime (Chapter 2), for example, takes great motivation from studies of the ecology and social geography of crime, such as appearing within the disciplines of environmental criminology and quantitative criminology; the analysis of the destruction of evidence (Chapter 4) takes inspiration from policy-oriented legal scholarship; and the analysis of victim resistance and reporting in the aftermath of victimization (Chapters 8 and 9) incorporates insights from studies by sociologists, psychologists, and public health scholars. For this reason, I hope this book will stimulate thinking and new research not just among scholars and graduate students in economics but also among scholars and students in criminology, criminal justice, or other social sciences interested in quantitatively rigorous yet intuitively meaningful analysis of crime and victimization.

Acknowledgments

THIS IS MY FIRST BOOK, and I have learned a great deal about the process of crafting and publishing a work of this length. Best of all, I learned some economics along the way. As always, no scholarly writing can succeed without good feedback and advice, and I have received copious amounts of them since I started this project. I particularly wish to thank Henning Curti, Eric Fong, Cynthia L. Gramm, Timothy D. Landry, Jonathan Lipow, Ilke Onur, Wafa Hakim Orman, John F. Schnell, Caron St. John, Allen Wilhite, Derek Yonai, seminar participants at the University of Alabama in Huntsville and the University of Arkansas, and my anonymous reviewers—all of whom provided valuable feedback on broad concepts and specific ideas, formally and informally. Special thanks to my friend and colleague Al Wilhite, not only for his continuous feedback on all things book but also for strongly urging me to pursue the project in the first place. You were right, man! I also have benefited greatly from the generous financial support of the Stephen P. Zelnak research fellowship, the expert research assistance of Christan Brady Yarbrough, and the technical assistance of Mary Morris at the Interuniversity Consortium for Political and Social Research and Seth Wilhite, liberator of important data sets once cruelly trapped inside a stricken computer. Finally, very special thanks to my editor at Stanford University Press, Margo Beth Crouppen. From the beginning, your hard work, encouragement, and wisdom have made this a delightful book-writing process and helped this first-time author feel not so much like a rookie. You are an absolute professional.

CRIMINALS AND VICTIMS

PART ONE

Offender Behavior

Who Are Criminals? A Review

An economic framework becomes applicable to, and helps enrich,
the analysis of illegal behavior.

—GARY S. BECKER

I. INTRODUCTION

Within the discipline of economics as a whole, crime economics occupies part of the large subdiscipline of law and economics, the application of economic analysis to matters of law. In law and economics, the formalized origins of which trace back to Coase (1960), researchers study the efficient formation of deterrence mechanisms, efficient bargaining and litigation, cost-benefit analysis of laws and legal rules, and the regulation of firms and industries—among other issues. Because crime constitutes such a pervasive and socially destructive problem, studying it demands critical thinking and careful analysis of the decisions and experiences of the economic agents involved—lawmakers and police, prosecutors and judges, and indeed criminals and victims. Viewed as a collective, crime economic research seeks to understand why crime occurs and, given that it does occur, seeks mechanisms that reduce its incidence or its consequences. By probing the determinants and processes by which criminals and victims make decisions, we can begin to formulate and evaluate specific policies and procedures toward this objective and learn more about human behavior in the process.

Part One of this book examines economic decisions made by potential and actual criminals, in a series of chapters containing original scholarly research on these decisions and their consequences. But before we look ahead to new research, we should take a look back at the research that has come before; this will give us a sharper perspective on the field as a whole even as we move forward within it. This is the objective of this initial chapter, a focused review of economic literature relating to criminal behavior.

As we shall see, crime economic research started with theoretical and empirical analysis conducted by the economists Gary S. Becker (the 1992 Nobel Laureate) and Isaac Ehrlich, usually working independently but occasionally working as collaborators. They and the many economists who followed broke new ground in economics by applying rigorous, objective analytical tools to the study of issues once solely the intellectual domain of sociologists, criminologists, and psychologists. Rather than viewing illegal activity as unpredictable, purely aberrant, or irrational behavior or behavior influenced primarily by external social or environmental factors, economists model offender and victim behavior as individual choices made under time, financial, informational, and even spatial constraints—the same sorts of constraints that regulate decision making in all applied microeconomic analysis. To the extent that these constraints reflect circumstances under the direct or indirect control of policy makers, economic models of crime can reveal concrete connections between policy mechanisms (e.g., policing, sanctioning, and employment availability) and important equilibrium outcomes pertaining to both offenders and victims.

To see how economists have methodically constructed this discipline of crime economics, let us take a brief tour through the major theoretical and empirical advances that have been made over the course of a generation of scholarly research.

II. THEORETICAL ADVANCES
A. *The Conceptual Foundation*

Most theoretical fundamentals in the economic analysis of illegal activity originate with the economic model of crime advanced by Becker (1968), who modeled crime alternately as an individual choice and as a broader social problem. Both approaches became highly influential to the great amount of crime economic research—theoretical and empirical—that followed.

Modeling crime as an individual choice involves specifying an economic agent's objective function, typically an expected utility expression that incorporates the probability of unsuccessful criminality (e.g., resulting in detection, apprehension, or sentencing) and an opposing probabil-

ity of successful criminality. This direct incorporation of factors capturing uncertainty reflects a "state-preference" approach to modeling illegal
activity. As discussed in Part Two of this book, such an approach underlies the theoretical analysis of crime *victim* behavior as well, although in
general economists have not studied the economic decisions of victims as
extensively as they have the actions of criminals. In the classic approach
to modeling criminal behavior, the hypothetical individual faces what
amounts to a time-allocation decision; that is, the individual must decide
how much scarce time to allocate to legal or illegal activity, given that
benefits exist with either choice. At the time Becker's analysis appeared,
this approach followed naturally from his own earlier development of
theories of home production (Becker 1965), a new approach to labor
economics that emphasized time allocation in general, that is, that economic agents allocate their time to a variety of activities beyond just ge-
neric labor and leisure, including marital courtship, child rearing, and meal
preparation.

Becker's (1968) analysis also illustrated how we can use familiar microeconomic tools—constrained optimization, the logic of consumer choice,
production theory, and others—to study crime from the perspective of
society as a whole. This approach to the phenomenon emphasizes that
society, as an aggregate or collective decision maker, has an incentive to
allocate some of its scarce resources to minimize the social "harm" created by crime. A society might allocate more resources to police, whose
greater presence can enhance the probability of detection or capture, or it
might alter the nature of penalties judges and juries can impose on criminals; as a society we might decide that fines suit our retributive objective
well enough or that imprisonment does a more efficient job, depending
on the perceived severity of the crime, its implied harm. This somewhat
more aggregated approach to the economics of crime has inspired major
strands of economic research concerned with the design of optimal sanctioning mechanisms, policing, and other policy aimed at improving deterrence. It even underlies the public-choice-oriented approach concerned
with individual and especially social costs of law enforcement itself, as
exemplified by Benson, Kim, and Rasmussen (1994) and Paul and Wilhite (1994). Although this book will emphasize the individual-based

analytical approach rather than this sociocentric approach, we shall on occasion encounter conceptual ideas and empirical results that have relevance to the more aggregated approach.

The extension and refinement of Becker's individual-based, state-preference approach to crime economics began with Ehrlich (1973). In this seminal article, Ehrlich applied and synthesized microeconomic concepts ranging from elasticity to occupational choice to the dynamics of human capital development, formulating hypotheses about how these factors come together not only to influence the decision to commit crime in the first place but also, very critically, to affect recidivism. Ehrlich's analysis, then and now, emphasizes the role of opportunities as they shape criminal outcomes—opportunities to engage in legal and illegal (or "illegitimate") activities, formed in part by a person's experiences in the legitimate labor market, illegal markets, and even prison itself. Many of Ehrlich's insights about recidivism become highly relevant in our study of this topic in Chapter 5. Just as important as his theoretical advancements are Ehrlich's empirical investigations of his hypotheses. Ehrlich became one of the first economists (of now *many*) to test the direct implications of the Beckerian economic model of crime using real crime data. We consider Ehrlich's empirical analysis in more detail later in this chapter. After Becker (1968) and Ehrlich (1973), it became clear that we could learn a great deal about crime, punishment, and deterrence by applying economic analytical tools to the study of these phenomena and that we could indeed assume that those who commit crime make decisions rationally, not necessarily because of psychological aberrance.

In the same era in which Becker and Ehrlich were establishing the conceptual foundation of crime economics, Sjoquist (1973) and Block and Heineke (1975) laid additional groundwork in important papers of their own. Sjoquist (1973) confronted head-on the notion that criminals act as economically rational (or what one might more accurately call *financially* rational) agents by studying whether those who commit property crimes—illegalities that offer quantifiable monetary rewards—do so in a manner consistent with that of other economic agents who make income-acquisition decisions under risky conditions. His empirical finding that higher probabilities of arrest and conviction reduce property crime lent support to a basic hypothesized implication of the model and provided early empirical evidence of the "deterrence hypothesis," a relationship replicated frequently and now virtually taken for granted in crime economics (understandably so, since it essentially reflects the law of demand). Block and Heineke (1975) further developed the notion of criminal behavior as the result of a time-allocation problem, emphasizing that the utility functions of prospective criminals contain more than just wealth considerations and that, because criminal utility is indeed "multiattributed," it becomes more difficult, short of overly simplifying assumptions, to make many definitive theoretical predictions about criminal behavior and deterrence. Ultimately, the most useful insights for policy would have to come from empirical analysis of criminal activity.

B. Further Extensions, New Emphases

1. Legitimate Income Opportunities Becker's economic model of crime in its basic form offers rich insights. A potential criminal identifies some psychic or monetary benefit available through illegal activity, faces a direct cost of this illegality in the form of an expected sanction, and potentially incurs an opportunity cost in the form of gains he could have obtained by doing something legal instead. As the earliest economic modelers demonstrated, we can address a number of issues, and predict a number of relationships, with little or no alteration of these essentials of the model. But where a model possesses basic, key elements, there exist at least as many opportunities for economists to develop certain elements further, revealing sometimes subtler, sometimes wider-ranging connections.

One strain of extensions to the model casts greater scrutiny on the role of legal gains, the rewards available from what Ehrlich (1973) called "legitimate" activities. In relation to this factor, the model's most intuitive prediction holds simply that a greater availability of legal, or licit, gains would deter the commission of crime, ceteris paribus. Not coincidentally, this connection bears great resemblance to the classic labor-leisure choice lying at the heart of the individual labor-supply decision. In that context, the available wage from work time represents the opportunity cost of leisure, the broadly defined alternative mode of time allocation; a higher wage offer makes leisure more expensive at the margin, thus encouraging the person to work more. In a crime economic context, wages or income or other gains available in licit work become the most immediate opportunity cost of engaging in criminal behavior, suggesting how their greater availability might deter crime. As the economic model of crime became part of the infrastructure of applied microeconomic research following the development of the conceptual foundation, the challenge became modeling the opportunity cost of crime in additionally creative ways so that we could learn something new about the coexistence of legal work and criminal activity in society.

Within the effort among economists to address this issue, Danziger and Wheeler (1975) imagined that individuals not only take into account their own absolute incomes in making a decision but furthermore consider their relative incomes compared to some standard. As such, in their framework, an individual's utility becomes a function not of the individual's own income but of an income *gap*, the excess of the individual's own income over that of a reference group, such as the individual's socioeconomic peers. This modeling approach allows one to explain how both poor individuals and wealthy individuals might commit property crime. If we imagined only that a person's income generates (indirect) utility, then we would have a hard time using the resulting model to explain why a wealthy person rationally steals things, whether money or property. But if we imagine that a person regards income *equality* as a good and that the marginal gains to a theft outweigh the usual marginal risks associated with enforcement, then we can predict the incidence of street crimes like burglary and larceny as well as "white-collar" crimes like embezzlement and insider trading using essentially the same theoretical structure.

Chiu and Madden (1998) developed these ideas further, in a somewhat more general-equilibrium setting, illustrating not only a distinct theoretical linkage between income inequality and crime (burglary in particular) but also how regressive taxation encourages crime and how crime can grow in wealthier neighborhoods, shades of the individual-level Danziger-Wheeler result. Models of this nature also inform economic analysis of the nexus between crime, poverty, and economic development. In many developing nations, great stratification of wealth as much as sheer poverty itself can create social tension that engenders crime and

8

slows economic growth. Along these lines, the theoretical model developed by Mehlum, Moene, and Torvik (2005) imagines that job creation spurred by economic growth at once reduces crime by increasing market labor demand but potentially increases crime by creating more output that thieves can then steal. Mehlum, Moene, and Torvik show that the crime-increasing effect dominates in less-modernized nations, potentially exacerbating a vicious cycle of growth, crime, and poverty rather than assisting an *escape* from poverty and crime. Their analytical results suggest that policy makers implement poverty-reducing measures methodically rather than hastily, so as to allow the gains to legal work to outpace the gains to illegal work. Related research by Soares (2004) and Demombynes and Özler (2005), discussed in greater detail in the following section on empirical advances, has given us further insights on the connection between wealth, inequality, and crime in the context of economic development.

The licit income element in the economic model of crime also lays bare the potential influence of legal earnings opportunities on the individual decision to engage in crime and, along the way, guides our thinking about crime committed by young people and possible means of deterrence. In his discussion of youth crime in the United States, Freeman (1996) observed that the returns to crime very much depend on legitimate earnings opportunities, among other things fundamental to the economic model of crime. He noted further that real earnings for the least educated had fallen dramatically from the mid-1970s through the 1990s, when his article appeared, suggesting a plausible reason why younger individuals (especially males) had turned to crime more prevalently.

Addressing the phenomenon of youth crime more directly, Grogger (1998) observed that, among a cohort of young men sampled in the National Longitudinal Survey of Youth, most worked licit jobs (in 1979) even as a quarter of them admitted to having committed crimes. The theoretical model presented by Grogger, drawing not only from the Beckerian crime economic model but also from the classic theory of home production advanced by Gronau (1977), illustrates how a person might engage in crime and work in the licit labor market simultaneously. In the model, a given individual encounters returns to crime in the form of a generalized function assumed to be concave in illegal time. As Grogger discusses, this function regulates how a person transforms illegal effort into illegal output ("stolen goods") and then into income, and its concavity ensures diminishing marginal productivity of illegal time. Two different individuals who face the same market wage might yet face different marginal returns—different degrees to which criminal activity helps them generate nonlabor income (i.e., accumulations of wealth)—implying variation in equilibrium illegal activity across individuals. Empirically, then, we should indeed observe a large number of criminals who also do licit work, and legal wage variation should influence the decision to engage in illegality.

Grogger's model blends elements of the economic model of crime with labor economic theory to shed more light on the role of legal income opportunities as a deterrent of crime in general and crime committed by youths in particular. His analysis has also influenced new research on this issue, exemplified in recent papers by Gould, Weinberg, and Mustard (2002), Williams and Sickles (2002), and Lin (2008). Like Grogger, these authors show empirical evidence of an inverse relationship between legitimate work opportunities and crime.

2. Enforcement Mechanisms   Economic research on criminal behavior carries inherent public-policy relevance: we seek clearer understanding of criminality in part to inform official efforts to deter it. Even research on legal work opportunities speaks to policy, adding intelligence to organized efforts in education, welfare provision, and enterprise development that can have socially favorable impacts on crime. It should come as no surprise, therefore, that many of the extensions of the economic model of crime have focused on the area most directly under the control of legislative policy makers: enforcement mechanisms. In its most basic form, the model suggests an expected utility objective function that contains, inter alia, a probability of detection (or apprehension) and a sanction of some form; together they form the criminal's *expected sanction*. The presence of an apprehension probability introduces police to the model; the presence of a sanction introduces lawmakers, judges, juries, and ultimately even voters to the model. Their joint presence in the model has motivated

CHAPTER I: WHO ARE CRIMINALS?

extended consideration by economists of the optimal use of law enforcement agents and sanctioning mechanisms.

To some degree the growth of research on enforcement mechanisms
reflects what Ehrlich (1981), writing about the frequent ineffectiveness of
incarceration, described as a movement toward finding effective modes
of rehabilitation of known criminals even as we seek deterrence of un-
known criminals. Ehrlich further developed (following some of his earlier work and Becker 1968) the notion of a "market for offenses" that
took into account not only the supply of offenses by criminals and the
effort at intervention through law enforcement but also the role of victims of crime and consumers of illegal goods and services; the actions of
victims and these consumers create the derived demand for crime itself
and for protection against crime (among other things). In many cases,
market forces make enforcement mechanisms and wage-determination
mechanisms more efficient deterrents to crime than imprisonment, as
both impact personal criminal *incentives*. For instance, if people spend
less on illegal drugs, some criminals will find other (perhaps legal) things
to sell; if victims protect themselves, or engage in resistance, or report
criminals more frequently (activities we study in Part Two), some criminals may find crime too costly to continue. None of these mechanisms
involves incapacitation of the offender. Taking a similar market-level approach, McCormick and Tollison (1984) devised a theory of law enforcement that explicitly modeled the implications of altering the number of
police officers in a society, incorporating the novel and realistic notion
that a given officer may or may not actually make an arrest given the
actual commission of a crime. They demonstrate a fundamental ambiguity of the relationship between enforcement efforts of this type and crime
(measured necessarily as an arrest probability), a fact that lies at the heart
of later research on crime and recidivism by Kim et al. (1993) and Allen
(2002).

Economic analysis of optimal sanctioning mechanisms stems from a
desire to improve the practical effectiveness of punishments, from a conceptually based realization that sanctions ideally redistribute lost income
(if not lost utility) to victims or to society in general, and from a desire to
make the sanction component of the model more accurately reflect the

reality of the criminal justice system. Consider the groundbreaking study of optimal sanctioning by Burnovski and Safra (1994). Rather than imagining (as is typically done) one hypothetical criminal committing one crime in one period, Burnovski and Safra imagine a criminal who intends all along to commit more than one crime (specifically two in their model) in a sequential manner. They show that, under reasonable assumptions about offender risk tastes, stiffening the penalty for the earlier crime leads to no greater crime and possibly even to deterrence, contrary to the practice of issuing stronger sanctions for the later crime (i.e., for repeat offenders). Essentially, imposing the stiffer sanction earlier obviates the need to capture the offender a second time in order to issue the type of sanction that presumably creates the greatest deterrent effect. Simply put, by the time we catch the offender a second (or later) time, he has already committed and society has already suffered harm from at least two crimes, and we would have deterred little or no criminal activity.

More recently, economic modelers have linked the use of optimal sanctions (fines, imprisonment, or both) to the wealth of offenders, a departure from one of Becker's (1968) notable results. Becker suggested that optimal sanctions (i.e., optimal fines), meant to reflect society's harm (or the social loss), do not depend on the economic positions, the wealth, of offenders. He viewed this as essential "if the goal is to minimize the social loss in income from offenses, and not to take vengeance or to inflict harm on offenders" (p. 195). In the classic treatment, imprisonment (of some form) substitutes for fines when the offender literally cannot afford to pay the prescribed fine. The complication arises from the fact that imprisoning offenders incurs nontrivial social costs. Suppose we observe offender wealth. Then, in principle, tying a fine to offender wealth allows a wealthier offender to make his socially acceptable retribution and at the same time allows society to avoid the expense of jailing him. Issuing a smaller fine to a poorer criminal can have the same effect if the fine still compensates society for the harm in question, but most likely this holds only for relatively minor crimes. If poorer criminals have lesser ability to earn income because of underdeveloped human capital skills (say), they may actually prefer imprisonment, suggesting insufficient compensation for society, an overly costly sanction, and underdeterrence. By the same logic, imprisoning a wealthier offender for the same illegal act may over-punish that offender, the sort of possibility investigated by Lott (1992).

In general, however, leaving a fine legislatively uncapped conceivably can aid deterrence because it allows the sanction to make a greater mar-ginal impact on the offender's utility and thus perhaps his future behavior. This and other possibilities emerge in a series of intriguing papers most notably by the economists Nuno Garoupa, A. Mitchell Polinsky, and Ste-ven Shavell. For a representative sampling, one should examine Polinsky and Shavell (1991, 1998) and Garoupa (2001). Very recently in this litera-ture, Polinsky (2006) considers these issues under the assumption that society does *not* observe offender wealth. In his model, the wealthiest criminals might still willingly pay an exorbitantly high fine (its larger size reflecting society's attempt to counteract a lower probability of receiving the accurate fine payment in the absence of wealth information), suggest-ing reasonable deterrence even without this information.

3. *Social Interaction and Space*   For the most part, theoretical variants on the economic model of crime have treated the activities of individual criminals as somewhat removed from the society and physical environ-ment in which criminals actually live and cause trouble. For this reason, these models, while frequently innovative in many other dimensions, have had little to say about how criminals interact among other crimi-nals, how they coexist with noncriminals, and how they make decisions within specific cultural or spatial settings. As a result, most of the theo-retical advancements we have considered so far have given us few insights about gang crime, organized crime (including terrorist networks), and urban crime, for example. But a newer strand of theoretical analysis in crime economics has begun to examine exactly these sorts of issues and indeed represents one of the more vibrant areas of research in applied microeconomics as a whole.

Social interaction, another phenomenon studied seminally by Becker (1974), lies at the heart of these models. Where social interaction exists, any given economic activity might incur not just the usual direct and oppor-tunity costs—many of them financial in nature—but also social costs, some of which may linger beyond some initial period of activity. Suppose you and I engage in a business deal, and I cheat you out of some of your money. In so doing, I risk capture and prosecution in the usual way, but I also risk damage to my reputation, which could hurt my ability to do any kind of business later, honest or otherwise. Frank (1988) develops this idea keenly in his treatise on the role of the emotions in economic activity.

Very much in this fashion, Rasmusen (1996) imagined that a convicted criminal incurs a direct, public-sector cost in the form of an official sanction as well as a private-sector cost in the form of social stigma. To varying degrees depending on society's expectations and tolerance of crime, other members of society may become reluctant to interact with that criminal, suggesting another, somewhat different avenue toward deterrence of crime. If some of those other members of society are potential employers, the situation emphasized by Rasmusen, then some employers may become reluctant to hire or pay competitive wages to known criminals. Because younger people generally have lower rates of employment, they may face relatively lower stigma costs of this nature, implying a marginally smaller disincentive to commit crime. In this way, Rasmusen's model provides an explanation for youth crime, a common motivating concern in crime economic research, grounded in an inherently *social*, though microeconomic, theoretical mechanism. The model also illustrates the importance of the government's publicizing accurate information about known criminals, because a reputation effect clearly depends on an efficient flow of information to potential victims.

In a similar study of crime rate variation across cities, punctuated by empirical analysis, Glaeser, Sacerdote, and Scheinkman (1996) assumed that economic agents make decisions by imitating the behaviors of their physical neighbors, implying the existence of social interaction at a "local" (as opposed to a "global") level of analysis. An approach emphasizing local interactions, also seen in Rasmusen (1996), allows for the possibility of information flow or other influences from person to person; an approach emphasizing global interactions would emphasize spillovers from system to system, such as between labor markets, neighborhoods, or nations. When one person decides to become a career criminal, or to commit an illegal act, he may influence someone he knows to do the same, who may in turn influence someone else, and so forth. Crime be-

comes contagious. But some agents, such as those who receive comparatively stronger influences from their parents or from schooling, may *not*
choose crime even though a neighbor did; the authors call these "fixed"
agents. Real communities differ in the amount of average physical distance between individuals (suggesting variation in the case of influence
between agents) and in the degree of prevalence of fixed agents (suggesting variation in the effectiveness of the customary economic and demographic factors that discourage crime), and of course each of these variables can also change over time. The model thus illustrates how we might
observe variation in crime rates across geography and time, traceable as
much to social interaction and physical space as to traditional exogenous
factors such as the benefits and costs of crime, as emphasized in earlier
expressions of the economic model of crime.

In placing hypothetical agents, some criminal and some not, on an
imaginary lattice and assuming that they make decisions in a heuristic,
imitative fashion (as compared to a purely optimizing fashion), Glaeser,
Sacerdote, and Scheinkman (1996) also set the stage for static and dynamic
analysis of crime using agent-based computational methods, such as by
Wilhite (2006) and Wilhite and Allen (2008), and more conventional approaches exemplified by Calvó-Armengol and Zenou (2004) and Calvó-
Armengol, Verdier, and Zenou (2007). An approach emphasizing criminal
interactions also distinguishes analysis by Silverman (2004), who incorporated the notion that economic agents embody different capacities
for—and develop different reputations for—committing criminal violence,
which in equilibrium leads to different cultures of violence across locations (across "streets," in his model). Taking the notion of criminal culture as a given, Allen (2005) illustrated how variation in this sort of culture
affects both the marginal benefit of illegality and an agent's accumulated
wealth, allowing for the possibility that an exogenous cultural change
(captured empirically by exploiting sports data and in-season player
trades) could indeed reduce individual-level criminality.

Where space matters, as it does in the Glaeser-Sacerdote-Scheinkman
model, distance and transportation inherently matter as well. This fact as
much as any other motivates research by Ihlanfeldt (2003), who presents
a "spatialized" economic model of crime. Ihlanfeldt characterized the

Beckerian economic model of crime as essentially "aspatial in the sense that all crimes are assumed to be committed by residents of the home community" (p. 235), an assumption inconsistent with the concept and the reality of geographically mobile criminals. Ihlanfeldt adds an element of space to the basic model structure by imagining that an individual makes a decision not merely whether or not to commit crime but indeed whether to commit crime in a particular place, specifically either inside or outside his home neighborhood. By further incorporating a parameter to account for travel costs and by allowing those costs to vary directly in travel time, Ihlanfeldt's model establishes a fundamental analytical tension between the net returns to crime, the physical location of the criminal target, and the probability of apprehension, at the same time motivating his accompanying empirical analysis of the link between mass transit and crime in Atlanta. (Mass transit appears to have increased central-city crime but reduced suburban crime.) Zenou (2003) presents a similar theoretical model that provides an additional foothold on the intuition of peer-influenced crime and on the role of residential location and physical distance to jobs in explaining the distribution of crime across space.

In an era in which international terrorism, aided by global networks of terrorist criminals, has become one of society's most serious threats, theoretical economic analysis of crime that directly confronts the interactivity and the interconnectedness of criminals and noncriminals—whether approached using neoclassical, game theoretic, or computational analytical methods or methods yet to be devised—possesses extraordinary policy and practical relevance and currently provides the setting for the most important new advances in crime economic theory.

III. EMPIRICAL ADVANCES

In this section we examine how economists have approached the empirical testing of specific hypotheses implied by the economic model of crime and its variants, summarizing along the way what researchers have found after nearly forty years of studies. In other words, what do we know (or at least think we know) about criminal activity, and how do we know it? As in Section II, we will concentrate on research that speaks to the role of legitimate income opportunities, enforcement mechanisms, and social interaction.

A. *Labor Markets, Income, and Inequality*

As noted above, one can trace empirical analysis of the model back to Ehrlich (1973), who besides making major contributions to theory became one of the first to present evidence of a positive relationship between income inequality and crime, among other regularities. Reflecting the paucity (if not the complete absence) of individual-level data available to researchers in the early 1970s, Ehrlich made use of aggregated data sets and drew inferences based on rates per unit of U.S. population. For example, Ehrlich used the number of offenses in a given crime category per person in a community as a measure of aggregate crime rate, the central dependent variable in his econometric models, whereas today we would generally prefer and tend to have greater access to data on individuals that would allow direct observation of whether a person engaged in crime or not (or was arrested or not) over some period of inquiry. Nevertheless, this early empirical effort, as well as that of Sjoquist (1973), showed compelling evidence that criminals respond to economic incentives, which ultimately may have been the most important initial contribution of researchers interested in testing the model. Real criminals did appear attracted to crime by greater economic gains, by lesser access to legitimate income, and by income inequality; they did appear deterred by official enforcement and sanctioning activities that make up the expected costs of crime. Although the empirical research that followed also frequently took motivation from the most basic theoretical questions (as seen in Mathur 1978 and Witte 1980), the earliest findings laid groundwork for later researchers to study subtler empirical questions using finer, micro-level data sets and sophisticated econometric methodologies that those data sets facilitated and often necessitated.

Grogger (1998) showed that young men appear responsive to variation in (legal) wage incentives in a manner predicted by the economic model of crime. Other things being equal, more favorable earnings opportunities discourage crime, and declining real wages may well have explained increasing youth crime during the 1970s and 1980s. Gould, Weinberg, and Mustard (2002) drew comparable conclusions about licit wage opportunities investigating a sample extending into the 1990s, and in a similar spirit Ralston (1999) and Lin (2008) showed evidence of a positive relationship between unemployment and crime. Just as intriguingly, the findings relating to wages imply that criminals may respond to wage *gaps* as well: if such gaps exist between blacks and whites (an issue of particular interest in Grogger's study), then this may help explain racial differences in youth crime, especially given the relatively limited development of legitimate human capital skills at young ages. Complementing and building on these results, several researchers have investigated the impact of income inequality on crime as a matter of concentration, much as suggested by Ehrlich (1973) and Danziger and Wheeler (1975). The subsequent studies have yielded mixed results on this relationship, but the disagreement itself may be revealing and instructive.

Motivated in part by the work of Grogger (1998), Doyle, Ahmed, and Horn (1999) studied the impact of labor markets, income distribution, and other variables on crime, but their analysis differed from most others' to that point because of their use of pooled cross-sectional, time series data, that is, panel data. Owing mostly to inherent costs of compiling and maintaining panel data sets, most empirical researchers in crime economics historically used, and today continue to use, cross-sectional data sets—most commonly, data on a sample of known offenders (e.g., prisoner populations or releasees) or, better than this, data on a sample consisting of known criminals and noncriminals. (Cornwell and Trumbull 1994 and Tauchen, Witte, and Griesinger 1994 also used panel data, but these authors did not pursue hypotheses specifically relating to wage- or income inequality.) Because panel data sets offer a repeated look at a fixed sample of individuals over time, they allow greater control for unobserved heterogeneity than typically possible with cross-sectional data and explanatory variables. In principle, variables that appear to influence crime cross-sectionally may prove spurious when we observe the individual or a given marginal effect on multiple occasions; effects that emerge as statistically significant in a panel data setting, subject to customary diagnostic tests, would thus seem all the more compelling.

Within this methodological setting but also linking their individual observations to variables aggregated at the state level, Doyle, Ahmed, and Horn (1999) found, consistent with Grogger (1998), that higher wages appear to reduce criminality (per capita incidents of crime), but they found no evidence that income inequality significantly influences either property or violent crime. Fajnzylber, Lederman, and Loayza (2002) reached a different conclusion. Using a comparable aggregated cross-*national* panel data set and comparable estimation techniques (generalized method of moments, suitable in panel data environments that feature the possibility of endogenous regressors, such as a market-level wage), they found evidence that greater income inequality increases crime, other things being equal. Soares (2004) similarly analyzed variation in crime rates across nations and found that developed countries have higher over-all rates of crime reporting, which accounts for the apparent positive rela-tionship (found in previous studies) between economic development and crime. Once Soares (2004) accounted for this factor, which of course hints at a key role played by crime *victims*, he found no evidence of such a rela-tionship; instead, criminality appeared more strongly associated with in-come inequality, slow growth rates, and low levels of education.

But three particularly recent studies yield results more consistent with those of Doyle, Ahmed, and Horn. Neumayer (2005), again using panel data at a level of aggregation comparable to that of the earlier research-ers, finds no robust evidence that income inequality influences crime, and he suggests that the Fajnzylber-Lederman-Loayza result largely reflects those authors' use of too few countries in their sample and too few mea-sures of country-specific fixed effects. Noting a specific motivation to use more micro-level data, not generally seen in this literature despite the frequent use of panel data, Demombynes and Özler (2005) linked their individual-level data with data aggregated at the South African police precinct level, a procedure that allowed an extensive control for hetero-geneity in a manner much like that suggested by Neumayer. Like Neu-mayer, they find evidence that income inequality influences some crimes (such as burglary and vehicle theft) but not others (such as rape and as-sault). (They find more compelling evidence of influential inequality *within* racial groups as opposed to *between* racial groups, intriguing in light of South Africa's seemingly greater vulnerability to crime associated with racial conflict.) Neumayer (2005, p. 110) observed that "there [may be] limits to identifying the effects of inequality on violent crime at the cross-national level, and more micro-oriented studies . . . [may be] more promising in this regard."

To this point we still have too few empirical studies to suggest any consensus about the crime/income-inequality relationship, but the best progress may yet come from research that employs data that can identify the *individual* criminal choice as a function of wage- or income inequality pertinent to that individual—a connection entirely relevant to the economic model of crime in its purest form but potentially obscured when we use aggregated data.

B. Enforcement and Deterrence

As observed earlier, all of the factors that make the economic model of crime functional as a theoretical approach, and all of the measurable variables that go into explaining crime empirically, one way or another speak to deterrence. From there lies a short step to policy. When we conclude that declining wages for inexperienced or low-skilled workers, say, encourage crime, we suggest by implication that higher wages—or policies that will facilitate them—could deter crime. If we decide that wage inequality or income inequality encourages crime, we suggest by implication that movements designed to narrow the gap might serve as a deterrent; if we decide (as some obviously have) that income gaps do not actually matter, then we imply that society should allocate its crime-deterrence resources more efficiently elsewhere, toward mechanisms that will work. But most discussions of deterrence, especially in empirical research, center on elements of the expected sanction faced by a hypothetical criminal: the likelihood of apprehension and the sanction potentially incurred thereafter. Economists have demonstrated in many studies, using a variety of empirical measures, that a greater probability of detection or apprehension does act as a deterrent to crime. Some researchers have gone even further, concluding that a greater *certainty* of punishment exerts a more powerful deterrent effect than the *severity* of punishment.

The most straightforward approach to investigating the influence of the certainty of punishment involves incorporating a measure of police presence or of other enforcement resources in regressions modeled to explain variation in either the individual crime choice or aggregated crime rates. Sjoquist (1973), using cross-sectional, municipality-level crime data from 1960, employed variables such as the number of arrests per number of crimes and the number of convictions per arrest to approximate the probability of incurring a sanction. Ehrlich (1972) used a similar, state-level ratio of monetary commitments to state and federal prisons per unit of known offenses for this purpose. These treatments again somewhat reflect data limitations of the era, but their empirical results nevertheless support the theoretical prediction that stronger enforcement discourages crime. Very recently, Lin (2009) has demonstrated the hypothesized inverse relationship between crime and the presence of police by econometrically controlling for the fact that jurisdictions sometimes deploy more police *because* of crime, which can otherwise make it seem as though the incidence of crime and the number of police vary directly.

The bulk of empirical studies published since the appearance of the earliest papers have made use of individual-level data sets, which present new opportunities for pinpointing the relationship between enforcement activity and criminal activity—most compellingly in the form of natural experiments in law enforcement. Natural experiments lend themselves to the testing of economic theory because they frequently (and ideally) involve the alteration of a single variable assumed to be influential in an economic agent's decision making. Because the alteration occurs exogenously— external to the specific behavior or choices made by the individuals under analysis—natural experiments allow cleaner inferences and clearer indications of the direction of causality. Studies designed around a natural experiment also possess inherent policy relevance, and their results can attract the attention of lawmakers and other public officials: because public resources went into adopting a given change, scholarly research can assist in evaluating the effect of that change on behavior, whether the change justified the costs, and the wisdom of expanded alterations of the policy instrument in question.

Levitt (1997) took a natural-experiment approach in his study of how police hiring affects crime. Where political turnover occurs via cyclical mayoral and gubernatorial elections, we may see, and Levitt documents, increases in the size of police forces in the associated cities and states. Using electoral timing essentially as an instrumental variable for police hiring—which is reasonable if one assumes that criminals react systematically more to changes in the presence of police than to political changes— Levitt finds evidence that these exogenous bumps in the presence of police significantly reduce crime, especially violent crime. McCormick and Tollison (1984), applying their model of enforcement that recognized the possibility of errors in enforcement, and Allen (2002), applying a straightforward rendering of the economic model of crime and a panel data set, took advantage of natural experiments in sports officiating to investigate a similar question. McCormick and Tollison found that an increase in the number of on-court officials in college basketball (from two to three) in the 1980s reduced the number of fouls called, evidence of what one could call a "dominant deterrent effect" of the greater presence of police. I found that an experimental increase in the number of on-ice referees (from one to two) in the National Hockey League in 1999–2000 increased the number of penalties assessed for particularly *violent* infractions, evidence of a dominant "apprehension effect" and a result similar in nature to Levitt's (1998) finding. More recently, Evans and Owens (2007) found that an increase in the hiring of police officers in selected U.S. cities—facilitated by the Violent Crime Control and Law Enforcement Act of 1994— significantly reduced the incidence of crimes such as auto thefts, burglaries, and assaults.

As a group, these studies illustrate how researchers interested in testing aspects of the economic model of crime can take advantage of naturally occurring changes in at least one factor central to the model as a way of further solidifying it as a framework for thinking about crime and deterrence. Indeed, Levitt (1998, p. 286) has suggested that a natural-experiment approach, by its nature, may yield "more reliable estimates than studies based on either cross-sectional or time-series variation." Along these lines, Owens (2009) recently exploited an exogenous change (reduction) in sentencing in the state of Maryland to examine the impact of variation in criminal sanctions on individual criminal activity. Beginning in mid-2001, Maryland began applying new, less harsh sentencing guidelines whereby judges no longer took into account an adult defendant's juvenile delinquency record in determining sentences. Using data on a sample of male offenders observed before and after the regime change, Owens demonstrates empirically that the incapacitation of offenders reduces crime and recidivism and that it justifies the social cost.

As noted in the section on theoretical advances, economists have since the 1990s begun to question the efficacy of imposing increasing sanctions for *repeat* crime, a notion that has origins in earlier assertions by Ehrlich regarding the likely systematic ineffectiveness of incapacitation as a means of criminal deterrence, especially for career offenders. On occasion, researchers in crime economics have found empirical evidence not only that the risk of apprehension deters crime but indeed that it does so more effectively than do sanctions. Witte (1980) found this in her important analysis of crime using individual-level data (among the first published studies to use such data), as did Grogger (1991), using a large micro data set that linked the individual criminal and work histories of men in California. In light of the general insignificance of the sanction variables—those measuring the severity of punishment, as opposed to the certainty of punishment—Grogger (p. 308) questioned "the economic rationality of a sanctioning strategy based on increasingly lengthy prison terms as a means of reducing crime," much in line with the purely conceptual discussions relating to optimal sanctioning. Subsequent research by Levitt (1998) provides further empirical evidence that arrest rates, rather than incapacitation, more effectively facilitate criminal deterrence, casting doubt on the long-term efficiency of sanctioning mechanisms such as the "three-strikes" law.

C. Social Interaction, Culture, and Space

Crime economic research that stresses social interaction as a fundamental premise does not depart radically from the Beckerian approach: the essentials of the economic model of crime—the gains to crime, apprehension probability, sanctioning, and licit income opportunities—still matter. The departure, where it exists, rests in modelers' conceptualizations of how these factors become relevant to the lives and decision making of actual and potential criminals, namely, through interaction with other people and with the physical space where they all live—an ecological (or environmental) approach to crime economics. Where information about these factors, or of course the influence of the factors themselves, has an opportunity to flow between groups of people, we may begin to observe interesting patterns of variation in crime across families, across neighborhoods, across cities, or across countries—especially in an increasingly mobile, electronically connected world—and we may witness the development of what one might regard as cultures of criminal activity.

In one of the first major economic studies of international variation in crime, Wolpin (1980), who had previously undertaken a comparative study of criminality in the neighboring countries of England and Wales (Wolpin 1978), placed the notion of differential cultures across nations at the forefront of his analysis. Wolpin (1980, p. 417) thought of culture in this context as "the set of unmeasured crime determinants that permanently differ across countries" and went on to test its effects using country-specific dummy variables (focusing on England, Japan, and the United States). In light of an empirical finding that countries with relatively high robbery rates also appeared to have low formal conviction rates and yet fairly severe penalty structures, Wolpin suggested that cultural differences may offer some explanation. He specifically considered the possibility of a culture effect that "reflects an omitted sanction external to the law enforcement system itself, . . . a private cost to the offender that is administered indirectly through what might be called social pressure or stigma" (p. 423), intriguingly foreshadowing Rasmusen's (1996) formal analysis of just such a possibility. As Wolpin acknowledged, however, if one accepts a culture-based explanation for crime, the challenge for researchers becomes measuring culture objectively and demonstrating that a given result truly reflects culture—learned social beliefs and behavior—and not just an artifact of the criminal justice system or other more traditional influences.

Economists have fleshed this out in a number of interesting ways. In a wide-ranging study of life outcomes among youths in low-income Boston neighborhoods, Case and Katz (1991) investigated determinants of whether a subject had engaged in a crime in the previous year. (They also studied outcomes like illegal drug use, church attendance, and the presence of a single parent.) Among other findings from probit models, Case and Katz showed evidence that criminality in one neighborhood— consisting by the authors' definition of a person's own neighborhood, the adjacent neighborhood, and the one adjacent to it—significantly increased the probability of youth crime. In their study of the role of social interaction in determining patterns of crime, Glaeser, Sacerdote, and Scheinkman (1996) directly acknowledged the fact that criminals *move* and at the same time that older criminals in particular have more personal autonomy in changing residential locations and have had more time to do so compared to younger criminals. These facts lend background to their empirical finding, based on data from New York City, that the lesser degree of migration among younger criminals tends to make local, or neighborhood, effects more influential in their criminal decisions and offers additional explanation for why younger criminals have a greater tendency to commit crimes in groups (gangs?)—a syndrome exacerbated among youths with less stable households. Glaeser and Sacerdote (1999) develop this element further in their study of urban crime, and Williams and Sickles (2002) and Loureiro et al. (2009) show additional evidence of the effects of peers and family on individual crime. Research that emphasizes continuous interaction among criminals and noncriminals also serves as foundational material for the recent study of dynamic crime patterns by Wilhite and Allen (2008) using agent-based computational methods.

Glaeser and Sacerdote (1999) immediately acknowledge and document the fact that more crime occurs in cities than in smaller towns. Using data from three different sources, including crime victimization data (a type of data used prominently in Part Two of this book), they attribute this to the greater existence of pecuniary benefits to crime (cities have altogether more loot to steal, more people on whom to prey) and to a lesser probability of arrest tied to the relatively greater anonymity of urban life, but they conclude that the disproportionate presence of female-headed households in cities—itself a reflection of out-migration and dwindling licit work opportunities for low- to medium-skilled men— influences urban crime just as much.

Cullen and Levitt (1999) provide empirical insights of a piece with those findings. They observe that increasing crime leads more to greater out-migration from cities than to lesser in-migration of new arrivals, and of course those with children and more advanced (and thus more portable) human capital skills exhibit the greatest responsiveness in this way. This dynamic process leads to smaller overall populations in cities, a less-skilled labor pool, and potentially worse crime for those who remain, as legitimate work opportunities dry up (especially for young minority men). Tilling similar ground, Ihlanfeldt (2002) demonstrates the empirical connection between lessened urban access to jobs and racial differences in crime across the city of Atlanta. Grogger and Willis (2000) demonstrate an empirical link between urban crime and the rise of crack cocaine, the addictive properties of which create a significant derived demand for criminal activity and incentives to create and violently enforce cartels in the sale of the drug.

IV. THE PRESENT WORK

With this body of theoretical and empirical economic analysis of criminals and crime as background, the remaining four chapters of Part One of this book seek to make new contributions in this area and, where appropriate, illustrate certain essentials of crime economic research to readers perhaps new to this field.

Chapter 2 focuses on the planning of crimes, a departure of sorts from most studies interested primarily in the commission of an illegality. I present a model developed within a traditional Beckerian state-preference, time-allocation theoretical framework but greatly informed by other social sciences, and I apply it to considerations that become relevant *prior to* the commission of a crime. Chapter 3 examines violence and damages emanating from crime, building especially on the consequences of property crime that provides the empirical environment in Chapter 2. Chapter 3 extends the model of criminal planning introduced in the preceding chapter and provides a glimpse into the *harm* caused by crime, scrutinized at a micro level. Chapter 4 presents a theoretical analysis of criminal evidence destruction, a behavior that potentially becomes relevant in the immediate aftermath of a crime. As discussed further there, this model retains the essential structure of the traditional economic model of crime but extends the analysis by considering an alternative connection between official enforcement activity and criminal deterrence. Could deterring the destruction of criminal evidence aid in deterring crime itself? Finally, Chapter 5 examines the recommission of crime—recidivism—a behavior relevant to the aftermath of a given crime *and* punishment. The chapter illustrates the essentials of how one can use the economic model of crime as a framework for thinking about repeat crime and considers the results of econometric models that estimate durations between crimes.

By examining behaviors that logically occur before, during, and after a crime, we can think about these various issues over the course of what amounts to a "life cycle" or time line of criminal activity, an orientation replicated in Part Two in the analysis of victim behavior.

CHAPTER 2

The Planning of Crime

The world of crime is a last refuge of the authentic,
uncorrupted, spontaneous event.
—DANIEL J. BOORSTIN

I. INTRODUCTION

The desire to deter crime reflects a desire to make crime somehow more costly and thus less attractive for potential offenders to undertake. Most deterrence mechanisms, as illustrated in many studies, involve either increasing or improving policing, so as to enhance the likelihood of criminal detection, or legislating stronger sanctions altogether—actions that collectively increase the expected cost of illegal activity. Polinsky and Shavell (2000) provide a valuable overview of research along these lines. But criminals incur some costs before they ever do anything formally illegal—as part of the planning process. Within a more general process of victim selection, criminals need to figure out whether to use a weapon, whether to recruit accomplices, even whether to take the time to plan at all. Resolving these planning decisions can make a criminal more efficient at crime, but these activities also cost time and money. The fact that we have laws governing *attempted* crime gives an indirect indication of society's concern with criminal-planning behavior and the social desire to prevent worse crimes. In the words of Landes and Posner (1975, p. 27), "we try to prevent [illegal] activities from occurring by intervening at the preparatory stages, rather than allowing the legal system's 'market' in crimes to determine their extent." These concerns motivate distinct research questions. How do criminals plan their crimes, and what impacts that planning? Can we discourage crime, or reduce its consequences, by making it harder, more costly, to plan?

We address these questions in this and the following chapter. To do so, it becomes useful to think about criminal-planning behavior as an economic activity separate from the actual commission of a crime. Much of what we know about the planning behavior of criminals comes from research in criminology, social environment, and other social sciences outside of economics. Authors of these studies, owing much to pioneering analysis by Cohen and Felson (1979), frequently take an "ecological" approach to the analysis of criminal behavior, emphasizing the importance of the physical environment in shaping the choices made by criminals (and victims). As examples, Pettiway (1982) and van Koppen and Jansen (1998) demonstrate the role of geography and offender mobility as they influence the choices of urban burglars and robbers. Similarly, D'Alessio and Stolzenberg (1990) illustrate the importance of "subneighborhood" factors that affect commercial robbery and other criminal activity: access to transportation routes, the extent of automobile traffic, the presence of other commercial establishments in the vicinity of a targeted establishment, and others. We have also seen the economic model of crime applied and extended to these sorts of settings and problems, especially those involving a central *individual* decision to engage in illegal activity. As noted in Chapter 1, Ihlanfeldt (2003) and Zenou (2003) demonstrate the importance of physical space, transportation, and criminal travel costs as they pertain to crime.

A few researchers have proposed intriguing, if not always rigorous, possibilities about the planning of crimes, which suggests the potential for a more formal, pointed analysis in this chapter. Komesar (1973) argued that offenders likely make decisions by evaluating what amounts to expected values of probability distributions (as of net benefits of crime) and that the offender search process can provide a criminal useful information. Komesar cited as an example how a burglar gains information by "casing" potential target locations. Pettiway (1982) characterized some criminal offenders as relatively calculating and others as "petty materialists" or opportunists. The latter type would regard any part of an area, like a city street or neighborhood, as a potential venue for a crime and lie in wait for the perfect moment to strike at a target that presents itself. This more opportunistic approach to criminal activity, in Pettiway's description, "lacks planning, and perhaps the only risk assessed is during the moment of the incident" (p. 263). D'Alessio and Stolzenberg (1990) similarly characterized the possibility that some offenders would act randomly and others more deliberately. Going further, van Koppen and Jansen (1998, p. 232) suggested that "to overcome security measures, [offenders] have to put more energy into preparations, have to plan more carefully, and divide up tasks." Such possibilities clearly indicate how time use and accomplice use may become important in criminal planning. In an analysis of the lethality of robberies using an economic approach, Zimring and Zuehl (1986) characterized robbery killings as "unplanned" but offered no specific evidence of this.

Precedent for scholarly analysis of criminal planning clearly exists, but we can certainly do more. As an effort toward a more structured conceptualization of criminal planning as an economic activity, and to motivate empirical analysis of the topic, the model developed in this chapter builds on the classic time-allocation approach to illegal activity, highlighting the three important criminal-planning decisions suggested above: the use of an accomplice, the use of a weapon, and the use of scarce planning time itself. The model casts the hypothetical offender as an expected-utility maximizer in the familiar fashion but also imagines that an offender who seeks to commit a crime essentially relies on a production function that regulates how efficiently he can undertake the crime in question. According to that function, the offender's ability to make the crime happen depends on allocations of scarce labor (his own and possibly that of accomplices) and capital (in the form of weapons), inputs typically seen in production functions used in many microeconomic applications, crime economics included. One encounters the notion of criminal production functions in Philipson and Posner's (1996) conceptualization of crime as a social disease and in Grogger's (1998) analysis of youth crime, as examples. Comparative-static analysis will reveal how exogenous variation in environmental and other factors—including those that impact criminal productivity or the expected sanction—influence the offender's utility-maximizing planning choices. These results function as empirically testable hypotheses.

In this chapter, convenience store robberies (one form of commercial robberies, as distinguishable from residential robberies) provide the setting for empirical investigation of the criminal-planning model and these hypotheses. I use a data set compiled under the auspices of the National

Institute of Justice (NIJ) containing information obtained from a sample of known convenience store robbery offenders on a large number of personal and environmental variables, including the three planning choices of central interest. These planning outcomes plausibly unfold simultaneously, and in practice the associated variables take binary form, as detailed below. Therefore, I model the outcomes empirically as a seemingly unrelated, multivariate system of three probit equations using a simulated maximum-likelihood approach. The empirical results support several of the hypothesized relationships, and further diagnostic statistics confirm the essential simultaneity of the three choices. These and other results give an indirect indication of the relative substitutability and complementarity of the various inputs in the "production" of a property crime, aiding our understanding of how criminals plan crimes. The empirical results discovered in this chapter also set the stage for probing the relationship between the offenders' planning behaviors and important practical consequences of these robberies, such as the incidence of injury and the amount of money actually stolen. We investigate these consequences in earnest in Chapter 3.

II. A TIME-ALLOCATION MODEL OF CRIMINAL PLANNING

A. Definitions and Assumptions

The model developed here allows a hypothetical criminal offender to allocate time separately to the planning and to the commission of a crime. Define t_P as the time potentially allocated to planning and t_M as the time potentially allocated to committing the crime; the sum $t_P + t_M = t_I$ then represents the total amount of time the criminal may allocate to the entirety of the illegal activity. Given the present focus on the offender's precrime or planning actions, we will not consider the offender's postcrime actions. However, to the extent that exiting a crime scene constitutes an important part of the illegal act, a modeler might readily separate t_M further into time allocated specifically to the commission of the crime and time allocated to leaving the crime scene. The offender may also have opportunities to allocate time in other ways, such as to licit activity (e.g., leisure, legal work) or to some other illicit activity. Denote this alternative time allocation as t_L, so that the total amount of time available to the offender becomes $t_I + t_L = T$.

The hypothetical offender in this model has a pecuniary motive. Suppose the offender has identified a potential target who presents an amount of money or property (loot), G, vulnerable to theft. This loot exists exogenous to the offender's actions, and its magnitude depends on factors associated with the target's wealth or profitability. Individual target wealth or expenditure would become important in the context of noncommercial (e.g., residential) robberies, as analyzed by Gould, Weinberg, and Mustard (2002), Ihlanfeldt (2003), and Demombynes and Özler (2005). Target profitability becomes particularly important in the context of commercial robberies, the eventual empirical focus of this chapter. Notwithstanding these distinctions, Ihlanfeldt points out that "residential and commercial loot" do tend to be positively correlated in practice.

Suppose the offender may steal a percentage g of the target loot, where g represents a production function indicating the offender's ability to complete the crime, comparable to the returns-to-crime function incorporated by Grogger (1998). Further suppose production varies directly in three scarce inputs: the criminal's own planning time (t_p), external labor (n) that can take the form of accomplices, and physical capital (k) in the form of weaponry usable in the commission of the crime. Thus, we can write the theft percentage as the production function $g = g(t_p, n, k; \gamma)$, where the parameter $\gamma > 0$ captures exogenous factors that increase g and enhance the marginal productivity of each of these inputs. This parameter might capture the offender's criminal human capital, such as personal experience committing this sort of crime, or environmental factors, such as the presence of efficient transportation modes (as in Ihlanfeldt 2003).

Because the offender might elect to use at least one accomplice—relying on a division of labor suggested by van Koppen and Jansen (1998)—the focus offender ultimately would earn a share $g/(n+1)$ of the loot G. Observe that if the focus offender uses no accomplices ($n = 0$), the share collapses to g; but if $n > 0$, the focus offender's share diminishes. I assume equally weighted shares for simplicity. (Because n represents the number of accomplices in this formulation, it takes the form of a nonnegative integer.)

The criminal's *effective loot* thus becomes $E(G) = gG/(n+1)$. Let $L = L(t_L; \lambda)$ represent the collective gains available to the criminal from alternative time allocation, such as in the form of wages from legal work or alternative returns available from other illegal activity. In this function, $\partial L/\partial t_L > 0$, indicating that allocating more time to these alternative activities increases these returns, and the parameter $\lambda > 0$ captures exogenous factors that increase these alternative gains. This parameter would capture, among other things, the offender's licit human capital skills, such as formal education. Greater such skills enhance the availability of these alternative returns, implying that $\partial L/\partial \lambda > 0$, and they enhance the extent to which the allocation of time toward these activities generates these returns, implying that $\partial^2 L/\partial t_L \partial \lambda > 0$. Observe that we can express the alternative-gains function equivalently as $L = L(T - t_P - t_M; \lambda)$ by incorporating the fact that $t_L + t_I = t_L + t_P + t_M = T$. This allows us to see how the planning and commission of the focus crime incur an opportunity cost in the form of lost alternative gains.

Let p represent the probability that police apprehend the offender in the aftermath of the crime, so that $1 - p$ represents the probability that the criminal commits the crime without capture. As only the actual commission of the crime creates a risk of apprehension for an illegal act, we can express the apprehension probability function as $p = p(t_M; \omega)$, where the parameter $\omega > 0$ captures exogenous factors that enhance the probability of apprehension. This parameter might capture the presence or efficiency of police who patrol the physical location where the crime may occur or who investigate the crime afterward. So, the assumed properties $\partial p/\partial \omega > 0$ and $\partial^2 p/\partial t_M \partial \omega > 0$ indicate, respectively, that a more effective police presence (however accomplished) enhances the probability of apprehension and enhances the extent to which the commission of the crime creates a risk of apprehension. Early research by Mathieson and Passell (1976) demonstrated a positive relationship between police patrol workload and the probability of offender apprehension in robbery cases. More recently, Evans and Owens (2007) have linked exogenous increases in policing to criminal deterrence. Apprehension probabilities may also increase exogenously to offenders when victims more readily report their crimes, as discussed by Goldberg and Nold (1980) and Allen (2007).

Denote the sanction for the crime as the function $F = F(t_M, t_P, n, k; \varphi)$. In practice, this sanction takes the form of a lost opportunity to earn income for a period of time associated with incarceration. The robbery sanction function has properties such that $F(t_M = 0) = 0$, $\partial F / \partial t_P \geq 0$, $F(n > 0) > F(n = 0)$, and $F(k > 0) > F(k = 0)$. That $F(t_M = 0) = 0$ indicates that the offender incurs no sanction if he does not commit the crime. The property $\partial F / \partial t_P \geq 0$ accounts for the possibility that greater planning creates evidence of premeditation, which can increase the sanction imposed. As documented below, states vary in the degree and nature of robbery sanctions; the properties $F(n > 0) > F(n = 0)$ and $F(k > 0) > F(k = 0)$ reflect the fact that many states officially call for enhanced sanctions when the offender uses a weapon or an accomplice. (Zimring and Zuehl 1986 characterized these sorts of provisions as "malice laws," and Mauser and Maki 2003 studied the passage, application, and impact of comparable provisions for weapon use in Canada.) The parameter $\varphi > 0$ captures exogenous factors that make the robbery sanction more severe at the margin. For example, we might observe variation across jurisdictions in the severity of sentences actually imposed, or we might observe legislative stiffening of a given sanction over time, as Evans and Owens (2007) analyze.

Given these component functions, we can express the criminal's objective function as expected utility

$$Z = L(T - t_P - t_M) + [1 - p(t_M)]U\left[\frac{g(t_P, n, k)}{n + 1} G\right] + p(t_M)U[F(t_M, t_P, n, k)],$$

$$(2.1)$$

where U is a quasi-concave utility function and $\partial U / \partial F < 0$ (a more severe sanction reduces utility). As a problem of planning, the criminal seeks levels of t_P, n, and k that maximize Z, subject to the implicit time constraint $t_P + t_M = t_I$. (The offender would also seek the utility-maximizing level of offense time t_M and alternate time use t_L; I do not analyze the economics of these choices as a matter of concentration for this chapter.) The first-order conditions for the focus problem imply that

$$\frac{\partial Z}{\partial t_P} = -\frac{\partial L}{\partial t_P} + (1-p)\frac{\partial U}{\partial E(G)}\frac{\partial g / \partial t_P}{n+1}G + p\frac{\partial U}{\partial F}\frac{\partial F}{\partial t_P} = 0; \qquad (2.2a)$$

$$\frac{\partial Z}{\partial k} = (1-p)\frac{\partial U}{\partial E(G)}\frac{\partial g / \partial k}{n+1}G + p\frac{\partial U}{\partial F}\frac{\partial F}{\partial k} = 0; \qquad (2.2b)$$

and

$$\frac{\partial Z}{\partial n} = (1-p)\frac{\partial U}{\partial E(G)}\frac{(\partial g / \partial n)(n+1) - g}{(n+1)^2}G + p\frac{\partial U}{\partial F}\frac{\partial F}{\partial n} = 0. \qquad (2.2c)$$

Using the envelope theorem and implicit differentiation of the first-order conditions, we can readily derive comparative statics that speak to how the utility-maximizing planning-time, weapon-use, and accomplice-use choices vary with key individual and environmental factors: loot, the robbery sanction, apprehension probability, criminal productivity, opportunity costs, and endogenous factors.

To illustrate the derivation of comparative statics, realize that in the present context, the offender's objective function has the general form $Z = Z(x; \theta)$, where the vector x contains the choice variables t_P, n, and k and θ contains the various shift parameters introduced above. Maximization of Z with respect to any of the choice variables in x yields the first-order conditions shown above, which we can express generally as $Z_x(x^*; \theta) = 0$, where x^* represents the equilibrium level of x. Totally differentiating this first-order condition, we obtain $Z_{xx}dx^* + Z_{x\theta}d\theta = 0$ for any choice variable x and any parameter in θ. Hence, the comparative-static effect of a change in any of these parameters (for example, the exogenous presence of police) on any given expected utility-maximizing choice becomes $\partial x^*/\partial\theta = -Z_{x\theta}/Z_{xx}$. Under the assumption of a quasi-concave utility function that can have a maximum, $Z_{xx} < 0$, leaving the sign of any given comparative-static effect dependent on the sign of the second cross-partial derivative $Z_{x\theta}$. For this reason, the specific components of these cross-partials become vitally important in making predictions about the relationships between key variables within a conceptual model and in illustrating the economic intuition embedded within those relationships. We will exploit these mathematical facts, described further in Chiang (1984) and Silberberg (1990), to derive comparative-static effects on generalized objective functions throughout this book, starting with this chapter.

B. Comparative Statics

1. Loot Recognizing the patterns traced above, an exogenously greater amount of loot (e.g., associated with a more profitable store or a heightened pecuniary motive within the offender) will affect the criminal's utility-maximizing planning time according to the derivative $\partial t_p{}^*/\partial G = -[\partial(\partial Z/\partial t_p)/\partial G]/(\partial^2 Z/\partial t_p{}^2)$. As suggested above, the shape of the utility function implies a negative denominator, and so the sign of $\partial t_p{}^*/\partial G$ will reflect the sign of the bracketed term in the numerator, which represents the derivative of the first-order condition $\partial Z/\partial t_p$ with respect to loot G. As seen within the first-order conditions, $\partial Z/\partial t_p = (1-p)[\partial U/\partial E(G)][\partial g/\partial t_p/(n+1)]G$; thus, $\partial^2 Z/\partial t_p \partial G = (1-p)[\partial U/\partial E(G)][\partial g/\partial t_p/(n+1)]G'$, where $G' > G$. Each component of this expression is positive, and so the effect $\partial t_p{}^*/\partial G > 0$, suggesting that a larger amount of loot motivates a longer equilibrium planning time. Variation in loot exerts a similar predicted effect on weapon use: $\partial k^*/\partial G = -(\partial^2 Z/\partial k \partial G)/(\partial^2 Z/\partial k^2)$ and $\partial^2 Z/\partial k \partial G = (1-p)[\partial U/\partial E(G)][(\partial g/\partial k)/(n+1)]G' > 0$. This suggests that a greater amount of available loot encourages weapon use, other things being equal. Within these comparative statics, one can see that exogenous variation in loot ultimately enhances the utility an offender derives from the crime, subject to how the choice in question, planning time or weapon use, enhances his share-adjusted theft productivity, subject to not getting caught by the police.

A greater amount of loot influences accomplice use (as described by the derivative $\partial n^*/\partial G$) less definitively than the other choices. In the same spirit as the derivation of $\partial t_p{}^*/\partial G$ and $\partial k^*/\partial G$, the key derivative in signing $\partial n^*/\partial G$ is $\partial^2 Z/\partial n \partial G = (1-p)[\partial U/\partial E(G)][(\partial g/\partial n)(n+1) - g]/(n+1)^2]G'$. If the term $[(\partial g/\partial n)(n+1) - g]/(n+1)^2 > 0$, then exogenously greater loot will encourage accomplice use, other things being equal. Otherwise, greater loot will encourage the offender to act alone, or at least with fewer accomplices. The sign of this term, which captures how the effective share $g/(n+1)$ varies in n, ultimately turns on the marginal benefit of accomplice use on robbery productivity. If, at the margin, accomplices contribute more to the primary offender's productivity than they reduce his loot share, then greater loot encourages the offender to use that external labor. Empirical investigation of these comparative statics can provide at least an indirect indication of how criminal offenders actually regard the use of other human resources in the commission of crime. The coexistence of criminals also will become important in the analysis of criminal evidence destruction in Chapter 4.

2. *The Robbery Sanction*   Exogenous variation in the robbery sanction, functioning through the parameter φ, affects the offender's optimal planning time according to the derivative $\partial t_p{}^*/\partial\varphi = -(\partial^2 Z/\partial t_p\partial\varphi)/(\partial^2 Z/\partial t_p)$, the sign of which mirrors that of $\partial^2 Z/\partial t_p\partial\varphi = p(\partial U/\partial F)(\partial^2 F/\partial t_p\partial\varphi)$. If a more calculated plan leads to a stronger sanction—for example, in the form of a penalty for evidence of premeditation—then $\partial F/\partial t_p > 0$ and $\partial^2 F/\partial t_p\partial\varphi > 0$, each indicating the exogenous reinforcement of this planning-sanction effect. Because $\partial U/\partial F < 0$, it must hold that $\partial^2 Z/\partial t_p\partial\varphi < 0$, and so $\partial t_p{}^*/\partial\varphi < 0$ as well, indicating that a greater sanction for robbery would motivate a shorter equilibrium plan. Absent evidence of planning, or absent judicial concern about premeditation in practice, $\partial F/\partial t_p = 0$, suggesting no predictable connection between robbery sanctioning and criminal-planning time.

Exogenous variation in the sanction exerts very similar marginal effects on k^* and n^*, represented as $\partial k^*/\partial\varphi$ and $\partial n^*/\partial\varphi$. Observe that $\partial k^*/\partial\varphi = -(\partial^2 Z/\partial k\partial\varphi)/(\partial^2 Z/\partial k^2)$. Because $\partial Z/\partial k = (1-p)[\partial U/\partial E(G)][(\partial g/\partial k)/(n+1)]G + p(\partial U/\partial F)(\partial F/\partial k)$, as indicated within the first-order conditions, $\partial^2 Z/\partial k\partial\varphi = p(\partial U/\partial F)(\partial^2 F/\partial k\partial\varphi)$. Thus, $\partial k^*/\partial\varphi = -p(\partial U/\partial F)(\partial^2 F/\partial k\partial\varphi)/(\partial^2 Z/\partial k^2)$. But because $\partial U/\partial F < 0$, necessarily $\partial k^*/\partial\varphi < 0$. For utility-maximizing accomplice use (n^*), very similarly $\partial n^*/\partial\varphi = -p(\partial U/\partial F)(\partial^2 F/\partial n\partial\varphi)/(\partial^2 Z/\partial n^2) < 0$. The negative signs of $\partial k^*/\partial\varphi$ and $\partial n^*/\partial\varphi$ suggest that a stronger sanction would discourage weapon use and accomplice use in the planning of the crime, other things being equal. In each of these relationships, the parameter φ analytically magnifies the sanction effect (captured as $\partial^2 F/\partial k\partial\varphi$ and $\partial^2 F/\partial n\partial\varphi$), to the detriment of offender utility; variation in this parameter might reflect variation in sanctions across jurisdictions, for example.

The hypothesized deterrence of weapon use along these lines formalizes a suggestion by Zimring and Zuehl (1986) that malice laws would have this effect. Zimring and Zuehl also recognized that if stronger sanctions or malice-law provisions essentially raised the price of using a firearm, offenders may react according to a substitution effect and use different weapons, possibly resulting in a minimal reduction in robbery rates. In Section III of this chapter we see some empirical support for such a substitution effect in relation to the state of Massachusetts. Later empirical analysis will allow us to examine whether stronger sanctions appear to affect these choices as hypothesized and whether robbery offenders use accomplices less frequently in states that officially call for stiffer penalties for the use of accomplices in robberies.

3. *Apprehension Probability*   To examine how an exogenously greater apprehension probability (e.g., associated with increased policing activity) affects the criminal's planning choices, we must study $\partial t_p^*/\partial\omega$, $\partial k^*/\partial\omega$, and $\partial n^*/\partial\omega$. Observe that $\partial t_p^*/\partial\omega = -(\partial^2 Z/\partial t_p\partial\omega)/(\partial^2 Z/\partial t_p^2)$. Because $\partial Z/\partial t_p = (1-p)[\partial U/\partial E(G)][(\partial g/\partial t_p^*)/(n+1)]G$, clearly $\partial^2 Z/\partial t_p\partial\omega = -(\partial p/\partial\omega)[\partial U/\partial E(G)][(\partial g/\partial t_p)/(n+1)]G < 0$, implying that $\partial t_p^*/\partial\omega < 0$: a greater probability of apprehension encourages a shorter planning time. Empirical analysis will allow us to investigate not only whether a greater apprehension probability makes a robbery offender act more impulsively but also (in Chapter 3) the consequences of offender impulsiveness, where it exists.

Observe that $\partial k^*/\partial\omega = -(\partial^2 Z/\partial k\partial\omega)/(\partial^2 Z/\partial k^2)$ and that $\partial^2 Z/\partial k\partial\omega = -(\partial p/\partial\omega)[\partial U/\partial E(G)][(\partial g/\partial k)/(n+1)]G + (\partial p/\partial\omega)(\partial U/\partial F)(\partial F/\partial k)$. Each term of this second cross-partial derivative is negative, implying that $\partial^2 Z/\partial k\partial\omega < 0$ and $\partial k^*/\partial\omega < 0$: a greater apprehension probability discourages weapon use. In this result, the component $\partial F/\partial k$, which captures how the robbery sanction varies with weapon use at the margin, accentuates this negative effect. This suggests that any weapon-use deterrence effect related to exogenously greater apprehension probability in general may be enhanced in jurisdictions that impose additionally more severe sentences for weapon use during robberies. Many state penal codes specify just such a provision. Similarly observe that $\partial n^*/\partial\omega = -(\partial^2 Z/\partial n\partial\omega)/(\partial^2 Z/\partial n^2)$ and that, inside this expression, $\partial^2 Z/\partial n\partial\omega = -(\partial p/\partial\omega)[\partial U/\partial E(G)]\{[\partial g/\partial n(n+1)-g]/$

$(n+1)^2\}G+(\partial p/\partial\omega)(\partial U/\partial F)(\partial F/\partial n)<0$, implying $\partial n^*/\partial\omega<0$ and suggesting that greater apprehension probability discourages accomplice use as well. Symmetrically, the term $\partial F/\partial n$, capturing the marginal impact on the robbery sanction of accomplice use, accentuates this effect. Empirical analysis will enable us to examine the extent to which a greater apprehension probability affects accomplice use and whether variation across jurisdictions in sanctions applicable to accomplices becomes additionally influential in this choice.

4. *Criminal Productivity*   Exogenous variation in the offender's productivity, functioning through the parameter γ, captures how criminal human capital affects the offender's planning choices. Analytically, such variation exerts a similar effect on each of the choices. As in the other comparative statics, how t_p^*, k^*, and n^* vary in γ depends on how the marginal expected utility of each choice varies with γ. For $\partial t_p^*/\partial\gamma$, the key derivative is $\partial^2 Z/\partial t_p\partial\gamma=(1-p)[\partial U/\partial E(G)][(\partial^2 g/\partial t_p\partial\gamma)/(n+1)]G>0$. For $\partial k^*/\partial\gamma$, the key derivative is $\partial^2 Z/\partial k\partial\gamma=(1-p)[\partial U/\partial E(G)][(\partial^2 g/\partial k\partial\gamma)/(n+1)]G>0$. For $\partial n^*/\partial\gamma$, the key derivative is $\partial^2 Z/\partial n\partial\gamma=(1-p)[\partial U/\partial E(G)]\{[\partial^2 g/\partial n\partial\gamma/(n+1)-\partial g/\partial\gamma]/(n+1)^2\}G$, which has an ambiguous sign. The positive signs for $\partial t_p^*/\partial\gamma$ and $\partial k^*/\partial\gamma$ suggest that greater criminal human capital (e.g., greater experience as a criminal) encourages a longer (i.e., less impulsive) equilibrium planning time and encourages weapon use, respectively. The former comparative static formalizes a suspicion raised by D'Alessio and Stolzenberg (1990, p. 267) that "experienced offenders are probably more highly attuned than novice offenders to the situational clues that indicates vulnerability [to apprehension]" and that, consequently, "novice offenders strike more randomly." A variable capturing offender experience will allow an empirical investigation of this factor applicable to the commission of convenience store robberies. The ambiguous sign for $\partial n^*/\partial\gamma$ makes it unclear, ex ante, how greater criminal human capital would influence the accomplice-use decision. The source of the ambiguity lies in the component $(\partial^2 g/\partial n\partial\gamma)/(n+1)-\partial g/\partial\gamma$. To the extent that the primary offender's human capital complements the marginal productivity of external labor (accomplices), represented in $\partial^2 g/\partial n\partial\gamma$, the use of accomplices exerts a marginal benefit; but because

the greater human capital by definition makes the offender himself more productive, he may more readily substitute his own planning actions for the actions of one or more accomplices.

5. *Opportunity Cost of Planning*   Allocating time to plan a crime incurs opportunity costs: the value of activities, legitimate or otherwise, that the offender could have pursued instead of planning the crime in question. Greater availability of these alternative benefits impacts the equilibrium planning time in an intuitive way, according to $\partial t_p{}^*/\partial \lambda$, whose sign mirrors that of $\partial^2 Z/\partial t_p \partial \lambda = -\partial^2 L/\partial t_p \partial \lambda$. This is clearly negative, indicating that a greater opportunity cost of criminal planning would encourage a shorter planning time, other things being equal. We might expect an offender to allocate less time to planning a given crime if he has other criminal opportunities available to him in that moment or if, in general, he possesses more valuable skills applicable to licit activity. As reviewed in Chapter 1, numerous studies indicate that higher wages available in legitimate work or greater access to such work tend to reduce illegal activity, other things being equal. The present result extends this prediction by showing that such factors would reduce the incentive to *plan* crimes as well.

6. *Endogenous Factors*   Finally, we consider how the various planning choices logically interact with each other. The criminal's use of an accomplice affects his use of a weapon according to the derivative $\partial k^*/\partial n$, the sign of which mirrors that of $\partial^2 Z/\partial k \partial n = (1-p)[\partial U/\partial E(G)]\{[(\partial^2 g/\partial k \partial n)(n+1) - \partial g/\partial k]/(n+1)^2\}G$. If the offender does not regard weapons and accomplices as complementary inputs in the production of the crime (i.e., if $\partial^2 g/\partial k \partial n \leq 0$), then $\partial^2 Z/\partial k \partial n < 0$, implying $\partial k^*/\partial n < 0$. Otherwise, $\partial k^*/\partial n$ has a chance to be positive and indeed will be if $(\partial^2 g/\partial k \partial n)(n+1) > \partial g/\partial k$. These theoretical results suggest that the offender will be reluctant to combine weapon use and accomplice use in the absence of such a complementarity and when the law heavily sanctions their combined use. Zimring and Zuehl (1986) asserted reasonably that "in many commercial settings, a handgun is nearly indispensable" (p. 38). If so, then it seems unlikely that an offender would regard other inputs as

substitutes to weapon capital, perhaps making it more sensible that $\partial k^*/\partial n \geq 0$.

The criminal's use of a weapon affects his planning time according to the derivative $\partial t_p^*/\partial k$, the sign of which mirrors that of $\partial^2 Z/\partial t_p \partial k = (1-p)$ $[\partial U/\partial E(G)][(\partial^2 g/\partial t_p \partial k)/(n+1)]G$. The use of an accomplice affects planning time according to the derivative $\partial t_p^*/\partial n$, the sign of which mirrors that of $\partial^2 Z/\partial t_p \partial n = (1-p)[\partial U/\partial E(G)]\{[(\partial^2 g/\partial t_p \partial n - \partial g/\partial t_p)/(n+1)^2]\}G$. Each of these effects will be positive only if weapon use and accomplice use, respectively, complement the criminal's planning time in the production of robbery. Empirical analysis of the three endogenous choices analyzed here will allow us to investigate directly how a sampling of known robbery offenders simultaneously made these choices and indirectly will suggest the degree of complementarity among the various inputs of the criminal production function internal to this criminal-planning model.

III. THE EMPIRICAL ENVIRONMENT OF ROBBERY AND PLANNING

Ultimately we want to test the extent to which the theoretical hypotheses implied by the comparative statics show up empirically. But let us first consider the empirical environment in which (1) robbery offenders make criminal-planning decisions, (2) robberies occur, and (3) states impose sanctions for this crime.

A. Aggregate Patterns

Several aggregated U.S. statistical patterns relate directly to the sociolegal environment of the crime of robbery and the planning choices under analysis. Uniform Crime Report statistics from the Federal Bureau of Investigation (FBI) (1995) offer a glimpse of the prevalence of robbery, weapon use, and law-enforcement resource allocation in the United States as a whole and for specific states in 1995, the last year covered by the offender-level NIJ data used for more formal econometric analysis later in this chapter. The NIJ data set, introduced more fully in the next subsection, provides information on convenience store robberies that occurred in the early 1990s in four states: Maryland, Massachusetts, Michigan, and South Carolina. In 1995, robbery rates (number of total robberies reported per 100,000 population) were highest in the South (34% of all violent crimes) and lowest in the Midwest (19%); by FBI definition, the South includes Maryland and the Midwest includes Michigan, meaning that eventually we can examine individual-level robbery planning behavior in areas representative of extremes in overall robbery incidence.

Of the four focus states, Maryland exhibited the highest robbery rate, 423.1, nearly double the national average of 220.9. Indeed, Maryland had the highest state robbery rate in the country. Michigan (187.3) and South Carolina (175.9) showed the second- and third-highest robbery rates among the focus states in 1995, while Massachusetts showed the lowest (150.4); in the entire United States, North Dakota had the lowest 1995 robbery rate (10.0). The employment of law-enforcement officers across the four states obviously gives an indication of the individual states' reactions to the severity of robbery (and other crimes) in those states. Many analysts have documented how jurisdictions commonly increase law-enforcement activity reactively, that is, as a consequence of crime; for useful discussions, see Doyle, Ahmed, and Horn (1999) and Evans and Owens (2007). While Maryland and Michigan exhibited the highest robbery rates, Maryland and Massachusetts showed the largest employment of law-enforcement officers (per 100,000 population), 351.7 officers and 305.2 officers, respectively. This may suggest that law-enforcement agencies were more effective at deterring robbery in Massachusetts than in Michigan. The pattern calls to mind Levitt's (1997) finding that larger police forces, tied to mayoral and gubernatorial electoral cycles, can reduce the incidence of certain types of crime.

The Uniform Crime Reports also show a rather distinct ranking, by state, in the prevalence of firearm use in robberies in 1995. Not surprisingly, robbers overwhelmingly favored firearms over any other weapon, as also documented by Zimring and Zuehl (1986) in their study of robbery-related injury and homicide. Robbers in Maryland showed the most prevalent use of firearms (52.3% of all robberies) among the four focus states, followed by robbers in Michigan (46.3%), South Carolina (37.3%), and Massachusetts (23.3%). Only in Maryland and Michigan did this percentage exceed the 1995 national average of 40.9%. Intriguingly, robbers in Massachusetts more prevalently used knives or other cutting instruments compared to robbers in the other states; the 18.4% rate in that state well exceeded the comparable rate for the other states and exceeded the national average (9.1%) by more than double. Factors that deterred robbery in general and armed robbery in particular in Massachusetts may have motivated robbery offenders to adopt knives as a substitute form of physical robbery capital, in a manner suggested by Zimring and Zuehl (1986).

How states officially code and impose sanctions for robbery and how they regulate the legal availability of firearms give further indications of the sociolegal environment criminals encounter when planning robberies. One can obtain details about a state's codification of sanctions for robbery and other crimes by studying the official laws of those states, as generally published online in LexisNexis or in sites maintained by state governments and legislatures. Among the four focus states, only Maryland and South Carolina specify any limit for legally purchasing firearms within a thirty-day period (specifically, no more than one such purchase), presumably a reflection of the problem of gun use in violent crimes such as robbery. Maryland and Massachusetts also specify a seven-day waiting period for the legal purchase of a firearm; South Carolina does not. Maryland and South Carolina formally specify fairly comparable sanctions for robbery: both states mandate a prison sentence of no more than fifteen years for robbery committed without a weapon, and both call for an increased penalty for robbery undertaken with a weapon, including a mandatory seven years of prison without the possibility of parole in South Carolina. Penal codes in Massachusetts and Michigan actually allow life sentences for robbery, armed or otherwise.

These official codifications notwithstanding, the formal specification of a sanction in a state or provincial penal code does not imply that convicted robbers will always receive sentences in line with that code. For example, in their study of 1977 gun law reform in Canada, Mauser and Maki (2003) observed that courts had by 1994 only infrequently applied special penalties for firearm use in robbery that the reformed law had allowed. Mauser and Maki suggest that more frequent application might have reduced armed robbery rates. One can observe a similar inconsistency of robbery penalty application in the focus states here. By 1995, Maryland had responded to robbery by imposing the longest average robbery sanction among the four focus states (10.47 years), while South Carolina imposed the *shortest* average sanction (5.83 years). Of these four states, Massachusetts imposed the second-highest robbery sentence (8.47 years) while exhibiting the lowest robbery rate, as documented earlier. Formal probit analysis will reveal whether these sentences appeared to discourage individual accomplice use or weapon use, as hypothesized.

To put these sentencing figures in perspective, by 2004, the most recent year of complete robbery sentencing data published by the U.S. Sentencing Commission, the average sentence imposed for robbery had declined appreciably in Maryland, to 8.33 years, and had increased appreciably in South Carolina, to 7.93 years. By comparison, the average robbery sentences imposed in Massachusetts and Michigan in 2004 were 8.10 years and 6.79 years, respectively, not appreciably different from their 1995 averages. Future research beyond our current scope may endeavor to determine why these changes occurred, whether the apparent trend toward greater uniformity in robbery sentencing occurred nationwide, and of course the extent to which these changes influenced the commission of robbery.

For accessories to robbery, Massachusetts and South Carolina officially mandate the same sentence as for the principal felon—perhaps a reaction to the relatively greater lethality of robbery committed by more than one offender—while Maryland and Michigan allow for lesser sentences for accessories. Among the four states, only Michigan officially mandates a monetary fine ($10,000) as part of the penalty for accessory to robbery. These patterns suggest that the cost of using an accomplice may vary across these states: assuming a reasonably efficient flow of information about sanctions for robbery accessories, principal offenders may find it relatively more difficult to recruit accomplices in states that mandate no lesser sentence for accessories than for the principal felon.

B. Individual-Level Patterns

To investigate criminal-planning behavior at the individual level, I use the aforementioned data set compiled by Wellford (2000) under the auspices of the Data Resources Program of the NIJ, the research arm of the

United States Department of Justice. Based on structured interviews with convenience store robbery offenders sampled from prison rolls (as well as interviews with unrelated victims), this data set tabulates information on convenience store crime that occurred in Georgia, Massachusetts, Maryland, Michigan, and South Carolina from 1991 to 1995. The present study uses data from the offender sample, which contains 147 usable observations. (In point of fact, the offender sample contained only one observation whose crime occurred in Georgia, which eliminates Georgia as a focus state in this chapter; also, due to missing or unusable data, some statistical analyses will employ a smaller sample of 130 offenders.)

The offender sample contains a considerable amount of data conducive to empirical investigation of the criminal-planning choices and their hypothesized determinants. Besides gathering data on various personal characteristics of the offenders and on the nature of the stores they robbed (described in detail in Section IV below), NIJ surveyors gathered information relating to the extent to which each offender planned the robbery in question, whether the offender used a weapon during the robbery (and, if so, what type of weapon), and whether the offender used accomplices.

When asked how far in advance they planned the robbery, some offenders reported having planned no more than six hours, others reported having planned for a longer time but still the same day, and others reported having planned the crime for more than one day. The variable Planning Time equals 1 for those who reported this longest planning time and 0 for the shorter planning periods. The variable Weapon Used equals 1 if the offender reported having used any type of weapon and 0 if the offender used no weapon. The variable Accomplice Used equals 1 if the offender reported having used an accomplice and 0 if the offender acted alone. In addition, the NIJ ascertained the offender's perception of the "likelihood of capture," as phrased in the survey, prior to the robbery, coded on a scale from 0 (meaning absolutely no chance) to 10 (meaning absolutely a chance); this allows construction of an offender-specific measure of the probability of apprehension. The variable No Chance of Apprehension equals 1 if the offender reported having perceived absolutely no chance of capture and 0 otherwise. These and other variables become useful in empirical comparisons of offenders across states and in more comprehensive probit analysis of the planning choices.

In light of the aggregated state patterns documented and described above, we might consider how the robbery offenders in the NIJ sample made choices and perceived the risk of apprehension in their specific legal environments. To address this, I conducted t-tests of mean differences, by state of offense, in the variables Weapon Used, Accomplice Used, Planning Time, and No Chance of Apprehension. These tests indicate that offenders who used an accomplice were significantly less likely to have committed their robberies in Maryland and were significantly more likely to have committed their robberies in Michigan. Sample offenders in Maryland used a firearm, and a weapon in general, significantly more often than not, while Michigan offenders showed the opposite proclivity. By state, Maryland offenders exhibited a significantly shorter planning time for their robberies; in no other state did Planning Time differ significantly. Together, the aggregate and individual-level data suggest a particularly vivid profile of convenience store robbery commonly committed in Maryland: lone offenders, acting impulsively, aided by firearms. With the economic model of criminal planning as a guide, probit analysis of these planning outcomes may reveal what makes an offender either relatively more impulsive or relatively more calculating when planning and committing robbery.

IV. ADDITIONAL VARIABLES AND EMPIRICAL METHODOLOGY

Testing the hypotheses implied by the comparative statics derived in Section II requires data that capture the planning choices, as introduced earlier, as well as variables that capture exogenous factors relating to loot, the robbery sanction, the probability of apprehension, opportunity costs of planning, and criminal human capital. The NIJ data on convenience store robberies, supplemented with data from other sources, allow measurement of these factors. I incorporate these variables in two sets of probit models that estimate determinants of the planning-time, accomplice-use, and weapon-use choices. The first set of models analyzes those choices as three separate univariate probit models, that is, uncorrected for the likely simultaneity of the choices. The second set of models treats the choices more properly as simultaneous and therefore analyzes them as a seemingly unrelated, three-equation multivariate (trivariate) system of probit equations. The two sets of models allow us to examine the extent to which the hypothesized relationships hold empirically and reveal how certain estimated relationships remain robust or even disappear when we formally account for simultaneity. Let us examine the explanatory variables and the econometric specifications more carefully.

A. Explanatory Variables

As a measure of loot availability or importance, the probit models will incorporate the dummy variable Robbed for Money & Drugs, equal to 1 if so and 0 otherwise. This variable results from the effort by NIJ surveyors to determine the sample offenders' objectives in robbing their targeted stores. Offenders who indicated a nonpecuniary motivation cited characteristics of the store itself rather than the desire to obtain money or drugs. Van Koppen and Jansen (1998) observed similar sets of motives in their study of commercial robberies in Great Britain. In light of the comparative-static results on variation in loot, we would anticipate that those who expressed this motivation would exhibit comparatively lengthier planning times as well as greater weapon and accomplice use. To measure the robbery sanction, the models will incorporate the variable Average Sentence 1995, introduced earlier, as well as the dummy variable Lesser Accomplice Sentence, set equal to 1 if a state's penal code specifies a sanction for accessory to robbery other than that specified for the principal felon. For offenders in the NIJ sample who committed their crimes in Maryland or Michigan, this variable equals 1; for offenders who operated in Massachusetts or South Carolina, it equals 0. As seen earlier, the criminal-planning model suggests that greater robbery sanctions should discourage accomplice use and weapon use but have no impact on planning time.

As an additional indicator of the nature of law potentially relevant to criminal planning, the models will also incorporate dummy variables that indicate the presence of a seven-day waiting period for the purchase of a firearm (equal to 1 for Maryland and South Carolina, equal to 0 for Massachusetts and Michigan). Because these variables, relevant only in probit models designed to explain weapon use, necessarily represent states' reactions to firearm-aided crime (among other reasons), they essentially capture the degree to which criminal firearm use appears problematic in the various states. One would expect positive coefficients for this reason. If instead we could observe a natural experiment in the strengthening of firearms law, as in Mauser and Maki (2003), we would anticipate a negative coefficient indicating deterrence.

The models will capture the probability of apprehension directly using the variable No Chance of Apprehension, introduced earlier, and indirectly with Likert-type environmental variables that capture the importance to the offender of the visible presence of video surveillance cameras at the store and the proximity of police near the store. In their natural form, these variables take on categorical values corresponding to whether the offender regarded such factors as "important," "very important," "moderately important," "slightly important," or "not important at all." The variables used for statistical analysis here equal 1 if the offender regarded those factors as either "important" or "very important" and 0 otherwise. Such factors presumably would become relevant to an offender because they indicate a marginally greater probability of apprehension. If the equilibrium planning time becomes shorter and accomplice use and weapon use become less likely with a greater such probability, as hypothesized, these variables would take on positive coefficients in probit models that cast these planning outcomes as dependent variables. The police-proximity importance variable serves the same purpose as Mathieson and Passell's (1976) measure of police density, which captured concentrations of police deployment in New York City.

Several variables will capture criminal human capital and productivity in the probit models. NIJ data collectors ascertained, among other offender-specific information, whether offenders had robbed similar stores prior to the incident in question. The variable Similar Robbery Experience equals 1 for those who indicated such experience and 0 otherwise. NIJ surveyors further ascertained, using additional Likert-type variables, the extent to which the offenders in the sample regarded certain other factors relating to the physical environment of the crime as important. A set of three such variables ascertains the importance of the store's exit location, the proximity of major roads near the store, and the volume of customers present at the store. Conceptually, these variables account for factors that might influence the offender's marginal productivity in robbery. A favorable exit location (e.g., relatively close to the cash register) and proximate roadways may facilitate an efficient departure from the crime scene, as discussed by researchers interested in geography, criminal travel, and transportation systems. A greater volume of customers may increase the level of "informal surveillance" of the store, as characterized by D'Alessio and Stolzenberg (1990), perhaps indirectly enhancing the probability of apprehension, but it may alternatively create a necessity for crowd control, thus reducing the offender's efficiency. The construction of this variable in the NIJ data set prevents a more definitive prediction.

As measures of opportunity costs of planning time, the models will include dummy variables indicating whether the offender had been involved in "normal" activity (as opposed to drinking, taking drugs, or partying) prior to the robbery and whether the offender indicated the availability of an alternative robbery target at that time. These variables allow us to investigate whether routine time allocation prior to a robbery, suggesting relatively inexpensive planning-time use, leads to less impulsive robbery behavior and whether the availability of other targets, suggesting relatively costlier planning-time use, reduces the offender's planning time, as suggested by the theoretical model. The variable Average Annual Pay 1991–1995 represents the mean annual income of workers in each of the four covered states over the sample period 1991–1995. This variable, comparable to legal-income variables used by Gould, Weinberg, and Mustard (2002) and others, serves as an additional measure of the opportunity cost of planning time. One would expect a negative coefficient. The models will control for the offender's race using a dummy variable capturing whether the offender was nonwhite. As all but one of the sample offenders were male, I do not control for gender.

B. Probit Specifications

Conceptually, the criminal-planning choices centrally at issue in this chapter reflect the hypothetical offender's perception that he could obtain greater expected utility by engaging in a lengthier rather than a shorter planning time, by using a weapon rather than not, and by using at least one accomplice rather than acting alone. In practice, of course, we observe not these latent evaluations of expected utility but merely the outcomes of these choices, here in the form of the indicator variables Planning Time, Accomplice Used, and Weapon Used. In a traditional univariate probit setting, letting y_i represent any of these dichotomous dependent variables, $i \in \{1, 2, 3\}$, we estimate the latent regression relationship $y_i = X_i'\beta + \varepsilon_i$ as a probit model such that $\mathrm{Prob}(y_i = 1) = \mathrm{Prob}(\varepsilon_i > -X_i'\beta) = 1 - F(-X_i'\beta)$ and where F is the normal cumulative distribution function. We obtain estimates of β for each dependent variable using customary iterative maximum-likelihood methods.

In the present analytical setting, however, the hypothetical offender plausibly makes these criminal-planning choices simultaneously rather than independently, suggesting interdependence among the disturbance terms in the probit equations. To account for this simultaneity, one can estimate the choices as a system of three multivariate probit equations for each binary outcome: $y_1 = X_1'\beta_1 + \varepsilon_1$; $y_2 = X_2'\beta_2 + \varepsilon_2$; $y_3 = X_3'\beta_1 + \varepsilon_3$. In this system, the vectors X_1, X_2, and X_3 contain the explanatory variables (including some endogenous variables) hypothesized to influence planning time, weapon use, and accomplice use, respectively, and each equation has its own error term capturing unobservable factors that matter conceptually. For example, the NIJ data set does not contain information on the criminal experience of accomplices that would allow a measure of *their* criminal productivity or on the focus offender's formal education level, which might have captured licit human capital skill.

As Greene (2008) discusses, simultaneous probit models involving more than two equations become notoriously difficult to estimate using standard maximum-likelihood (ML) algorithms because of the necessity of evaluating generally intractable higher-order multivariate integrals of the normal distribution. For this study, the coefficient vectors β_1, β_2, and

β_3 are estimated using simulated maximum likelihood, which approximates the underlying joint probabilities $\text{Prob}(Y_1 = y_{i1}, Y_2 = y_{i2}, Y_3 = y_{i3} | X_1, X_2, X_3, \rho_{12}, \rho_{13}, \rho_{23})$ by taking random draws from the implied trivariate normal distribution, where the parameters ρ_{12}, ρ_{13}, and ρ_{23} represent the covariance-of-error terms for each possible pair of component probit equations. I specifically make use of the multivariate probit routine developed by Cappellari and Jenkins (2003) for the Stata system, which uses the Geweke-Hajivassiliou-Keane (GHK) smooth recursive simulator for this purpose. In this routine, the simulator calculates a likelihood contribution for each observation, and the simulated likelihood contribution becomes the average value calculated over the various draws (or replications). The routine then maximizes the simulated likelihood function using standard ML methods. Given the hypothesized simultaneity of the three criminal-planning choices, this multivariate probit analysis permits an econometrically efficient testing of the hypotheses advanced in Section II pertaining to the determinants of these choices.

Greene (2008) provides a valuable overview of the GHK simulator and simulated maximum-likelihood estimation, but one can find additional details on the derivation of the simulator in Geweke (1989), Hajivassiliou (1990), and Keane (1994). The use of simulated maximum-likelihood approximation to estimate multiple-equation probit models emanates from an initial suggestion by Lerman and Manski (1981). Keane and Moffitt (1998), Golob and Regan (2002), and Allen (2009) incorporated similar procedures to analyze simultaneous binary choices.

The theoretical model of criminal planning suggests structural inclusions and exclusions of explanatory variables that enable identification of the probit system. As suggested by the model, the planning-time equation will contain the other two endogenous variables (accomplice use and weapon use) under the assumption that the offender requires planning time to make those choices; it will additionally contain the sanction variable Average Sentence 1995 but not the variable Lesser Accomplice Sentence. The weapon-use equation will contain the accomplice-use endogenous variable, and the accomplice-use equation will contain no other endogenous variables. To be clear, the theoretical model does not specifically indicate that the accomplice-use endogenous variable should appear as an explanatory variable in the weapon-use equation, or vice versa. Either specification would enable testing of how the offenders under analysis use the two inputs together, but we can estimate only one to ensure identification of the system. Each equation also will contain certain exogenous variables uniquely relevant to its dependent variable, as suggested by the model. The planning-time equation will uniquely contain the time-allocation and opportunity cost variables Normal Activity Prior, Alternate Target Available, and Average Annual Pay 1991–1995. The accomplice-use equation will uniquely contain the variable Lesser Accomplice Sentence, capturing a presumably important marginal cost of using an accomplice. The weapon-use equation will uniquely contain the firearms-availability indicators.

In this modeling environment, a test of the null hypothesis H_0: $\rho_{12} = \rho_{13} = \rho_{23}$ ascertains the significance of the correlation between the three structural error terms. In principle, $\rho_{12} = \rho_{13} = \rho_{23}$ would indicate that the sample offenders essentially did not make the planning choices simultaneously and that one could make valid statistical inferences using separate probit equations for each planning outcome. Estimates of each ρ and the result of this test will appear among the multivariate probit results.

V. PROBIT RESULTS

A. Univariate Probit Results

Table 2.1 displays results of three separate (or "naive") univariate probit models estimating Planning Time, Accomplice Used, and Weapon Used. Although these models do not yet control for the simultaneity of these choices, the results do provide an instructive starting point for assessing the hypothesized relationships.

First consider the planning-time equation. The use of an accomplice does not appear to influence planning time significantly. We see mild evidence in this model that weapon use increases the planning time, significant at the 15% level. More compellingly, and as hypothesized, offenders who robbed for money and drugs allocated significantly more time to planning these robberies than those who expressed a nonpecuniary motive. To put this result in perspective, the coefficient estimate of 0.712 translates to a 0.237 increase in the probability of a lengthy plan in the

TABLE 2.1 *Univariate Probit Analysis of Planning Time, Accomplice Use, and Weapon Use*

	Planning Time			Accomplice Used			Weapon Used		
	$\hat{\beta}$	SE	p	$\hat{\beta}$	SE	p	$\hat{\beta}$	SE	p
Intercept	−0.292	1.52	0.85	1.831	0.55	0.01	−2.39	1.64	0.15
Accomplice Used	0.205	0.29	0.48	—	—	—	0.394	0.32	0.22
Weapon Used	0.746	0.51	0.15	—	—	—	—	—	—
Robbed for Money & Drugs	0.712	0.30	0.02	−0.181	0.25	0.47	−0.318	0.36	0.37
Average Sentence 1995	−0.233	0.10	0.02	−0.169	0.07	0.02	0.222	0.27	0.41
Lesser Accomplice Sentence	—	—	—	−0.078	0.26	0.76	—	—	—
Firearm Waiting Period	—	—	—	—	—	—	0.225	0.91	0.80
30-Day Firearm Limit	—	—	—	—	—	—	0.757	0.34	0.02
No Chance of Apprehension	−0.524	0.30	0.08	−0.303	0.24	0.21	1.091	0.33	0.00
Video Cameras Important	0.504	0.33	0.13	0.711	0.29	0.01	−0.074	0.42	0.86
Exit Location Important	−0.192	0.35	0.59	0.099	0.30	0.74	−0.531	0.41	0.19
Police Proximity Important	0.290	0.32	0.36	−0.068	0.27	0.80	0.555	0.39	0.16
Road Proximity Important	0.109	0.34	0.75	−0.076	0.30	0.80	0.304	0.42	0.47
Customer Volume Important	0.717	0.28	0.01	−0.131	0.23	0.57	0.205	0.32	0.52
Similar Robbery Experience	0.671	0.29	0.02	0.120	0.23	0.61	0.550	0.35	0.12
Normal Activity Prior	0.611	0.35	0.08	—	—	—	—	—	—
Alternate Target Available	−0.148	0.30	0.62	—	—	—	—	—	—
Average Annual Pay 1991–1995	−0.000	0.00	0.96	—	—	—	—	—	—
Offender Nonwhite	−0.426	0.30	0.15	−0.487	0.24	0.04	0.529	0.31	0.09
Likelihood ratio chi-square (H_0: $\beta = 0$)	33.21		0.00	23.89		0.01	35.82		0.00
Number of observations		130			147			147	

Note: SE = Standard Error.

presence of such a motive, calculated by capturing the change in the cumulative normal probability as described by Greene (2008). Elsewhere, this model suggests that offenders who had experience robbing similar stores allocated significantly more time to planning than their less experienced counterparts, the probability increasing by 0.216 given such experience; this pattern is consistent with the hypothesized positive relationship between criminal human capital and planning time. We also see mild evidence that offenders involved in normal activity prior to the robbery planned longer ($p = 0.08$), as did offenders who regarded the volume of present customers as particularly important. Somewhat contrary to expectations, those who expressed minimal precrime worry of the likelihood of apprehension exhibited shorter plans ($p = 0.08$). The multivariate probit specification will reveal whether these various patterns hold when we account for the simultaneity of the planning choices.

Very few variables emerge as significant determinants of the use of an accomplice in the naive probit model. However, the negative, statistically significant coefficient on Average Sentence 1995 does support the hypothesis that a stronger robbery sanction would discourage accomplice use. The coefficient estimate of −0.169 translates to a 0.067 reduction in the probability of using an accomplice. Results also suggest that offenders who regarded the presence of video surveillance cameras as particularly important (in committing robberies) were more likely to use an accomplice. The probability of accomplice use increases by about 0.267 given this assessment. (The NIJ data set also contains information on the actual number of accomplices used, which in the sample ranged from 0 to 3 with a mean of 0.833. Analysis of the determinants of the number of accomplices using ordinary least squares, Poisson regression, and negative binomial regression yielded qualitatively similar results to the dichotomous probit model of accomplice use.)

The weapon-use probit equation suggests no significant relationship with the use of an accomplice. But the positive, significant coefficient on No Chance of Apprehension in that equation is consistent with the hypothesis that a greater likelihood of apprehension would discourage weapon use in robberies, other things being equal. The positive, significant coefficient for 30-Day Firearm Limit (translating to a 0.134 increase in the probability of weapon use) likely reflects the fact that offenders more likely used weapons in states that had responded to firearms crimes (and possibly other circumstances) by instituting such a limit. In each of the univariate probit models, Offender Nonwhite emerges as reasonably statistically significant; we see this most strongly in the accomplice-use model, which suggests a 0.189 reduction in the probability of accomplice use among nonwhite offenders. Taken collectively, the respective signs in the three models suggest that nonwhite offenders tended to act more impulsively (i.e., use a relatively short planning time), act alone, and use a weapon—consistent with the earlier profile suggested particularly for offenders in Maryland, based on sample means. The multivariate probit model will allow us to see whether this demographic pattern persists when we account for simultaneity and, more importantly, will allow more statistically sound tests of the central hypotheses.

B. Multivariate Probit Results

Table 2.2 displays results from the simultaneous multivariate probit analysis of the three criminal-planning choices. Overall, the model reveals several relationships consistent with the theoretical hypotheses and indeed provides statistical evidence of the essential simultaneity of these choices.

In the naive probit model of planning time, neither of the other endogenous variables emerged as compellingly significant determinants. In the multivariate probit equation for planning time, Accomplice Used emerges as positive and statistically significant, consistent with the hypothesized positive relationship between the use of an accomplice and the allocation of time to criminal planning. In the context of the theoretical model, this result gives an indirect indication that the offenders under analysis essentially regarded the time allocation of accomplices as complementary to their own planning actions in the production of these robberies. Weapon Used retains its positive coefficient with improved significance from the initial model ($p = 0.12$ from $p = 0.15$), providing mild support for the hypothesis that the use of a weapon lengthens the planning time as well.

The hypothesized positive estimate for Robbed for Money & Drugs emerges as positive and significant, as in the naive model, suggesting

TABLE 2.2   *Multivariate Probit Analysis of Planning Time, Accomplice Use, and Weapon Use*

	Planning Time			Accomplice Used			Weapon Used		
	$\hat{\beta}$	SE	p	$\hat{\beta}$	SE	p	$\hat{\beta}$	SE	p
Intercept	−2.254	1.36	0.10	1.467	0.60	0.02	−0.747	1.65	0.65
Accomplice Used	1.311	0.44	0.00	—	—	—	1.167	0.82	0.15
Weapon Used	1.028	0.67	0.12	—	—	—	—	—	—
Robbed for Money & Drugs	0.672	0.29	0.02	−0.194	0.26	0.46	−0.520	0.42	0.22
Average Sentence 1995	−0.144	0.12	0.21	−0.156	0.07	0.03	0.010	0.23	0.97
Lesser Accomplice Sentence	—	—	—	−0.227	0.24	0.34	—	—	—
Firearm Waiting Period	—	—	—	—	—	—	0.532	0.69	0.44
30-Day Firearm Limit	—	—	—	—	—	—	1.953	0.60	0.00
No Chance of Apprehension	−0.414	0.30	0.16	−0.182	0.25	0.48	0.819	0.40	0.04
Video Cameras Important	0.185	0.32	0.56	0.539	0.30	0.07	0.152	0.60	0.80
Exit Location Important	−0.225	0.33	0.49	0.241	0.34	0.48	−0.895	0.50	0.07
Police Proximity Important	0.163	0.30	0.58	0.145	0.29	0.61	0.211	0.48	0.66
Road Proximity Important	0.138	0.31	0.66	−0.050	0.33	0.88	0.857	0.53	0.10
Customer Volume Important	0.646	0.27	0.02	−0.111	0.24	0.64	0.012	0.39	0.97
Similar Robbery Experience	0.480	0.27	0.08	0.148	0.25	0.56	0.134	0.40	0.74
Normal Activity Prior	0.452	0.31	0.14	—	—	—	—	—	—
Alternate Target Available	−0.175	0.25	0.48	—	—	—	—	—	—
Average Annual Pay 1991–1995	−0.000	0.00	0.66	—	—	—	—	—	—
Offender Nonwhite	−0.216	0.27	0.43	−0.304	0.25	0.23	0.054	0.43	0.90
ρ_{12}				−0.760 ($p = 0.00$)					
ρ_{13}				−0.245 ($p = 0.57$)					
ρ_{23}				−0.090 ($p = 0.84$)					
Chi-square (H_0: $\rho_{12} = \rho_{13} = \rho_{23}$)				8.220 ($p = 0.04$)					
Wald chi-square (H_0: $\boldsymbol{\beta} = 0$)				103.99 ($p = 0.00$)					
Number of observations				130					

Note: SE = Standard Error.

again that greater monetary "stakes" motivated a more calculated plan, other things being equal. To investigate the loot effect further, I estimated additional probit models that incorporated a variable called Average Sales per Store 1997 as an alternative measure of loot availability. This variable captures the actual dollar volume of sales earned in convenience stores in 1997 divided by the total number of stores in a given focus state. The raw data come from the North American Industry Classification System (NAICS), updated every four years by the U.S. Census Bureau. The year 1997 was the closest year to the time period covered by the NIJ convenience store robbery data in which convenience store sales data were available. Results of these models indicate that a greater volume of sales significantly encouraged a lengthier planning time but had no significant effect on accomplice use or weapon use. This pattern mirrors that of the NIJ variable Robbed for Money & Drugs and provides further evidence of the positive relationship between loot and planning.

Elsewhere, the positive, significant coefficient for Similar Robbery Experience ($p = 0.08$) again provides evidence, albeit milder than before, that more valuable criminal human capital encourages a lengthier planning time, as hypothesized. Whereas a perceived minimal likelihood of apprehension initially appeared mildly significant as a determinant of a lengthier planning time, this variable and most other previously significant variables lose significance in the multivariate setting. However, Customer Volume Important remains positive and significant, suggesting that a relatively larger presence of customers makes these offenders take longer to plan these crimes.

In the accomplice-use equation, the significance level of Video Cameras Important declines from $p = 0.01$ to $p = 0.07$ from the naive to the multivariate model. However, in general, the essential significance of this variable may suggest that offenders who recruited accomplices did so in part to diversify the relatively greater risk of apprehension presumably associated with the presence of surveillance cameras at their targeted stores. Elsewhere in this equation, the hypothesized negative coefficient for Average Sentence 1995 remains statistically significant, consistent with the hypothesis that a more severe robbery sanction would discourage the use of accomplices at the margin.

As in the initial models, No Chance of Apprehension and 30-Day Firearm Limit emerge as positive and significant determinants of weapon use. Indeed, only as a determinant of weapon use does No Chance of Apprehension ever emerge as significant, suggesting that the perception of a marginally greater risk of apprehension—whatever the specific source of that perception—exerted the greatest deterrent effect on the planning choice that potentially creates the greatest degree of fear and threat of physical danger in convenience store robberies. The analysis in Chapter 3 will allow us to see whether this perception translates moreover to a lesser incidence of victim injury in these robberies or indeed if any of these factors reduce injury likelihood. Unlike the naive probit models, the multivariate probit model shows no significant relationship between offender race and the outcomes of these planning choices.

Finally, the estimates of the error-covariance parameters ρ_{13} and ρ_{23} individually do not emerge as significantly different from zero, while the estimate of $\rho_{12} = -0.760$ is statistically significant. This suggests that these offenders may well have made the weapon-use choice *prior to* the planning-time and accomplice-use choices, which themselves strongly appear to have occurred simultaneously. Possibly, the offenders under analysis would not have even considered robbing a convenience store without using a weapon, which microeconomically would suggest minimal substitutability between weapons and other inputs in the robbery production function, a circumstance suggested by Zimring and Zuehl (1986). We already see evidence of fairly substantial complementarity between offender planning time and accomplice use. At the same time, the test of H_0: $\rho_{12} = \rho_{13} = \rho_{23}$ generates a statistic of 8.220, the significance of which enables rejection of this hypothesis. Together, these error-covariance estimates suggest that the essential simultaneity of the planning-time and accomplice-use choices lies at the heart of the *overall* empirical simultaneity of the three planning choices under analysis.

VI. CONCLUSION

This chapter illustrates the use of an economic model of crime to analyze the *planning* of crime, behavior that occurs logically before the commission of a crime itself. Although researchers have frequently commented on matters that speak to criminal planning—raising possibilities such as criminal "opportunism" or criminal "preparations"—these issues have gone largely undeveloped in the crime economics literature. But we can study criminal planning as a matter of concentration if we model individual criminal activity theoretically as a problem of time allocation and production; certain planning activities (accomplice use, weapon use) offer benefits and costs that impact these problems in microeconomically tractable and intuitive ways. Using econometric methodology that accounts for the simultaneity of the planning choices under analysis, we get a reasonable empirical indication that loot availability, various elements of the risk of apprehension, and criminal human capital affect the planning of crimes in ways predicted by this model.

Future researchers interested in the economics of criminal planning might examine more closely how criminal planning unfolds in the context of other activities undertaken by criminals, an avenue not explored at length here. Recall that we narrowed the focus of the conceptual discussion to the hypothetical criminal's utility-maximizing planning-time decision and essentially took his other time-allocation choices (offense time and noncriminal time) as given; we also paid no special attention to the end of the criminal event, the exit from the crime scene. These assumptions allowed a better tailoring of the model to the ensuing empirical analysis and the associated NIJ data set, which contains minimal information about the offenders' activities outside the planning and commission of the commercial robberies in question. But we might learn more by examining how criminal planning influences time allocated to these other activities, and this altered emphasis might yield interesting hypotheses testable with a data set containing more information about the broader lives of criminal offenders. A sufficiently broad-based data set might also facilitate a direct examination of whether greater costs of planning truly deter crime, a question obviously unaddressable with a sample of offenders.

While we cannot address deterrence in this context (we do so in other ways in later chapters), we can address how the criminal-planning behaviors analyzed in this chapter influence some of the *consequences* of crime, as these offenders exhibit variation not only in their robbery planning activities but also in the outcomes of their crimes. In Chapter 3, we address two particular types of criminal consequences: physical violence and monetary losses. In so doing, we build on our analysis of planning from this chapter and allow the totality of the results from both chapters to speak to distinctly practical concerns.

Violence and Damages

Violence is good for those who have nothing to lose.

—JEAN-PAUL SARTRE

I. INTRODUCTION

No matter how extensively criminals plan their crimes, those crimes fundamentally impose hardships on individual victims and society in general. Perhaps the most dramatic consequences of crime take the form of physical violence resulting in injury and emotional trauma, but crime also can affect day-to-day outcomes like victims' work patterns, a connection we explore as a matter of concentration in Chapter 10. Now, one might speculate that a criminal's planning behavior, as studied in Chapter 2, could actually help the criminal reduce the need for resorting to physical violence during the commission of a crime, which in turn might reduce the likelihood of victim injury. Criminal planning activity, combined with fixed factors related to the environmental setting of the crime or the specific target of the crime, might also help an offender engaged in a property crime come away with more stolen property. But the connection between criminal planning and the consequences of crime becomes less definitive once we recognize that crime victims themselves—particularly through the act of resistance—can also influence the productivity of criminals and the incidence of injury. This realization presents a new question of how the actions of criminals before and during their crimes affect the consequences of those crimes. In this chapter we build on the theoretical and empirical analysis presented in Chapter 2, aided by insights from previous research, to examine two such consequences: physical violence and monetary damages.

As intimated in Chapter 2, probing the determinants of criminal violence and damages as an extension of the analysis presented in that chapter offers both conceptual and practical benefits. Having established a basic economic model that helps us think about how criminals make planning choices leading up to a crime, we can turn our attention to the hypothetical criminal's essential goal: the acquisition of utility from the commission of the crime. This "bounty" from a crime takes different forms across different crime types, but in the context of robbery—the empirical environment in which we study criminal planning and consequences in these first two analytical chapters—it takes the form of some quantifiable amount of stolen money or property. Recall that the offender's criminal productivity—shaped by the offender's personal criminal human capital, aided by the use of the criminal inputs discussed in Chapter 2, but also potentially sensitive to interference by victims who offer resistance—assists the offender in extracting some proportion of an available amount of loot, its magnitude primarily determined by environmental factors out of the offender's immediate control. In this chapter we will use these essential elements of the model, as well as refinements motivated by lessons learned in Chapter 2, to study analytically connections between criminal actions, the extraction of loot, and the incidence of victim injury as an artifact of property crime.

As it happens, commercial robbery lends itself well to the economic analysis of this process and represents a significant form of robbery as classified by the FBI in its annual Uniform Crime Reports. As documented in the 2008 report, the most recently available, commercial robbery (including convenience store robberies, gas and service stations, and other places of business) accounted for 24% of all robberies, compared to 16% for residential robbery (see FBI 2008). Although the FBI officially classifies robbery as a violent crime, the crime has elements of both pure violent crimes like assault and pure property crimes like larceny, a fact recognized and exploited by many researchers. Because robbery, by definition, involves the illegal taking of *property* by *force* (or threat of force), it inherently involves the presence of some monetary bounty *and* the potential for physical violence and injury. Indeed, as Zimring and Zuehl (1986) pointed out in their pioneering study of robbery and its consequences, robbery violence tends to be more severe than violence associated with the comparable crimes of theft and burglary, undoubtedly due to the presence in robberies of a human victim who may stand between the offender and the loot and may even fight to protect it. From a more practical perspective, theoretical and empirical analysis of the determinants of violence and damages in crime gives us, as researchers, the opportunity to clarify circumstances that either eliminate or at least reduce the consequences of injuries to victims that may occur as part of commercial robberies.

With this in mind, we will study these issues in the context of commercial robberies as was done in Chapter 2. We begin with a conceptual analysis of the consequences of crime, robbery in particular, by applying aspects of the criminal planning model; this helps us frame the essential logic of criminal violence and damages and suggests testable hypotheses. We then move on to modeling outcomes relating to victim injury and monetary damages using probit analysis and the NIJ data set introduced in Chapter 2.

II. CONCEPTUAL FOUNDATION

To consider the various postcrime outcomes that could occur as a consequence of robbery, we can modify components of the criminal-planning model developed in Chapter 2, focusing in particular on the amount of effective loot potentially stolen by a hypothetical offender and on the possible connection to victim injury incidence.

As developed earlier, an offender has an opportunity to rob some portion g of a fixed quantity of loot G, the percentage g capturing the offender's criminal production function and G assumed unalterable by the offender's actions. We can think of the potential amount stolen as $\$gG$; in the phrasing of Ihlanfeldt (2003), this becomes the offender's "expected bounty" from the crime. In the initial formulation of the model in Chapter 2, we cast g as a function of the criminal inputs planning time (t_p), accomplice use (n), and weapon use (k), and we adjusted it by the accomplice-share factor $(n+1)$. Consider two refinements now. First, in light of the empirical results observed in Chapter 2, suppose we cast t_p itself as a positive function of n and k in recognition of the empirical evidence that accomplice use and weapon use appear to lengthen criminal planning time. Second, suppose we introduce a victim resistance factor, denoted r, that potentially imposes a cost for the offender in the form of a criminal productivity loss. Specifically, let $r = r(n, k)$ and stipulate a range such that $r \in [0, g]$, thus allowing for the complete absence of victim resistance in one extreme, resistance that completely nullifies the offender's production g in another extreme, or resistance between these extremes. Given these refinements, and incorporating full functional notation, we can rewrite effective loot, the potential amount stolen, as $E(G) = \{[g[t_p(n, k), n, k] - r(n, k)]/(n+1)\}G$. To the extent that robbery victims, including the employees of commercial targets, value the prevention of personal injury and even the prevention of property loss, resistance may become a viable option when encountering an offender. Kleck and Gertz (1995) and Tark and Kleck (2004) provide useful criminological discussions of the connection between property loss and victim resistance, and we will examine the victim resistance decision in greater detail in Chapter 8.

The refined expression for effective loot allows us to study (1) how variation in the criminal inputs affects the potential amount stolen, while recognizing the possibility of victim resistance, and (2) how various scenarios involving the use or nonuse of accomplices and weapons carry different implications for the possible incidence of victim injury as an artifact of the crime. The conceptual analysis also helps us frame the ensuing empirical analysis of victim injury incidence and the amount actually stolen in robberies.

Variation in the use of accomplices (n), weaponry (k), and planning time itself (t_p) alters the effective loot availability according to the derivatives $\partial E(G)/\partial n = \{[(\partial g/\partial t_p)(\partial t_p/\partial n) + \partial g/\partial n - \partial r/\partial n]/(n+1)^2\}G$, $\partial E(G)/\partial k = \{[(\partial g/\partial t_p)(\partial t_p/\partial k) + \partial g/\partial k - \partial r/\partial k]/(n+1)\}G$, and $\partial E(G)/\partial t_p = [(\partial g/\partial t_p)/(n+1)]G$, respectively. Within the first two of these marginal effects, $\partial t_p/\partial n$ and $\partial t_p/\partial k$, respectively, capture how accomplice use and weapon use influence criminal planning time. With reasonable statistical confidence, empirical results from Chapter 2 suggest that $\partial t_p/\partial n > 0$ and $\partial t_p/\partial k > 0$, illustrating avenues by which accomplice and weapon use contribute positively to the marginal productivity of those inputs in the commission of the crime. Given positive derivatives of g (reflecting positive marginal products of the criminal inputs), one would conclude that, in the absence of victim resistance, the use of these inputs potentially aids the offender's ability to extract loot in this crime. After all, the absence of resistance renders $\partial r/\partial n = \partial r/\partial k = 0$, making each of these marginal effects unambiguously positive. But the possibility of victim resistance complicates this conclusion and introduces an analytical connection to victim injury.

The complication lies in the fact that the offender does not know the extent to which his criminal actions—his employment of the various criminal inputs of interest in this model—will either encourage or discourage victim resistance where relevant. More formally, the offender does not know the signs of the derivatives $\partial r/\partial n$ and $\partial r/\partial k$. (Actually, the offender may not even know exactly how he himself will react to any resistance, a consideration underlying the analysis of Cook [1986] and that presented in Chapter 8. If one models criminal actions and victim resistance more fully as an information problem, one could interpret the offender's use of a weapon as a means of signaling what may be his true criminal type [e.g., willing to inflict injury] to victims otherwise uncertain of that type and thus unsure about whether to resist; the degree of violence contained in the resulting equilibrium outcome would then depend in part on the credibility of the offender's threat signal.)

To put this in perspective, realize that the offender's information gap becomes less relevant in the context of the robbery of a home or business the offender knows to be unoccupied (i.e., a burglary), because the offender would know that active victim resistance could not occur. Other, more passive forms of self-protection, such as alarms, may exist, but these do not carry the risk of victim injury. Where human victims do exist, the presence of accomplices and weapons in practice may plausibly encourage or discourage resistance. If resistance occurs ($\partial r/\partial n > 0$, $\partial r/\partial k > 0$, or both), the offender's productivity g declines by the factor r, possibly reducing the amount of loot the offender can effectively steal. As Kleck and DeLone (1993) observe, resistance can delay the offender's actions, physically injure the offender, or in some other way increase the costs of committing the crime. Given an empirical sample of robbery offenders, this possibility may make the estimated impact of accomplice use or weapon use on the amount actually stolen statistically milder, if not insignificant, because some of these offenders would likely encounter resistance.

By contrast to the role of criminal inputs in the extraction of loot, the use of accomplices and weapons has clearer implications for the incidence of victim injuries as an artifact of the crime. Consider four possible scenarios involving the use of a weapon and an accomplice in the context of a robbery. In Scenario 1, the offender uses a weapon and an accomplice $(k > 0, n > 0)$. As such, the offender exhibits presumably the greatest threat of victim injury and property loss by virtue of the presence of the weapon and at least one other offender who can act as an "enforcer" or as a monitor of any resistance or law enforcement. As we shall see in Chapter 8, real victims do appear less likely to resist multiple offenders. In Scenario 2, the offender uses a weapon but not an accomplice $(k > 0, n = 0)$. In this scenario, the weapon presents a threat of injury, but the offender does not have the benefit of an enforcer or secondary lookout. At the margin, given the absence of an accomplice, the model suggests that the offender would exhibit less criminal productivity to some degree relative to Scenario 1. Does the presence of an accomplice indeed aid the amount actually stolen? Does an accomplice's presence discourage resistance and the incidence of victim injury, or does that presence escalate the level of violence, as discovered by Zimring and Zuehl (1986)? These become key empirical questions here. In Scenario 3 the offender uses no weapon but does use an accomplice $(k = 0, n > 0)$. The implied *group* of offenders may rely in part on strength in numbers to compensate for the absence of a weapon. Finally, in Scenario 4, the primary offender uses neither a weapon nor an accomplice.

Among the four scenarios, the offender would seem the most vulnerable to resistance in Scenario 4, so much so that we might only rarely observe this combination of circumstances in equilibrium. Recall Zimring and Zuehl's (1986) very sensible comment about the indispensability of handguns in robbery. Because the offender uses none of the inputs in this scenario, one would predict the least amount of criminal productivity among the four outlined here. But to the extent that the absence of offender weapons, accomplices, or both encourages resistance at the margin, and resistance invites victim injury, we might in practice ironically observe a greater incidence of injury in the absence of these circumstances, as suggested in economic and criminological research by Cook (1986), D'Alessio and Stolzenberg (1990), and Kleck and DeLone (1993).

III. DATA AND EMPIRICAL METHODOLOGY

Empirically, what then influences the incidence of victim injury and the amount of money actually stolen in commercial robberies? To address this question here, I use the NIJ data on convenience store robberies introduced in Chapter 2. Whereas previously we focused on the circumstances that influenced the planning of crimes, robberies providing the empirical setting, in this chapter we focus on two dependent variables that speak to violence and damages as artifacts of robbery. The dependent variable Injuries Occurred equals 1 if a victim sustained an injury as a consequence of the robbery and 0 otherwise. Familiar binomial probit analysis will allow estimation of determinants of the victim injury outcome. The dependent variable Amount Stolen captures the amount of monetary loot the offenders under analysis stole. However, limitations with the NIJ data set necessitate measuring Amount Stolen as a set of five ordinal, categorical outcomes rather than as actual monetary amounts. Specifically, the variable accounts for stolen amounts ranging from $0 to $60, $61 to $100, $101 to $200, $201 to $800, and over $800, as coded in the NIJ data. In their study of burglary outcomes, Goldberg and Nold (1980) modeled a similar, six-category loot variable using multinomial logit analysis, a methodology that accounts for the categorical nature of the dependent variable but not its ordinality. I will estimate multinomial logit models to study various unordered categorical crime victimization outcomes in Chapters 7, 8, and 9, but in this chapter I will use ordered probit models, which retain the ordinality of the Amount Stolen variable. The probit models estimated for this study will incorporate regressors as seen in Chapter 2 in the analysis of the offender's planning outcomes.

One does not frequently encounter ordered probit models in the crime economics literature because empirical studies seldom feature ordered, categorical dependent variables. Where categorical variables exist, they typically have a binary, unordered form, such as indicating the commission or noncommission of crime, the presence or absence of recidivism, conviction versus acquittal, or a distinct economic choice made by a criminal, victim, or other agent. However, one might well encounter such variables in archival data that have limitations of the type encountered here. A data set might indicate categories of punitive sentences, each category more severe than another by implication, rather than the number of years sentenced, or it might feature Likert-type variables ascertaining the extent of an offender's or a victim's opinion on a key issue rather than a numeric measure—to cite two additional examples.

As pioneered by Zavoina and McKelvey (1975) and discussed extensively by Greene (2008), ordered probit estimation falls into a wider class of ordered-response econometric models that includes ordered logit. As with most limited-dependent-variable models, ordered probit starts with an assumption that we can characterize as the latent dependent variable Y_i according to the familiar regression relationship $Y_i = X_i \beta + \varepsilon$. In the present context Y_i would represent the actual dollar amount of loot stolen by the ith offender. But instead of observing Y_i completely as a continuous dependent variable, we observe it only as a set of dependent variable categories such that $y_i = 0$ if $Y_i \leq 0$, $y_i = 1$ if $0 < Y_i \leq \kappa_1$, $y_i = 2$ if $\kappa_1 < Y_i \leq \kappa_2$, and so on for J total categories and where the cut-points κ_1 through κ_{J-1} are parameters to be estimated. If we assume a normal distribution for the error term ε, then we have the probabilities $\Pr(y_i = 0 | X_i) = \Phi(-X_i \beta)$, $\Pr(y_i = 1 | X_i) = \Phi(\kappa_1 - X_i \beta) - \Phi(-X_i \beta)$, $\Pr(y_i = 2 | X_i) = \Phi(\kappa_2 - X_i \beta) - \Phi(\kappa_1 - X_i \beta)$, and so forth for our five Amount Stolen categories. One then maximizes the implied likelihood function to obtain estimates of β; Maddala (1983) provides detail on this optimization process. Assuming the logistic distribution for ε yields the comparable ordered logit model, which Greene (2008) notes tends to produce similar results as ordered probit.

In the primary sample used for the binomial and ordered probit models in this chapter, not surprisingly robbery Scenario 1 (weapon and accomplice use) and Scenario 2 (weapon use but not accomplice use) occur most frequently, accounting for 63 and 44 of the 124 total usable cases, respectively. Only seven of the sample cases reflect Scenario 3 (accomplice use without weapon use), and only ten reflect Scenario 4 (neither weapon use nor accomplice use). Overall, then, the present sample exhibits an accomplice-use rate just over 50%, very comparable to rates observed in data used by Zimring and Zuehl (1986) and van Koppen and Jansen (1998).

In a simple univariate statistical setting, the incidence of victim injury varies demonstrably across the four scenarios. A victim injury occurred in 17.5% of the Scenario 1 cases but in only 9.1% of the Scenario 2 cases, a statistically significant difference suggesting that the presence of accomplices created a serious danger of injury in the present sample. But accomplice use shows much less impact on the amount of loot stolen. For the sample of 113 cases that have usable Amount Stolen data, crimes reflecting Scenario 1 exhibit a mean Amount Stolen of 3.05, while those reflecting Scenario 2 exhibit a mean of 2.98; not surprisingly, these means, which reflect the monetary range $101 to $200, do not differ significantly. These preliminary observations suggest that the presence of accomplices may have had a more dramatic effect on victim injury outcomes than on the amount of money stolen in the commercial robberies under analysis, a possibility suggested by the conceptual model refined from Chapter 2.

The probit analysis will allow us to see whether either accomplice use or weapon use significantly affects the injury and amount stolen outcomes when we account for other variables that might influence violence and damages in these robberies.

IV. EMPIRICAL RESULTS

A. Determinants of Amount Stolen

Consider results pertaining to the Amount Stolen ordered-probit model, displayed in Table 3.1. The model first indicates that offenders with experience robbing similar stores managed to steal significantly more loot than less experienced offenders. Recall that the experience variable captures criminal human capital. One might reasonably wonder whether experience alone facilitates this more productive robbery or whether more experienced offenders exhibit longer planning periods, which then facilitate more bountiful robberies. After all, we saw in Chapter 2 that those with similar robbery experience did exhibit significantly longer planning times—a result that emerged in the context of univariate and multivariate probit analysis, in support of the theoretical model.

	Amount Stolen			Injuries Occurred		
	Coefficient	SE	p	Coefficient	SE	p
Intercept	—	—	—	—	—	—
Planning Time	−0.245	0.248	0.32	−0.344	0.500	0.49
Accomplice Used	0.071	0.220	0.75	0.701	0.388	0.07
Weapon Used	0.037	0.318	0.91	−0.766	0.545	0.16
Robbed for Money & Drugs	−0.0001	0.238	0.99	−0.401	0.476	0.00
Average Sentence 1995	0.120	0.082	0.15	−0.372	0.196	0.06
Lesser Accomplice Sentence	−0.482	0.254	0.06	−0.032	0.477	0.95
30-Day Firearm Limit	—	—	—	3.431	0.559	0.00
No Chance of Apprehension	0.465	0.227	0.04	−0.139	0.440	0.75
Video Cameras Important	0.493	0.267	0.07	0.235	0.487	0.63
Exit Location Important	0.072	0.270	0.79	−0.388	0.486	0.43
Police Proximity Important	−0.200	0.254	0.43	0.107	0.435	0.81
Road Proximity Important	0.625	0.267	0.02	0.628	0.528	0.23
Customer Volume Important	−0.154	0.217	0.48	−1.356	0.485	0.01
Similar Robbery Experience	0.489	0.221	0.03	4.394	0.436	0.00
Normal Activity Prior	0.200	0.273	0.46	−0.814	0.563	0.15
Alternate Target Available	−0.117	0.236	0.62	−0.157	0.414	0.70
Average Annual Pay 1991–1995	−0.0001	0.000	0.11	0.0004	0.000	0.00
Offender Nonwhite	−0.238	0.223	0.29	0.332	0.429	0.14
Cutpoint 1	−1.948	1.260	—	—	—	—
Cutpoint 2	−1.115	1.261	—	—	—	—
Cutpoint 3	−0.515	1.258	—	—	—	—
Cutpoint 4	0.285	1.254	—	—	—	—
Likelihood ratio chi-square (H_0: $\beta = 0$)	36.23		0.00	31.35		0.03
Number of observations	119			124		

However, when we estimate the Amount Stolen ordered-probit model incorporating an interaction between the variables Planning Time and Similar Robbery Experience, the experience variable remains positive and significant while the interaction shows no significant effect on Amount Stolen. This suggests that criminal human capital assists in the extraction of loot on its own terms, not because more experienced offenders use more calculated plans. The result resembles a finding by van Koppen and Jansen (1998) that "more professional" robbers, in their phrasing, tended to come away with significantly more loot than other robbers.

The Amount Stolen ordered-probit model also reveals that greater concern among offenders about the presence of video cameras at convenience stores significantly increases the amount of loot stolen. Given that this same concern significantly motivates the use of accomplices, as seen in Chapter 2, one might question whether this result simply reflects that stores with more loot to steal ("richer" stores, if you will) may also have a greater incentive and ability to protect themselves with cameras, implying a greater *availability* of loot at such stores. (One might raise a similar question about wealthier victims of residential robbery, concerning, for example, the presence of alarm systems or other self-protective mechanisms.) Examining this possibility more closely, we have seen in Chapter 2 that greater importance placed on the presence of video cameras significantly motivates offenders to use an accomplice, a result that holds even after we control for simultaneity. However, the current sample shows no evidence that "richer" stores elicit a significantly different opinion about the importance of video cameras. First, a *t*-test of the difference in mean 1997 state-level sales per store in the current sample reveals no significant difference along these lines. Similarly, the motivation of robbing for money or drugs, a regressor used in Chapter 2 and in this chapter to capture the presence of a specifically pecuniary motivation for the crime, does not differ significantly between those who viewed cameras as particularly important and those who did not. Unfortunately, the data set that surveyed offenders contains no information on the actual presence or absence of video surveillance at a given targeted store. But neither the average available loot in comparable stores in the relevant state nor the pecuniary motivation appears sensitive to the offender's perception of the importance of video cameras. Possibly, offenders who expressed greater concern about video cameras simply executed their crimes more carefully and more effectively, resulting in a greater extraction of loot.

Results from the Amount Stolen model also indicate that a greater concern among offenders about the proximity of roads significantly increases the amount of loot stolen, as does an offender belief that there existed "no chance" of apprehension. The empirical analysis in Chapter 2 revealed evidence that greater concern about the proximity of roads significantly encouraged weapon use among the offenders under analysis. One might then speculate that the criminals in question used a weapon as a facilitator for escaping the crime scene in the presence of relatively unfavorable road conditions (from their perspective). Conceivably, the offenders were able to steal more loot because of roadway circumstances generally associated with greater loot availability, such as an interstate highway adjacent to a heavily trafficked commercial area. Possibly, too, offenders who regarded roadway circumstances as especially important may have had to travel nontrivial distances to the locations of their crimes. Ihlanfeldt (2003) has suggested that criminals face an inverse relationship between the net returns to crime and travel times, an idea consistent with Glaeser, Sacerdote, and Scheinkman's (1996) suspicion that the probability of offender arrest increases with the travel time necessary to commit a crime. A greater extraction of loot in association with greater importance placed on roadway circumstances, as found here, may reflect the offenders' desire to obtain a greater return to their crimes as compensation for the greater expected cost implied by these possibilities. Similarly, we have also previously observed that the No Chance of Apprehension variable significantly encourages weapon use. An offender who sincerely expresses this opinion obviously exhibits a relatively high degree of confidence, which could impact his criminal productivity, but more tangibly this opinion could make the offender less worried about the risk of detection when using a weapon, thus facilitating a more bountiful robbery.

Neither a longer planning time, nor accomplice use, nor weapon use exerted a statistically significant impact on the amount of loot stolen, not an especially surprising result in light of the univariate statistical observations. In the context of the conceptual model, this finding suggests the possibility that a nontrivial number of the robbery offenders under analysis encountered resistance by victims that may have reduced the monetary productivity of their crimes. The offender sample within the NIJ data set does not contain a variable that accounts for the extent of any resistance, but the companion sample of (unrelated) robbery victims ($n = 80$) does ascertain such information. Within this sample, 31% indicated that they engaged in some form of self-protection (sounding an alarm, firing a weapon, or retaliating physically) during the commission of at least one robbery at a store where they worked. When we study victim resistance more fully in Chapter 8, we will see more vivid evidence, from within a much larger sample of crime victims, that a significant number of victims do engage in resistance—including physical resistance that possibly creates the greatest danger of victim (if not offender) injury even as it potentially interferes with an offender's criminal productivity. If some resistance does indeed exist, then our criminal-planning model suggests that at least one of the criminal-input variables should positively impact the incidence of victim injury. We investigate this hypothesis within the probit analysis of injury incidence.

B. Determinants of Victim Injury

Exactly along the lines suggested above, perhaps the most provocative result emanating from the probit model of the incidence of injury (Table 3.1) indicates that the presence of an accomplice significantly increases the probability of a victim injury. Among the criminal-input variables, only accomplice use emerges as statistically significant in the injury-incidence model. The data set does not allow us to discern exactly what events led to any victim injuries, but it does contain information on whether the primary felon or the accomplice used a weapon when the crime involved an accomplice and a weapon. Making use of variables that account for these circumstances, extended probit models do not reveal a significant relationship between the accomplice's (as opposed to the primary felon's) use of a weapon and the incidence of injury, suggesting that *other* factors related to the presence of multiple offenders and the incidence of injury must have come to bear. Either the victims of these commercial robberies systematically offered resistance in these occasions despite the obvious danger, or the presence of multiple offenders made the primary felon, the accomplice, or both more physically aggressive in the conducting of these crimes. Economic logic and strong empirical evidence give greater credence to the latter explanation, as we shall see in Chapter 8. The latter interpretation also makes more sense in light of Cook's (1986) observation about the gratuitousness of most robbery violence.

A longer average sentence assessed to robbery offenders in various states significantly reduces the incidence of injury, other things equal. The empirical analysis in Chapter 2 revealed that longer such sentences tend to discourage the use of an accomplice. From a public-policy perspective, this combination of results suggests that stronger enforcement of robbery may assist in the reduction of the severity of robbery on at least two fronts. Stronger sanctions obviously increase the expected cost of committing crime, including robbery, which may aid in deterring this crime; future research may investigate the extent to which this has indeed occurred. At the same time, perhaps not even by design, stronger sanctions appear to discourage accomplice use, which our results reveal as a key antecedent to the incidence of robbery injury.

Finally, greater offender concern about the volume of customers significantly reduces the incidence of injury relevant to the crimes studied here. Our earlier analysis showed that this concern leads to significantly longer planning times. Such a concern may correlate with lesser injury incidence because of a greater number of potential witnesses or a greater likelihood of effective resistance (or possibly both). Recall D'Alessio and Stolzenberg's (1990) cogent point about how a greater concentration of customers can facilitate what they call "informal surveillance" of a commercial robbery target. At the same time, longer, more carefully considered plans may create more controlled crime scenes that result in less physical danger. Regardless, we may have reason to conclude that an altogether busier store helps in preventing injuries in robberies and motivates offenders to take longer before striking. Operators of convenience stores or other commercial establishments concerned about the safety of their employees and customers may have sound justification for closing relatively isolated, low-traffic stores. Short of this, they may have justification for using increased security measures at such stores or calling for an enhanced police presence at lower-traffic times at all stores.

V. CONCLUSION

These first two analytical chapters demonstrate the development and application of an economic model of crime planning and then the minor modification of that model as a way of linking planning activity to two major consequences of property crime: victim injury and monetary losses. As noted in Chapter 2, the model invites further alteration and modification by those interested in other theoretical questions or who wish to motivate a different set of empirical questions, but in the present context this framework allows us to formalize and justify hypotheses relating to the planning and consequences of crime that we can test empirically using a data set that provides useful information about these outcomes.

Empirical evidence indicates that stiffer sentences for robbery translate to a lesser likelihood of victim injury in robberies that do occur. Although we cannot speak to the cost of this greater sanctioning in this study, the result nevertheless bodes well for its practical benefits, as it appears to discourage accomplice use (a particularly significant source of violence in these robberies) even as it presumably makes robbery a costlier crime to commit. On balance, however, we see more compelling empirical evidence regarding determinants of the amount of loot stolen than of injury outcomes.

That more experienced offenders steal significantly more loot attests to the effect of their greater criminal productivity and perhaps argues for stronger sanctions for first-time robbery offenders; if this serves as a greater deterrence, as suggested within the optimal sanctioning literature, then perhaps fewer individuals would have a chance to become experienced offenders. That offenders more concerned about video surveillance steal more loot calls into question the degree to which this sort of surveillance prevents losses of property, but one should interpret this result cautiously. Overt video surveillance might still deter the crime from occurring at all, and in any case we have not really shown how the presence or absence of video surveillance affects the extent of monetary damages; future researchers might address these issues by adapting the criminal planning model further and incorporating wider-ranging data. Offenders expressing greater precrime confidence in their ability to commit the crime without apprehension came away with more loot as well, accentuating the importance of having a regular, visible police presence at particularly vulnerable targets of commercial robbery. Finally, the results give an indirect indication that victim resistance may actually reduce the amount of property loss sustained in robberies, but this appears to hold only in lone-offender crimes.

As noted at the outset of this book, the violence and other damages that occur as a consequence of crime bear directly on individual victims and on society at large. The fact that they do gives us the incentive to engage in various personal and collective behaviors that might deter crime. But while violence and damages extend outward, away from the criminal, other products of crime, like the incriminating evidence it creates, bear inward, pointing harm toward the criminal. Just as a victim may have recourse that he or she may pursue, a criminal has recourse of his own: destroy the evidence that threatens to impose that harm. But evidence destruction constitutes an illegality in its own right, and as such imposes a social harm of its own. What would make a criminal destroy evidence, then, and what might we do about it? These are questions for Chapter 4, as we move along this "life cycle" of crime and criminal behavior.

The Destruction of Evidence

One crime has to be concealed by another.

—LUCIUS ANNAEUS SENECA

I. INTRODUCTION

People who engage in illegal activity—including but not limited to the property crime we have emphasized to this point—presumably gain utility from that behavior. The classic model of Becker (1968) certainly suggests so. But criminals likely get disutility from the evidence their actions create, especially if it threatens to incriminate them. The fact that such evidence exists might then create an incentive for criminals to destroy, or *spoliate*, that evidence—but even this action constitutes an illegality that calls for a distinct sanction if detected and prosecuted. The potential for evidence destruction motivates important research questions for economists, criminologists, and legal scholars. How do criminals decide whether to destroy postcrime evidence, and what might discourage this behavior? Can deterrence of spoliation help deter crime in general? This chapter departs somewhat from the preceding chapters by addressing these issues solely from a theoretical perspective, suggesting how we might first *think* about the problem. Having addressed the behavior conceptually, we will also consider ways future researchers might study issues of evidence destruction empirically.

As with illegal activity in general, evidence destruction creates costs well beyond the risks of detection and punishment incurred by the individual who spoliates. A form of obstruction of justice, spoliation interferes with the ability of aggrieved parties to obtain legal redress in court actions, potentially undermining the deterrence of the primary crime. As Porat and Stein (1997) and Gorelick, Marzen, and Solum (2002) (henceforth: GMS 2002) discuss, the destruction of evidence implies the destruction of information and the creation of uncertainty, resulting in an indirect increase in standards of proof required of plaintiffs, the very same victims of crime that occupy our attention in these pages. This can reduce the likelihood that plaintiffs, whether individuals or the state, can recover damages for the primary crime. Spoliation also can impose costs on society at large. As Sommers and Seibert (1999) illustrate, if a malpracticing physician, for example, destroys evidence of personal negligence that caused the injury of a patient, ultimately both the patient and society in general become vulnerable to increased health-care costs. As emphasized by Solum and Marzen (1987) and Kreimer and Rudovsky (2002), evidence destruction also undermines fairness, as it prevents all parties in a legal matter from having equal access to material that would help reveal truth.

Recognizing the personal and social consequences of evidence destruction, and the emergence of new, especially electronic, forms of evidence and spoliation, many legal scholars criticize existing U.S. spoliation law and its practical application. Current law specifies primarily procedural rather than substantive sanctions: rather than fining spoliators or awarding financial damages to plaintiff-victims, courts tend to rule only that the evidence destruction constitutes a prima facie indication that the destroyed material would have damaged the spoliator's case, with court actions proceeding from there. As GMS (2002) discuss, this treatment reflects the "spoliation inference," based on the ancient legal doctrine *contra spoliatorem omnia praesumuntur*, or that "everything most to [the defendant's] disadvantage is to be presumed against the destroyer (spoliator)," as cited by the court in *White v. Office of Public Defender*, 170 F.R.D. 138 (1997). Within this doctrine, courts assume that spoliators possess "consciousness of guilt" from their actions, which allows the law to target intentional or bad-faith spoliation rather than merely accidental (negligent) spoliation. This sort of inferential judgment becomes punitive because it prevents a defendant from formally challenging that evidence in court and exposes him to a greater risk of an erroneous judgment, potentially increasing the likelihood of conviction for the primary crime. But some legal scholars question whether this approach effectively deters spoliation and thus advocate either more severe, truly substantive sanctions (often calling for a formalized spoliation *tort*) or that judges begin exercising greater discretion, from case to case, in levying sanctions for general violations of evidentiary rules, spoliation included.

Spoliation torts do exist. The earliest one in the United States appeared in California in 1984. Several other states have adopted spoliation torts since then, and Canadian legal scholars have begun to call for spoliation torts in Canada. As the tort continues to evolve, its acceptance and its application suffer from a lack of uniformity across jurisdictions, especially relating to the basis on which courts should assess damages. One can find fuller discussions of these issues in legal scholarship by Porat and Stein (1997), Eng (1999), Sommers and Seibert (1999), GMS (2002), and Sanchirico (2004). Legal scholars also suggest, often quite vociferously, that ineffectively applied *spoliation* law, tort or not, can undermine the efficiency of *substantive* law, implying that strengthening spoliation law might increase deterrence not only of evidence destruction but also of crime in general. This possibility makes criminal evidence destruction centrally relevant to our broader analysis of criminals and victims in this book.

To see what might deter evidence destruction and to demonstrate potential connections to the commission or deterrence of primary crimes, we must understand the act of evidence destruction as an economic choice. As reviewed in Chapter 1, researchers have applied and extended Becker's (1968) economic model of crime to many settings and problems, especially those involving an *individual* decision to commit an illegality. The model developed in this chapter similarly focuses on the individual decision to destroy evidence, embedding the decision within a traditional analytical approach emphasizing illegal activity as a time-allocation choice. We first consider key components of a hypothetical solo criminal's objective function relevant to the commission of a primary crime and the possible destruction of evidence. Analysis of the criminal's incentives then reveals how utility-maximizing spoliation behavior might vary in key exogenous parameters, particularly those relating to elements of substantive law (i.e., relating to the primary crime) and elements of spoliation law. Later we study a two-criminal version of the model to consider the equilibrium formation of a spoliation conspiracy and how elements of each mode of law might impact the sustainability of such an arrangement.

The results emanating from the analysis support or refine provocative points raised by economists and legal scholars who have written extensively about evidence as a concept, the logic of evidentiary rules and their reform, and the legal, social, and philosophical implications of evidence destruction. The results also suggest implications for how legal authorities might efficiently approach the prevention of spoliation. A formal economic model of evidence-destruction behavior has not previously appeared in the broader crime-economics literature, but the analysis here does accompany a related and growing literature devoted to economic analysis of individual *avoidance* of law. Key papers in this literature include Malik (1990), Innes (2001), Jost (2001), Friehe (2008), and Nussim and Tabbach (2009), who study issues of screening, self-reporting, and optimal enforcement in the context of avoidance; Gordon (1989) and Crocker and Slemrod (2005), who study tax evasion; Freeborn (2009), who studies how avoidance of drug law affects cocaine prices; and Ognedal (2005), who studies how lowering standards of proof might affect illegal activity. In studying implications of redefining what we actually mean by *evidence*, Ognedal (2005) conceptualized a hypothetical agent who "cannot manipulate or destroy evidence to make it less incriminating," but she also recognized that a criminal who engaged in such activity would incur nontrivial costs and would leave evidence of the spoliation itself. These and other issues become prominent in the model developed here. This chapter attempts to add to this literature by specifically modeling the *postcrime* act of evidence destruction for the purpose of avoiding punishment; a criminal literally may use one illegal act to try to cover up another.

II. ONE-CRIMINAL ANALYSIS

A. Definitions and Assumptions

The one-criminal variant of the model embeds a hypothetical solo criminal's evidence destruction decision into a broader time-allocation model of illegal activity structured along traditional lines. Suppose an individual allocates an amount of time t_I to the commission of illegality. The offender must devote part of this time, denoted as t_M, to the commission of the primary crime. Suppose this crime creates residual physical evidence, denoted as e. Following commission of the primary crime, the offender might devote an additional amount of time, t_E, to its destruction, so that $t_I = t_M + t_E$ would represent the total amount of time potentially allocated to these combined illegal activities. The individual may also allocate time, t_L, to the commission of legal activities, so that $t_I + t_L = T$, the total amount of time that the individual has the opportunity to allocate. Suppose legal activity offers a gain according to the function $L(t_L)$ and the primary crime offers a gain according to the function $G(t_M)$; note that legal time allocation contributes to legal gains and illegal time allocation contributes to illegal gains.

I assume that the offender can physically destroy evidence at a rate $\delta \in (0,1)$, representing his proficiency at spoliation. To illustrate, suppose at time $t = 0$, when the criminal has completed commission of the primary crime, 10 units of evidence exist, and suppose $\delta = 0.1$. Then, at $t = 1$, after completion of some spoliation, 9 units of evidence would remain. In principle, an offender who possessed greater spoliation proficiency (a higher δ) could have destroyed more of the residual evidence in the same period and could destroy more in any future period. I further assume that the residual evidence, e, does not undergo significant natural degradation over the period of time that the criminal makes the spoliation decision. This model does not allow the option of confessing, or self-reporting, such as that modeled by Innes (1999, 2001). Innes noted that certain torts may offer reduced sanctions for self-reporting that might reduce a given defendant's incentive to engage in avoidance behavior. However, in practice, neither spoliation law nor the spoliation tort appears to offer "remediation" for bad-faith (i.e., intentional) spoliation, the present focus. See GMS (2002) for further discussion.

I assume that the criminal's spoliation proficiency depends on exogenous factors that impact the criminal's ability to destroy evidence: the criminal's existing (accumulated) human capital skill, h, applicable to evidence destruction, and technology, γ_c, that reinforces the criminal's marginal ability to destroy evidence. (Spoliation technology definitely exists: a company known as Electronic Fantasy World sells a software product called Terminus, a document-destruction program touted as "the most powerful data-destruction toolkit ever built.") Given these components, we can write the spoliation proficiency function as $\delta = \delta(h, \gamma_c)$, where $\partial\delta/\partial h > 0$ and $\partial\delta/\partial\gamma_c > 0$ (greater criminal human capital and more advanced spoliation technology enhance the criminal's proficiency at spoliation). The product $\delta t_E e$—incorporating the criminal's spoliation proficiency, spoliation time allocation, and the amount of evidence that actually exists—thus represents the amount of evidence destroyed. As evidence destruction constitutes an illegality in itself, it leaves its own evidence, known in legal terms as *spoliation evidence* and denoted here as n. Spoliation thus alters the evidence of the primary crime so that $e - \delta t_E e + n$ remains, where $n = n(t_E)$ and of course more time spent spoliating creates more spoliation evidence ($\partial n/\partial t_E > 0$). In practice, legal authorities establish the incidence of evidence destruction through direct or circumstantial spoliation evidence, such as proof that the material existed, that it no longer exists, or that it ordinarily would have existed. See Solum and Marzen (1987).

Suppose law-enforcement authorities will apprehend the offender who commits the primary crime with probability p_1, so that the individual can commit that offense uncaptured with probability $1 - p_1$. This apprehension probability depends directly on the offender's commission of the primary crime, spoliation itself, the magnitude of the postcrime evidence, and the level of investigative activity, v, undertaken by authorities. We can then write this probability functionally as $p_1 = p_1(t_I(t_E), \max[e(t_E), \Delta e], v; \gamma_p)$, where γ_p represents factors exogenous to the criminal that enhance investigative efficiency, that is, the marginal productivity of investigators in apprehending criminals. Without spoliation, the undisturbed evidence e contributes to the threat of apprehension; if spoliation occurs, the remaining postspoliation evidence (the amount $\Delta e = e - \delta t_E e + n$) threatens apprehension.

Spoliation affects the probability of primary-crime detection according to the derivative $\partial p_1/\partial t_E = (\partial p_1/\partial t_I)(\partial t_I/\partial t_E) + (\partial p_1/\partial\Delta e)(\partial\Delta e/\partial t_E)$, which importantly has an ambiguous sign. Within this expression, the component $\partial p_1/\partial t_I > 0$ indicates that engaging in the illegal activity as a whole creates a risk of getting caught having committed the primary crime. The component $\partial t_I/\partial t_E > 0$ indicates that time allocated to evidence destruction logically increases the time spent engaging in the illegality overall. The effect $\partial p_1/\partial\Delta e > 0$ indicates that authorities will more likely detect an

offense that has left more residual evidence. But because the act of spoliation destroys evidence (of the primary crime) and creates new evidence
(spoliation evidence), the effect $\partial\Delta e/\partial t_E$ ultimately may take on any sign,
leaving the entire effect $\partial p_1/\partial t_E$ ambiguous in sign. Specifically, because
$\Delta e = e - \delta t_E e + n(t_E)$, $\partial\Delta e/\partial t_E = -\delta e + \partial n/\partial t_E$; clearly $\partial\Delta e/\partial t_E > 0$ if $\partial n/\partial t_E > \delta e$
(the criminal creates more evidence anew than he or she destroys) and
$\partial\Delta e/\partial t_E < 0$ if $\delta e > \partial n/\partial t_E$ (the criminal destroys more evidence than he or
she creates).

The possibility that spoliation activity will increase p_1 helps explain
why a criminal might find evidence destruction less than appealing. As
Porat and Stein (1997) note, *evidence*, as a formal legal concept, necessarily involves human *inferences* about some potentially probative material.
When spoliation backfires, criminals leave themselves open to an increased
risk of judicial or prosecutorial error in interpreting or inferring from such
material; see GMS (2002) or Risinger et al. (2002) for additional discussion.
The possibility that destroying evidence will decrease p_1, or that spoliation
works, of course helps explain the appeal of spoliation. Observe also that
because $t_I = t_M + t_E$, one could alternatively write $p = p(t_M + t_E, \max[e(t_E),$
$\Delta e], v; \gamma_p)$, allowing one to establish that $\partial p/\partial t_M > 0$: more time allocated to
the commission of the primary crime also increases the risk of its detection,
consistent with a classical assumption.

From a legal perspective, the ambiguity of the relationship between
spoliation and the probability of primary-crime detection reflects the fact
that spoliation creates multiple and conflicting forms of uncertainty—
destructions of information—that at once threaten and benefit the criminal. As discussed by Solum and Marzen (1987) and Porat and Stein (1997),
spoliation creates uncertainty as to *probative value* of some material (the
extent to which it has informational value, or relevance, in a legal matter) and uncertainty as to *inferential vector* (the direction to which the
evidence points). Here I assume that the evidence has probative value to
the potential detriment of the criminal and that the criminal determines
this without undue error. (One could extend the model by formally incorporating the criminal's potential inability to judge the relevance of any residual evidence, thus allowing for the intriguing possibility that criminals
overlook incriminating evidence and destroy harmless evidence.) Thus,

in the present model a spoliating criminal creates uncertainty as to inferential vector, taking an action that calls into question the extent to which one can infer his culpability for the primary crime.

As observed by Solum and Marzen (1987), uncertainty of this type may take the form of "risk" or "ignorance." Evidence destruction creates uncertainty-as-*risk* to the extent that it undermines the accuracy of known evidence. For example, prior to spoliation, an article of evidence may carry 95 percent accuracy in determining the culpability of the criminal; after spoliation, it may carry only 50 percent accuracy in this determination. Evidence destruction creates uncertainty-as-*ignorance* when, after spoliation, there exists *no basis* for assigning any probability to the accuracy of an article of evidence, possibly because officials never know of the material's existence. If we view spoliation as a form of strategic avoidance behavior—which may plausibly be unobserved, as noted by Malik (1990) and Innes (2001)—unobserved spoliation would reflect the creation of uncertainty-as-ignorance. When spoliation reduces p_1, the criminal essentially engages in behavior that creates more uncertainty-as-ignorance (henceforth: *ignorance*) that at the margin benefits him than uncertainty-as-risk (henceforth: *risk*) that threatens him.

Investigative efficiency affects p_1 conditionally as well. I assume that if spoliation increases this probability, then an exogenous enhancement of investigative efficiency, such as an advancement in technology that aids police, will reinforce this marginal increase in risk. Formally, this implies that $\partial^2 p_1/\partial t_E \partial \gamma_p > 0$ if $\partial p_1/\partial t_E > 0$. I assume that if spoliation reduces the probability of primary-crime detection, greater investigative efficiency *lessens* that probability reduction. That is, $\partial^2 p_1/\partial t_E \partial \gamma_p < 0$ if $\partial p_1/\partial t_E < 0$. By contrast, unambiguously $\partial p_1/\partial v > 0$ (more investigative activity enhances the probability of apprehension), and so $\partial^2 p_1/\partial v \partial \gamma_p > 0$ unambiguously, indicating that greater investigative efficiency reinforces the positive impact of investigative activity on the probability of detection.

If authorities apprehend the criminal for commission of the primary crime, the criminal faces a sanction for that crime if subsequently convicted. Express the sanction (utility cost) as $F = F(t_M \, ; \, \varphi)$, such that time allocated to the commission of the primary crime maps directly into the sanction (i.e., $\partial F/\partial t_M > 0$). In the event of primary-crime detection and conviction, the criminal, consistent with a fine or incarceration, faces the sanction F in the form of a loss of a future stream of income, discounted at rate r and represented by $A(t) = \int_{T_c}^{T_r} a(t)/(1+r)dt$. In this expression, $a(t)$ represents time-dependent earnings that the criminal could earn from future illegal or legal activity during a period of incarceration that begins at the point of conviction (T_c) and ends at the point of release (T_r). (If the sanction takes the form of a fine, then essentially the convicted criminal incurs a one-period rather than a multiperiod loss of income.) The parameter $\varphi > 0$ represents an exogenous factor through which this sanction might become stiffer, so that $\partial^2 F/\partial t_M \partial \varphi > 0$. This parameter essentially captures the state of the law governing the primary crime in question, presumably alterable only as a matter of public policy. Because a higher φ reinforces the positive marginal impact of the primary crime on the sanction, φ essentially captures the *severity* of the primary crime. I assume that the amount of postcrime evidence has no bearing on the primary-crime sanction, and so evidence e does not enter the F function.

Express the probability of primary-crime conviction functionally as $p_2 = p_2(t_I, \max[e, \Delta e]; \Omega)$, which specifies the conviction probability as a direct function of the amount of time allocated to the commission of the illegality as a whole and of the postcrime evidence, subject to the extent of any spoliation. GMS (2002) note that when courts invoke the spoliation inference, the inference serves as a penalty because it increases the risk of an erroneous judgment against the spoliator, potentially manifesting as a higher conviction probability. The parameter $\Omega > 0$ captures exogenous factors through which the conviction probability might change, such as due to greater prosecutorial resources or expertise or perhaps lowered standards of proof (see Pyne 2004 and Ognedal 2005). The criminal thus faces an expected primary-crime sanction $E(F) = p_1 p_2 F$.

As Sommers and Seibert (1999) discuss, U.S. courts typically adjudicate the main part of a case separately from any spoliation charge, and indeed some courts have required that plaintiffs lose the first cause of action before allowing pursuit of spoliation cases. But when courts have heard spoliation cases, they have generally ruled spoliation evidence as admissible, as documented by GMS (2002). Given this precedent, and because evidence destruction constitutes a violation separate from the primary crime, we must account for an additional expected cost faced by the criminal, associated with the potential detection of and punishment for spoliation.

Any spoliation sanction depends on whether legal authorities detect the spoliator and courts convict the spoliator. Suppose authorities detect spoliation with probability $q_1 = q_1(t_E; \omega)$, where $\partial q_1/\partial t_E > 0$ (a greater amount of spoliation increases the likelihood of spoliation detection) and $\omega > 0$ captures external variation in q_1 such that $\partial^2 q_1/\partial t_E \partial \omega > 0$. Essentially, ω captures the degree of monitoring of the evidence, and the latter property indicates that greater monitoring reinforces the positive marginal impact of spoliation activity on the probability of spoliation detection by authorities. In general, an illegality that occurs with a greater number of witnesses or whose evidence otherwise attracts significant attention from authorities would exhibit greater monitoring relative to other crimes. To put this in perspective, the crime of insider trading, for example, exhibits relatively limited monitorability. Ognedal (2005) notes that authorities consistently have trouble proving insider trading because convictions require "uncertain inferences from telephone calls, meetings," and other concealed or indirect evidence. Mookherjee and Png (1992) and Innes (2001) in fact incorporate endogenous monitoring by government in their studies of optimal enforcement mechanisms. In the context of q_2 here, such monitoring would provide information to court officials prior to any spoliation offense, consistent with Mookherjee and Png's (1992) definition of monitoring.

Suppose court officials convict spoliators with probability $q_2 = q_2(t_E; \chi)$, where $\partial q_2/\partial t_E > 0$ (a greater amount of spoliation increases the likelihood of conviction for spoliation) and $\chi > 0$ captures external variation in q_2 such that $\partial^2 q_2/\partial t_E \partial \chi > 0$. The parameter χ captures factors such as the extent to which spoliation is reported to authorities (see Solum and Marzen 1987) or the aggressiveness with which courts, in practice, apply any existing spoliation sanction. A higher magnitude for $\partial^2 q_2/\partial t_E \partial \chi$ would imply a stronger (positive) connection between the act of spoliation, if detected, and the probability of receiving punishment for it.

If authorities detect spoliation, the spoliator faces the sanction (utility cost) S. The widely prevalent procedural sanction in most U.S. jurisdictions implies that $S = \underline{S}$, a constant whereby a greater degree of spoliation incurs no greater sanction. Alternatively, given a more substantive sanction, the spoliator might face $S = S(t_E; \sigma)$, where $\partial S / \partial t_E > 0$ and $\sigma > 0$ captures exogenous factors that influence the state of spoliation law (e.g., spoliation tort creation or reform, judiciary attitudes about the seriousness of spoliation), such that $\partial^2 S / \partial t_E \partial \sigma > 0$. That is, under the substantive sanction, spoliators face an increasing penalty for more demonstrative or successive commissions of spoliation, and the strength of the sanction may increase exogenously through σ. Economists have not studied optimal spoliation sanctioning mechanisms in a manner comparable to the analysis of primary-crime sanctioning by Garoupa, Polinsky, Shavell, and others. I make the simplifying assumption here that reform of spoliation law would impose this essential form on the spoliation sanction, but this does not necessarily mean that such a form would be socially optimal. No matter the specific form of the spoliation sanction, the criminal faces an expected spoliation sanction $E(S) = q_1 q_2 S$, subject to the probability of primary-crime detection p_1.

Given the component functions introduced above, the hypothetical solo criminal seeks levels of t_L, t_E, and t_M that maximize the assumed concave expected utility

$$
\begin{aligned}
Z = {}& p_1(t_I, \max[e(t_E, \Delta e)], v; \gamma_p) \, U[(G(t_M) + L(t_L) + \delta(h, \gamma_c)t_E \, e - n(t_E) \\
& - p_2(t_I, \max[e, \Delta e]; \Omega)F(t_M; \varphi) - q_1 (t_E; \omega)q_2 (t_E; \chi)S(t_E; \sigma)] \\
& + [1 - p_1 (t_I, e, v; \gamma_p)]U[G(t_M) + L(t_L) + \delta(h, \gamma_c)t_E \, e - n(t_E)], \quad (4.1)
\end{aligned}
$$

subject to the implicit time constraints $t_I = t_M + t_E$ and $t_I + t_L = T$. Assuming the optimal legal activity, $t_L^* = \text{argmax}(Z)$, predetermined, we focus on the selection of the illegalities $t_M^* = \text{argmax}(Z)$ and $t_E^* = \text{argmax}(Z)$. In this one-criminal setting, the criminal may only allocate *time* resources. As the criminal does not purchase spoliation services in a market, the criminal

faces no relevant income or wealth constraint. Within the two-criminal setting developed later, we will study third-party spoliation, wherein the criminal may spend *non*time resources (a monetary or in-kind fee) to engage an
outside agent not involved in the primary crime to spoliate on the criminal's
behalf.

Suppressing functional arguments other than the time-allocation variables, the necessary condition for maximization of Z with respect to t_M
implies that $Z_M = \partial Z / \partial t_M = 0$, or

$$
Z_M = -\frac{\partial p_1}{\partial t_M} p_1(t_I) F(t_M) + q_1(t_E) q_2(t_E) S(t_E) - p_1(t_I) \left[\frac{\partial p_2}{\partial t_M} F(t_M) + p_2(t_I) \right]
$$

$$
+ \frac{\partial U}{\partial G} \frac{\partial G}{\partial t_M} = 0. \tag{4.2}
$$

The necessary condition for maximization of Z with respect to t_E similarly implies that

$$
Z_E = \frac{\partial Z}{\partial t_E} = -\frac{\partial p_1}{\partial t_E} [p_1(t_I) F(t_M) + q_1(t_E) q_2(t_E) S(t_E)]
$$

$$
+ \frac{\partial U}{\partial \Delta e} \delta e - \frac{\partial U}{\partial t_E} \frac{\partial e}{\partial t_E} - \frac{\partial U}{\partial n} \frac{\partial n}{\partial t_E}
$$

$$
- p_1(t_I) \left\{ \left[\frac{\partial p_2}{\partial t_I} F(t_M) - \frac{\partial U}{\partial E(S)} \left[\frac{\partial q_1}{\partial t_E} q_2(t_E) S(t_E) \right. \right. \right.
$$

$$
+ q_1(t_E) q_2(t_E) \frac{\partial S}{\partial t_E} \right] \right\} = 0. \tag{4.3}
$$

Necessarily, $Z_M(t_M^*; \theta) = 0$ and $Z_E(t_E^*; \theta) = 0$, where the vector θ contains
the exogenous factors incorporated in the model. Using the envelope
theorem and these first-order conditions in a fashion comparable to that
seen in Chapter 2, we can investigate how comparative-static variation in
key exogenous factors, particularly relating to elements of substantive

and spoliation law, influences the criminal's allocation of time to the primary crime and spoliation.

B. Primary-Crime and Spoliation Deterrence

The present model highlights three essential elements of spoliation law:
the probability of spoliation detection, the probability of spoliation conviction, and the spoliation sanction. Each potentially provides an avenue
to spoliation deterrence because authorities have the ability to manipulate each of these variables. The model highlights three comparable elements of substantive law: the probability of primary-crime detection,
the probability of primary-crime conviction, and the primary-crime sanction. These factors similarly provide avenues to primary-crime deterrence. Propositions 1 and 2 formalize how variation in these elements—as
might occur as matters of public policy—potentially impact the offender's behavior.

PROPOSITION 1: *Strengthening spoliation law discourages commission
of the primary crime.*

Proof. We must show that $\partial t_M^*/\partial\omega < 0$, $\partial t_M^*/\partial\chi < 0$, and $\partial t_M^*/\partial\sigma < 0$.
(1) By the envelope theorem, $\partial t_M^*/\partial\omega = -Z_{M\omega}/Z_{MM} = -(\partial^2 Z/\partial t_M\partial\omega)/(\partial^2 Z/\partial t_M^2)$. After differentiating Z_M (Equation 4.2) with respect to ω, we
obtain $\partial t_M^*/\partial\omega = -(-\partial p_1/\partial t_M)(\partial q_1/\partial\omega)q_2 S/Z_{MM}$. The shape of Z ensures
$Z_{MM} < 0$, and the numerator is positive, rendering $\partial t_M^*/\partial\omega < 0$. (2) Simi-
larly, $\partial t_M^*/\partial\chi = -Z_{M\chi}/Z_{MM}$. $Z_{M\chi} = -(-\partial p_1/\partial t_M)(\partial q_2/\partial\chi)q_1 S$, so that $\partial t_M^*/\partial\chi = -(-\partial p_1/\partial t_M)(\partial q_2/\partial\chi)q_1 S/Z_{MM} < 0$. (3) $\partial t_M^*/\partial\sigma = -Z_{M\sigma}/Z_{MM}$. Observe that
$\partial Z_M/\partial\sigma = -(\partial p_1/\partial t_M)(\partial S/\partial\sigma)q_1 q_2$, so that $\partial t_M^*/\partial\sigma = -[(-\partial p_1/\partial t_M)(\partial S/\partial\sigma)q_1 q_2]/Z_{MM} < 0$.

PROPOSITION 2: *(1) Strengthening spoliation law and (2) strengthening substantive law unambiguously discourage spoliation only if spoliation creates more risk than ignorance.*

Proof. (1) We must show that $\partial t_E^*/\partial\omega < 0$, $\partial t_E^*/\partial\chi < 0$, and $\partial t_E^*/\partial\sigma < 0$
unambiguously only if $\partial p_1/\partial t_E > 0$. (*i.*) By the envelope theorem, $\partial t_E^*/\partial\omega = -Z_{E\omega}/Z_{EE}$. Making use of Z_E (Equation 4.3), we have

$$\frac{\partial t_E^*}{\partial \omega} = \frac{-Z_{E\omega}}{Z_{EE}}$$

$$= \frac{\dfrac{\partial p_1}{\partial t_E}\dfrac{\partial q_1}{\partial \omega}q_2 S + p_1 \dfrac{\partial U}{\partial E(S)}\left(\dfrac{\partial^2 q_1}{\partial t_E \partial \omega}q_2 S + \dfrac{\partial q_1}{\partial \omega}\dfrac{\partial q_2}{\partial t_E}S + \dfrac{\partial q_1}{\partial \omega}q_2 \dfrac{\partial S}{\partial t_E}\right)}{Z_{EE}}.$$

(4.4)

The shape of Z implies $Z_{EE} < 0$. The second term in the numerator of Equation (4.4) is positive. In the first term of the numerator, $\partial q_1/\partial \omega > 0$ and $q_2 S > 0$, but $\partial p_1/\partial t_E$ has an ambiguous sign. If $\partial p_1/\partial t_E > 0$, the numerator is unambiguously positive, consistent with $\partial t_E^*/\partial \omega < 0$ unambiguously. However, if $\partial p_1/\partial t_E < 0$, then the numerator may take on any sign, leaving the sign of $\partial t_E^*/\partial \omega$ ambiguous. (*ii.*) Similar analysis reveals that

$$\frac{\partial t_E^*}{\partial \chi} = \frac{-Z_{E\chi}}{Z_{EE}}$$

$$= \frac{\dfrac{\partial p_1}{\partial t_E}\dfrac{\partial q_1}{\partial \chi}q_2 S + p_1 \dfrac{\partial U}{\partial E(S)}\left(\dfrac{\partial q_1}{\partial t_E}\dfrac{\partial q_2}{\partial \chi}S + q_1 \dfrac{\partial^2 q_2}{\partial t_E \partial \chi}S + q_1 \dfrac{\partial q_2}{\partial \chi}\dfrac{\partial S}{\partial t_E}\right)}{Z_{EE}},$$

(4.5)

which will be unambiguously negative only if $\partial p_1/\partial t_E > 0$. (*iii.*) Finally, observe that

$$\frac{\partial t_E^*}{\partial \sigma} = \frac{-Z_{E\sigma}}{Z_{EE}}$$

$$= \frac{\dfrac{\partial p_1}{\partial t_E}\dfrac{\partial S}{\partial \sigma}q_1 q_2 + p_1 \dfrac{\partial U}{\partial E(S)}\left(\dfrac{\partial q_1}{\partial t_E}q_2 \dfrac{\partial S}{\partial \sigma} + q_1 \dfrac{\partial q_2}{\partial t_E}\dfrac{\partial S}{\partial \sigma} + q_1 q_2 \dfrac{\partial^2 S}{\partial t_E \partial \sigma}\right)}{Z_{EE}},$$

(4.6)

which will be unambiguously negative only if $\partial p_1/\partial t_E > 0$.

(2) We must show that $\partial t_E^*/\partial \gamma_p < 0$, $\partial t_E^*/\partial \Omega < 0$, and $\partial t_E^*/\partial \varphi < 0$ unambiguously only if $\partial p_1/\partial t_E > 0$. (*i.*) Observe that $\partial t_E^*/\partial \gamma_p = -(\partial Z_E/\partial \gamma_p)/(\partial^2 Z/\partial t_E^2)$ and that $-\partial Z_E/\partial \gamma_p = (\partial^2 p_1/\partial t_E \partial \gamma_p)(pF + q_1 q_2 S) - (\partial p_1/\partial \gamma_p)\{-\partial p_2/\partial t_E - [\partial U/\partial E(S)]$

$[E(S)']$}, where $E(S)' = \partial E(S)/\partial t_E = (\partial q_1/\partial t_E)q_2 S + q_1(\partial q_2/\partial t_E)S + q_1 q_2(\partial S/\partial t_E)$. Because $Z_{EE} < 0$, a deterrent effect $(\partial t_E^*/\partial \gamma_p < 0)$ will prevail if the numerator of $\partial t_E^*/\partial \gamma_p$ is positive. If $\partial p_1/\partial t_E > 0$, then $\partial^2 p/\partial t_E \partial \gamma_p > 0$ as well; as all other terms inside $-\partial Z_E/\partial \gamma_p$ are positive, $\partial t_E^*/\partial \gamma_p < 0$ unambiguously. However, if $\partial p_1/\partial t_E < 0$, then $\partial^2 p/\partial t_E \partial \gamma_p < 0$ as well, thus adding a negative quantity to the numerator of $\partial t_E^*/\partial \gamma_p$ and creating the possibility that $\partial t_E^*/\partial \gamma_p \geq 0$. (*ii.*) $\partial t_E^*/\partial \Omega = -Z_E \Omega/Z_{EE}$, where $Z_E \Omega = \partial Z_E/\partial \Omega = [(\partial p_1/\partial t_E) (\partial p_2/\partial \Omega) + p_1(\partial^2 p_2/\partial t_E \partial \Omega)]$. If $\partial p_1/\partial t_E > 0$, then the bracketed term is positive, rendering $\partial t_E^*/\partial \Omega < 0$ unambiguously. However, if $\partial p_1/\partial t_E < 0$, the numerator may take on any sign, making the deterrent effect less definitive. (*iii.*) $\partial t_E^*/\partial \varphi = -Z_E \varphi/Z_{EE} = (\partial F/\partial \varphi)[(\partial p_1/\partial t_E)p_2 + (\partial p_2/\partial t_E)p_1]/Z_{EE}$. If $\partial p_1/\partial t_E > 0$, the numerator is positive, rendering $\partial t_E^*/\partial \varphi < 0$ unambiguously. But if $\partial p_1/\partial t_E < 0$, the numerator may take on any sign, making the deterrent effect less definitive.

C. Discussion

What are the economic implications of Propositions 1 and 2? As we see in Chapter 1, theoretical and empirical economic analysis of crime has long demonstrated mechanisms that contribute to the deterrence of crime in general. We know that, for a given crime, society might allocate more resources toward policing so as to increase the likelihood of criminal detection or apprehension, or it might legislate stronger sanctions; these and other actions related to the enforcement of substantive law can increase the expected cost of engaging in illegal activity. In this present extension of the economic model of crime, which considers part of the *aftermath* of a crime (in contrast to the model in Chapter 2, which considered the moments leading up to a crime), Proposition 1 reveals an additional mechanism that can act as a deterrent to crime: the strengthening of *spoliation* law. Furthermore, Proposition 1 formalizes a connection between the application of evidentiary rules (particularly relating to spoliation) and criminal deterrence, a possibility suggested by legal scholars and economists. Solum and Marzen (1987, p. 29) argued that deterring the destruction of materials evidencing unlawful activity "directly increases the cost of law-breaking itself," citing as an example how controlling the destruction of pricing data might deter corporate wrongdoing such as predatory pricing. Porat and Stein (1997, p. 51), in their analysis of evidential damage in general, suggested that deterring such abuses leads to "more accurate fact determination and consequently more effective execution of the substantive law." More recently, Demougin and Fluet (2006), who analyze the efficient use of evidence and evidentiary rules in the context of negligence, strongly suggest that deterrence of a primary illegality "depends on the quality of the evidence" relating to the injurer's actions.

It becomes clear, however, that such a deterrence mechanism relies greatly on the interactive effectiveness of spoliation law in its application. As visible in Parts 1 and 2 of the proof of Proposition 1, hypothetical increases in the probability either of spoliation detection or of spoliation conviction—policy actions that may involve greater allocations of court resources to monitoring and prosecution, respectively—reduce the amount of time the rational criminal allocates to illegality only to the extent that he faces a nontrivial spoliation sanction (i.e., $S > 0$). As visible in Part 3 of that proof, increasing the spoliation sanction, such as through the adoption of a stronger or more systematized penalty (e.g., a widespread spoliation tort), exerts a deterrent effect on the primary crime so long as $q_1 > 0$ and $q_2 > 0$, that is, if legal authorities have a chance of detecting spoliation and convicting those who spoliate. That the elements of spoliation law apparently must function interactively to influence the individual decision to commit the primary crime supports an assertion by Porat and Stein (1997) that tort law mechanisms (as governing primary crimes) and evidence law mechanisms should "complement each other." Realistically, however, if legal jurisdictions face scarce enforcement resources, we might in practice observe tradeoffs rather than complementarities between the two modes of enforcement, possibly complicating policy aimed at strengthening both simultaneously.

Proposition 2 reveals that broad reform (strengthening) of spoliation law may not offer deterrence of evidence-destruction behavior as definitively as perhaps is desired by many courts and legal scholars. Solum and Marzen (1987) note that the court in *Smith v. Superior Court*, 198 Cal. Rptr. 836 (1984), which created California's spoliation tort, pointedly emphasized the importance of *deterring* spoliation so as not to allow spoliators to "profit" from their actions. Because the effectiveness of such a strengthening depends on whether the act of spoliation creates relatively more risk or ignorance, effective reform along these lines would appear to depend on factors essentially out of the control of policy makers, namely, the amount of evidence created by the primary crime and the proficiency with which criminals destroy it and create relatively minimal spoliation evidence.

Part 2 of Proposition 2 implies that a higher expected sanction for the primary crime might actually *encourage* spoliation if spoliation creates more ignorance than risk. Nussim and Tabbach (2009) demonstrate a comparable possibility in their analysis of criminal deterrence and avoidance generally. In such a case, a particular kind of "avoidance" behavior, as viewed from the criminal's perspective, may be worthy of the individual costs of avoidance that Innes (2001) discusses. Similarly, Malik (1990) argues that maximum fines create the incentive to engage in avoidance behaviors, which impose significant social costs of their own. Clearly the disproportionate creation of ignorance through spoliation would involve the creation of such costs, in the form of a lost social opportunity to discover truth. The result also complements Solum and Marzen's (1987) argument that the two types of uncertainty created by spoliation greatly complicate and possibly prevent the efficient formation of a single, general rule intended to govern and deter evidence destruction. Finally, like Proposition 1, Proposition 2 also reveals the importance of strong and interactive application and adjudication of spoliation law. Overall, the two propositions suggest that stronger spoliation law may offer as much potential for discouraging primary crimes as for discouraging spoliation itself, but perhaps not simultaneously.

III. TWO-CRIMINAL ANALYSIS

In a two-criminal modeling context, both criminals, neither criminal, or only one of the criminals may destroy evidence, and the various possibilities carry both conceptual and practical relevance. Researchers in crime economics, including the economics of legal avoidance, have frequently demonstrated that criminals may have an incentive to collaborate with each other; Malik (1990), Jost (2001), Benoît and Dubra (2004), and Chang, Lu, and Chen (2005) provide key examples of such analysis. If gains to collaborative crime may exist, then conceivably gains to collaborative spoliation may exist. Indeed, Solum and Marzen (1987), Kowal (1999), GMS (2002), and Kreimer and Rudovsky (2002) document many cases of spoliation conspiracies, including those where lawyers or other professionals have engaged in *third-party* spoliation, destroying evidence on behalf of culpable clients or even advising clients to take this action. Advising illegal activity often violates professional codes of conduct, if not formal laws, and certainly can become sanctionable on that basis.

As in the models of Jost (2001) and Benoît and Dubra (2004), one criminal in this environment must account for uncertainty about how the second criminal might respond to the first criminal's action. Within this analytical setting, we study conditions under which two hypothetical criminals rationally cooperate (i.e., form a conspiracy) to destroy evidence, which includes third-party spoliation as a special case. These results allow us to examine how hypothetical variation in enforcement activity, including the strengthening of spoliation law, might affect the sustainability of a spoliation conspiracy.

A. *The Second Criminal*

Suppose an individual, labeled Criminal 1 (C1; masculine), has a partner, labeled Criminal 2 (C2; feminine), who may assist C1 in committing the primary crime, destroying evidence, or both. As before, the primary crime creates evidence e, and spoliation creates spoliation evidence. In the two-criminal setting the evidence transforms to $e - \delta_1 t_{E1}$ $e + n_1$ if C1 alone destroys evidence; it transforms to $e - \delta_2 t_{E2}$ $e + n_2$ if C2 alone destroys evidence; it transforms to $e - \delta_1 t_{E1}$ $e - \delta_2 t_{E2}$ $e + n_1 + n_2$ if both destroy evidence. Here, δ_1 and δ_2 represent the individual spoliation proficiencies of C1 and C2, respectively, such that $\delta_1 = \delta_1(h_1, \gamma_c)$ and $\delta_2 = \delta_2(h_2, \gamma_c)$, h_1 and h_2 represent C1's and C2's respective spoliation human-capital skills, t_{E1} and t_{E2} represent their respective evidence-destruction activities, and n_1 and n_2 represent spoliation evidence created by each criminal. Because δ_1 and δ_2 merely represent the spoliation *proficiencies* of each criminal, one criminal's spoliation human-capital skill does not enter the other's proficiency function. But this does not preclude the possibility of gains to collaborative spoliation or equilibrium collaborative spoliation, as explored below. In this formulation, C1 moves first and C2 reacts.

If C1 destroys evidence, C2 may also destroy (assist), or she may not destroy. If C1 does not destroy, C2 may destroy evidence unilaterally, or she may follow C1 in not destroying. To analyze the two criminals' actions in this setting, we can study the situation as a simple sequential model of cooperation similar to the approach taken by Feess and Walzl (2004) in their analysis of self-reporting and by Chang, Lu, and Chen (2005) in their analysis of organized crime. We first consider the general condition under which the two hypothetical criminals will create and sustain a conspiracy to spoliate evidence. We then consider the special case of third-party spoliation, wherein C2 has *not* participated in the primary crime and the two criminals determine a mutually advantageous fee for C2's cooperation. Finally, we examine how enforcement activity and variation in offender characteristics impact these outcomes.

Because of C1's uncertainty, he must assign conditional probabilities to C2's possible subsequent actions. Define $\lambda \equiv \Pr(\text{C2 destroys}|\text{C1 destroys})$, $1 - \lambda \equiv \Pr(\text{C2 does not destroy}|\text{C1 destroys})$, $\alpha \equiv \Pr(\text{C2 destroys}|\text{C1 does not destroy})$, and $1 - \alpha \equiv \Pr(\text{C2 does not destroy}|\text{C1 does not destroy})$. The shorthand notations $Z_{1d,2d}$, $Z_{1d,2nd}$, $Z_{1nd,2d}$, and $Z_{1nd,2nd}$ represent C1's payoffs (expected utilities) if C2 destroys or does not destroy as a reaction to C1's action; $Z_{2d,1d}$, $Z_{2d,1nd}$, $Z_{2nd,1d}$, and $Z_{2nd,1nd}$ represent C2's payoffs if C1

TABLE 4.1   *Two-Criminal Evidence Destruction*

Outcome	Payoffs (Expected Utilities) to: Criminal 1 (C1), Criminal 2 (C2)
C1 destroys, C2 destroys (λ)	$p_1 U_1(\delta_1 t_{E1} e + \delta_2 t_{E2} e - n_1 - n_2 - p_2 F - q_1 q_2 S - M t_{E2}) + (1 - p_1) U_1(\delta_1 t_{E1} e + \delta_2 t_{E2} e - n_1 - n_2 - M t_{E2})$, $p_1 U_2[M t_{E2} + \delta_1 t_{E1} e + \delta_2 t_{E2} e - n_1 - n_2 - p_2 F - q_1 q_2 S - \eta Y(t)] + (1 - p_1) U_2(M t_{E2} + \delta_1 t_{E1} e + \delta_2 t_{E2} e - n_1 - n_2)$
C1 destroys, C2 does not destroy ($1 - \lambda$)	$p_1 U_1(\delta_1 t_{E1} e - n_1 - p_2 F - q_1 q_2 S) + (1 - p_1) U_1(\delta_1 t_{E1} e - n_1)$, $p_1 U_2[M t_{E2} + \delta_2 t_{E2} e - n_2 - p_2 F - q_1 q_2 S - \eta Y(t)] + (1 - p_1) U_2(M t_{E2} + \delta_2 t_{E2} e - n_2)$
C1 does not destroy, C2 destroys (α)	$p_1 U_1(\delta_2 t_{E2} e - n_2 - p_2 F - q_1 q_2 S - M t_{E2}) + (1 - p_1) U_1(\delta_2 t_{E2} e - n_2 - M t_{E2})$, $p_1 U_2[M t_{E2} + \delta_2 t_{E2} e - n_2 - p_2 F - q_1 q_2 S - \eta Y(t)] + (1 - p_1) U_2(M t_{E2} + \delta_2 t_{E2} e - n_2)$
C1 does not destroy, C2 does not destroy ($1 - \alpha$)	$p_1 U_1(-p_2 F)$, $p_1 U_2(-p_2 F)$

destroys or does not destroy. Table 4.1 shows details of the respective payoffs for each criminal given the various contingencies, as developed below.

To derive the general condition for a spoliation conspiracy, which constitutes the equilibrium {C1 destroys, C2 destroys}, we must first characterize the relevant payoffs. A spoliation conspiracy first requires that C1 destroy evidence, which will occur if C1's expected utility from destroying evidence exceeds that from leaving the evidence undestroyed. These payoffs greatly resemble the solo criminal's payoffs in the one-criminal variant seen earlier, except that C1 now must account for the fact that C2 may or may not assist him in destroying evidence, according to the probabilities λ and α. Making use of these probabilities and the shorthand notation introduced above, C1 will destroy evidence if $\lambda Z_{1d,2d} + (1-\lambda) Z_{1d,2nd} > \alpha Z_{1nd,2d} + (1-\alpha) Z_{1d,2d}$; the component expected utilities appear in Table 4.1.

If C1 indeed does destroy evidence $(t_{E1} > 0)$, a conspiracy outcome then depends on how C2 responds. C2 will destroy (assisting C1) if her expected utility from destroying exceeds that from not destroying, conditional on C1 having destroyed. If C1 destroys, C2's payoff from not destroying is simply

$$Z_{2nd,1d} = p_1 U_2 \left(\delta_1 t_{E1} e - p_2 F \right) + (1 - p_1) U_2 \left(\delta_1 t_{E1} e \right). \tag{4.7}$$

By not destroying, C2 would face no expected spoliation sanction $q_1 q_2 S$. In principle, if C2 were a nonparticipant in the primary crime, then $F = 0$ (C2 would face no primary-crime sanction) and the payoff Equation (4.7) would simplify to $Z_{2nd,1d} = U_2(\delta_1 t_{E1} e)$; the implied utility would emanate solely from any empathy C2 carries for C1's destruction of the evidence, and even this may be zero.

If C2 destroys evidence alongside C1, then C2's payoff becomes

$$Z_{2d,1d} = p_1 U_2 \left[M t_{E2} + \delta_1 t_{E1} e + \delta_2 t_{E2} e - n_1 - n_2 - p_2 F - q_1 q_2 S \right.$$

$$\left. - \eta \int_{T_{2p}}^{T_{2f}} \frac{y(t)}{1 + r_2} dt \right] + (1 - p_1)(M t_{E2} + \delta_1 t_{E1} e + \delta_2 t_{E2} e - n_1 - n_2) \tag{4.8}$$

This expected utility incorporates additional factors that become relevant depending on whether C2 acts as C1's partner in the commission of the primary crime or as an outside agent who spoliates on behalf of C1. Specifically, let M represent monetary or (monetized) in-kind compensation the criminal must pay to engage the agent. As ever, any individual who destroys evidence risks incurring the spoliation sanction S subject to spoliation detection and conviction probabilities q_1 and q_2. Suppose C2 also risks, with probability $\eta \in [0, 1]$, the loss of a future stream of earnings over a duration $T_{2f} - T_{2p}$, discounted at rate r_2 and represented by

$$Y(t) = \int_{T_{2p}}^{T_{2f}} y(t) / (1 + r_2)dt,$$ where $y(t)$ represents time-dependent earnings from potential future illegal or legal activity. One can see this term in (4.8). In practice, spoliation sanctions typically do not call for incarceration (see Solum and Marzen 1987 and Eng 1999), and so a spoliating agent would not likely lose income opportunities due to a loss of personal freedom to work in markets. But if the agent's spoliation activity becomes exposed, she may lose these income opportunities due to loss of reputation (e.g., losses of clients among attorneys, accountants, or financial advisors; losses of voters or supporters among politicians), professional sanctions (e.g., suspensions, decertifications, or disbarments), or reductions in employability due to having a history of illegal activity. In this way, the factor η analytically resembles the reputation cost incorporated by Gordon (1989) in his model of tax evasion. Along these lines, if C1 employs a career criminal to act as his spoliating agent, then logically η approaches 0.

B. Spoliation Conspiracies

In light of the payoffs, Equations (4.7) and (4.8), C2 will destroy evidence alongside C1 if

$$p_1 U_2 \left[Mt_{E2} + \delta_1 t_{E1}e + \delta_2 t_{E2}e - n_1 - n_2 - p_2 F - q_1 q_2 S - \eta \int_{T_{2p}}^{T_{2f}} \frac{y(t)}{1 + r_2} dt \right]$$

$$+ (1 - p_1)U_2 \left(Mt_{E2} + \delta_1 t_{E1}e + \delta_2 t_{E2}e - n_1 - n_2 \right) > p_1 U_2 (\delta_1 t_{E1}e - p_2 F)$$
$$+ (1 - p_1)U_2 \left(\delta_1 t_{E1}e \right), \tag{4.9}$$

irrespective of her culpability in the commission of the primary crime. Study of this condition reveals how variation in the model's primary enforcement variables (relating to spoliation law and substantive law) impacts the sustainability of a conspiracy to destroy evidence—an issue similar to the collective or coordinated attempts by Swiss handicraft producers to violate environmental law, studied by Jost (2001). Proposition 3 summarizes these results, with proofs demonstrated within the subsequent discussion.

PROPOSITION 3: *Suppose C1 spoliates. (1) Strengthening spoliation law reduces the sustainability of the spoliation conspiracy equilibrium, {destroy, destroy}. (2) Strengthening the probability of primary-crime detection reduces the sustainability of {destroy, destroy}. (3) Strengthening the probability of primary-crime conviction and the primary-crime sanction exerts no systematic effect on the sustainability of a spoliation conspiracy.*

Factors that reduce the sustainability of a spoliation conspiracy make the condition shown by Equation (4.9) more difficult to hold. As seen previously, strengthening spoliation law implies increasing one or more of the components of the expected spoliation sanction $E(S) = q_1 q_2 S$. With respect to Part 1 of Proposition 3, variation in q_1, q_2, and S impacts only the left side of Equation (4.9), representing C2's expected utility from spoliating given that C1 has spoliated. Variation in q_1, functioning through the parameter ω, affects this payoff according to the derivative $p_1[\partial U_2/\partial E(S)]$ $(\partial q_1/\partial \omega)q_2 S$. Variation in q_2, functioning through the parameter χ, affects this payoff according to the derivative $p_1[\partial U_2/\partial E(S)]q_1(\partial q_2/\partial \chi)S$. Variation in S, working through the parameter σ, affects this payoff according to the derivative $p_1[\partial U_2/\partial E(S)]q_1 q_2(\partial S/\partial \sigma)$. Within each of these effects, the component derivative $\partial U_2/\partial E(S) < 0$ (a greater expected spoliation sanction reduces utility) while all other terms are positive, rendering each effect negative, consistent with reductions in C2's expected utility from spoliating alongside C1. Hence, just as stronger spoliation law may reasonably discourage a solo criminal from destroying evidence, it also discourages a spoliation conspiracy in the event C1 does spoliate.

Part 2 of Proposition 3 formalizes a link between the sustainability of a spoliation conspiracy and the enforcement of substantive law. Variation in p_1, acting through the parameter γ_p, affects the left side of Equation (4.9) according to $\partial p_1/\partial \gamma_p[U_2(M+\delta_1 t_{E1}e+\delta_2 t_{E2}e-n_1-n_2-p_2F-q_1q_2S$

$-\eta\int_{T_{2p}}^{T_{2f}} y(t)/(1+r_2)dt)]$ and affects the right side of Equation (4.9) accord-

ing to $\partial p_1/\partial \gamma_p[U_2(\delta_1 t_{E1}e-p_2F)-U_2(\delta_1 t_{E1}e)]$. But how these relative pay-offs change depends on the extent of C2's participation in the primary crime.

If C2 did not participate in the primary crime, then $F=0$ and the right-side effect simplifies to $\partial p_1/\partial \gamma_p[U_2(\delta_1 t_{E1}e)-U_2(\delta_1 t_{E1}e)]=0$. Intuitively, variation in the probability of primary-crime detection could not impact C2's payoff from not spoliating; she would neither have participated in the primary crime nor spoliated, leaving her invulnerable to legal punishment. However, the left-side effect would remain negative. Specifically, within the brackets of the left side of Equation (4.9), $U_2[(Mt_{E2}+\delta_1 t_{E1}e+\delta_2 t_{E2}e-n_1$

$-n_2-q_1q_2S-\eta\int_{T_{2p}}^{T_{2f}} y(t)/(1+r_2)\,dt]-U_2(Mt_{E2}+\delta_1 t_{E1}e+\delta_2 t_{E2}e-n_1-n_2)<0$

because C2 still faces the expected spoliation sanction q_1q_2S and risks the loss of the future income stream (i.e., $\eta>0$). These facts imply that the left side of Equation (4.9) declines, consistent with a higher detection probability discouraging C2's spoliation and thus threatening the viability of the conspiracy.

If C2 *did* participate in the primary crime, then $F>0$ while $M=\eta=0$. That is, C2 would face the primary-crime sanction, would require no fee M to persuade her to spoliate, and would have no career concerns related to her spoliation. This reflects an assumption that if C2 participates in the commission of the primary crime, she is enough of a career criminal to be unconcerned with any reputational effect of having spoliated. In this case, variation in p_1 affects the left side of Equation (4.9) according to $\partial p_1/\partial \gamma_p$ $[U_2(\delta_1 t_{E1}e+\delta_2 t_{E2}e-n_1-n_2-p_2F-q_1q_2S)-U_2(\delta_1 t_{E1}e+\delta_2 t_{E2}e-n_1-n_2)]$, which is negative, consistent with a lesser payoff to C2 for spoliating alongside C1. The right side of Equation (4.9) changes according to $\partial p_1/\partial \gamma_p[U_2(\delta_1 t_{E1}e-p_2F)-U_2(\delta_1 t_{E1}e)]$, also negative, which by itself would tend to encourage C2 to spoliate alongside C1. Through some algebraic manipulation of these effects, one can discover that if $M=\eta=0$, C2's expected payoff from spoliating changes according to $U_2(-p_2F-q_1q_2S)$, while C2's expected payoff from not spoliating changes according to $U_2(-p_2F)$. Each expression is negative, describing a reduction in C2's utility, but U_2 $(-p_2F - q_1q_2S) < U_2(-p_2F)$, indicating that for a nonzero expected spoliation sanction q_1q_2S, an exogenously higher probability of primary-crime detection indeed discourages the sustainability of a spoliation conspiracy.

Because we study C2's behavior essentially by studying variation in her incentive conditions rather than through formal comparative statics, the role of risk versus ignorance in C2's decision emerges somewhat more obliquely than in the one-criminal variant. As observed above, regardless of C2's culpability in the primary crime, an exogenously higher p_1 reduces her incentive to spoliate: she compares a lower utility involving some sort of income loss to a higher utility that involves no income loss, resulting in a reduced incentive to spoliate. But note that whether culpable or not, C2 would possess a lesser incentive to spoliate if $\delta_2 t_{E2}e < n_2$ than if $\delta_2 t_{E2}e \geq n_2$, that is, if she created more new evidence than she destroyed (more risk than ignorance).

Beyond illustrating a possible connection between an important element of substantive law and spoliation behavior in a two-criminal setting, Part 2 of Proposition 3 suggests that an exogenously higher probability of primary-crime detection might discourage *third-party* spoliation conspiracies relatively more effectively than conspiracies involving two culpable partners in crime. Given an exogenously higher p_1, a culpable, partnered criminal C2 may have an increased incentive to spoliate alongside C1 because declining to spoliate increases the risk of receiving sanctions for the primary crime. Because no such worry exists for a nonculpable third-party agent C2, that individual could decline to spoliate at a lesser cost.

To demonstrate Part 3 of Proposition 3, consider how the conspiracy condition varies in p_2 (through Ω) and in F (through φ). Suppose C2 participated in the primary crime, so that again $F > 0$ and $M = \eta = 0$. Variation in Ω affects both sides of Equation (4.9) according to $p_1(\partial U_2/\partial p_2 F)$ $(\partial p_2 F/\partial \Omega)$, negative because $\partial U_2/\partial p_2 F < 0$ (a stronger expected primary-crime sanction reduces utility) and all other terms are positive. As these reductive effects have equal magnitudes, variation in p_2 exerts no net effect on C2's spoliation decision. If C2 did *not* participate in the primary crime ($F = 0$, $M > 0$, $\eta > 0$), then $p_2 F$ disappears from Equation (4.9), and variation in Ω does not affect C2's decision. Similarly, for a culpable criminal C2, exogenous variation in F impacts both sides of Equation (4.9) according to the derivative $p_1(\partial U_2/\partial p_2 F)(\partial p_2 F/\partial \varphi) < 0$, implying no net impact on C2's decision. For a nonculpable third-party agent C2, $p_2 F$ does not appear in Equation (4.9), making any variation in F irrelevant to this choice. These results suggest that variations in criminal conviction rates, punishments, or degrees of severity associated with the primary crime would exert no predictable systematic impact on the sustainability of spoliation conspiracies, whether involving culpable partnered criminals or third-party arrangements.

C. Third-Party Spoliation and Endogenous Spoliation Fees

The relationships summarized in Proposition 3 pertaining specifically to *third-party* spoliation arrangements also emerge in the context of the spoliation fee the criminal must pay a third-party spoliator. Because a third party's evidence destruction does not legally subject a criminal defendant to the spoliation inference, the criminal clearly may benefit from recruiting such a person; however, as GMS (2002) point out, third parties generally do not carry inherent incentives to destroy evidence, suggesting a third party would require an inducement to spoliate. In such a setting, the criminal (the principal) and the spoliator (an agent) essentially take on the roles of employer and employee, respectively, in a labor market for spoliation services. Because each party must agree on a mutually advantageous level of compensation, the implied equilibrium fee becomes endogenous to the model in the two-criminal variant. Study of this fee can reveal how characteristics of criminals or law enforcers might impact the formation of an equilibrium third-party spoliation arrangement.

Consider the purely monetary implications of a third-party spoliation arrangement for both the criminal and agent. Having committed the primary crime and generated probative evidence, the criminal (C1) arrives at the spoliation decision carrying some initial, or accumulated, wealth V_1. If he chooses not to employ an outside spoliating agent, his expected income becomes $V_1 - p_1 p_2 \int_{T_c}^{T_r} a(t) / (1 + r_1)dt$, where r_1 represents C1's discount rate. If he employs a spoliating agent, his expected income instead becomes $V_1 - Mt_{E2} - (p_1 - \Delta p_1)(p_2 - \Delta p_2) \int_{T_c}^{T_r} a(t) / (1 + r_1) dt$. That is, a criminal who employs a spoliating agent must pay the total spoliation cost Mt_{E2} but in exchange gains an opportunity to receive a higher expected lifetime income due to the agent's spoliation activity, which I assume reduces p_1 by Δp_1 and reduces p_2 by Δp_2. Necessarily, $\Delta p_1 \leq p_1$ and $\Delta p_2 \leq p_2$. Because p_1 and p_2 represent existing primary-crime detection and conviction probabilities, the agent's spoliation could not reduce them beyond their initial levels. Therefore, Δp_1 could not exceed p_1, and Δp_2 could not exceed p_2. In the seemingly unlikely case that the agent's spoliation completely nullifies these risks, then $p_1 = \Delta p_1$ and $p_2 = \Delta p_2$. The criminal will employ the agent if $V_1 - Mt_{E2} - (p_1 - \Delta p_1)(p_2 - \Delta p_2) \int_{T_c}^{T_r} a(t) / (1 + r_1) dt$

$\geq V_1 - p_1 p_2 \int_{T_c}^{T_r} a(t) / (1 + r_1) dt$, which implies that $M \leq [p_1 p_2 - (p_1 - \Delta p_1)$

$(p_2 - \Delta p_2)] \int_{T_c}^{T_r} a(t) / (1 + r_1) dt / t_{E2}{}^d$ where $t_{E2}{}^d$ denotes the quantity of spoliation activity demanded by the criminal. A fee acceptable to the criminal must lie at or below the critical maximum on the right side of this inequality, denoted as $M_{critmax}$.

The agent, not culpable in the commission of the primary crime, arrives at the spoliation decision carrying accumulated wealth V_2. If she elects not to spoliate on behalf of the criminal, despite any fee offer, she retains V_2 and loses nothing. If she spoliates, her expected income becomes $V_2 + (1 - q_1) Mt_{E2} + q_1 [M - q_2 \int_{T_{2p}}^{T_{2f}} y(t) / (1 + r_2) dt] t_{E2}$. Spoliating exposes the agent to the risk of spoliation detection q_1. If she spoliates undetected (with probability $1 - q_1$), she earns Mt_{E2}. If detected, she earns Mt_{E2} but also faces the potential loss of the income stream $\eta \int_{T_{2p}}^{T_{2f}} y(t) / (1 + r_2) dt$, subject to the spoliation-conviction probability q_2. This income loss would stem entirely from reputational effects, as discussed earlier: the agent would face no formal punishment associated with participating in the primary crime, and present law does not widely specify loss of freedom as a spoliation sanction. The agent will accept the offer

to spoliate if $V_2 + (1-q_1)Mt_{E2} + q_1\left[M - q_2\eta\int_{T_{2p}}^{T_{2f}} y(t)/(1+r_2)dt)\right]t_{E2} \geq V_2$,

which implies that $M \geq q_1 q_2 t_{E2}{}^s\eta\int_{T_{2p}}^{T_{2f}} y(t)/(1+r_2)dt)]/(1-q_1+q_1 t_{E2}{}^s)$,

the factor $t_{E2}{}^s$ denoting the quantity of spoliation activity undertaken by the agent. A fee acceptable to the agent must lie at or above the critical minimum on the right side of this inequality, denoted as $M_{critmin}$.

The equilibrium spoliation fee M^* thus prevails if $t_{E2}{}^d = t_{E2}{}^s$, or

$$\frac{[p_1 p_2 - (p_1 - \Delta p_1)(p_2 - \Delta p_2)]\int_{T_c}^{T_r}\frac{a(t)}{1+r_1}dt}{M^*} = \frac{M^*(1-q_1)}{q_1 q_2 \eta\int_{T_{2p}}^{T_{2f}}\frac{y(t)}{1+r_2}dt}. \qquad (4.10)$$

Variation in the components of Equation (4.10) disturbs the equality, implying greater difficulty for the criminal principal and the spoliating agent to find a mutually advantageous spoliation fee and thus discouraging the conspiracy.

Strengthening spoliation law clearly upsets this equality. Exogenous variation in q_1, acting through ω, affects the right side of Equation (4.10), according to the derivative

$$\frac{\partial t_{E2}^S}{\partial\omega} = \frac{-M\frac{\partial q_1}{\partial\omega}\left[q_1 q_2\eta\int_{T_{2p}}^{T_{2f}}\frac{y(t)}{1+r_2}dt\right] - M(1-q_1)\left\{\frac{\partial q_1}{\partial\omega}\left[q_2\eta\int_{T_{2p}}^{T_{2f}}\frac{y(t)}{1+r_2}dt - M\right]\right\}}{\left[q_1 q_2\eta\int_{T_{2p}}^{T_{2f}}\frac{y(t)}{1+r_2}dt - Mq_1\right]^2}, \qquad (4.11)$$

which despite its ungainliness is unambiguously negative if $q_2\eta\int_{T_{2p}}^{T_{2f}} y(t)/(1+r_2)dt \geq M$, that is, if the spoliation fee paid by the criminal does not exceed the agent's expected lifetime income, which would seem likely even for an especially wealthy criminal. Variation in q_2, acting through χ, affects the right side of Equation (4.10) according to the derivative

$$\frac{\partial t_{E2}^S}{\partial \chi} = \frac{-M(1 - q_1)q_1 \dfrac{\partial q_2}{\partial \chi} \displaystyle\int_{T_{2p}}^{T_{2f}} \dfrac{y(t)}{1 + r_2} dt}{\left[q_1 q_2 \eta \displaystyle\int_{T_{2p}}^{T_{2f}} \dfrac{y(t)}{1 + r_2} dt \right]^2}, \tag{4.12}$$

also negative. Intuitively, higher probabilities of spoliation detection and conviction increase the critical minimum fee the agent would accept in equilibrium, reducing the spoliation activity she undertakes and making a mutually agreeable spoliation fee more difficult to obtain.

A strengthening of substantive law has the same effect, along the lines of Part 2 of Proposition 3. Variation in p_1, acting through γ_p, affects the *left* side of Equation (4.10), according to the derivative $(\partial p_1/\partial \gamma_p)$ $[p_2 - (p_2 - \Delta p_2)) \int_{T_{2p}}^{T_{2f}} y(t)/(1 + r_2)\,dt]/M$, which is positive because $\Delta p_2 \leq p_2$. Variation in p_2, acting through Ω, affects the left side of (4.10) according to the derivative $(\partial p_2/\partial \Omega)[p_1 - (p_1 - \Delta p_1)) \int_{T_{2p}}^{T_{2f}} y(t)/(1 + r_2)\,dt]/M$, also positive because $\Delta p_1 \leq p_1$. Intuitively, stronger substantive law (higher probabilities of primary-crime detection, conviction, or both) increases the critical maximum spoliation fee acceptable to the criminal to initiate a third-party spoliation arrangement; this increases the quantity of spoliation he requires, again making an equilibrium spoliation arrangement (and fee) more difficult to obtain.

Study of the formation of an equilibrium third-party spoliation fee also reveals the role of criminal and agent career concerns and as such suggests a general profile of circumstances that might make third-party spoliation conspiracies particularly resistant to deterrence. It further reveals how a fundamental tradeoff between the enforcement of substantive and spoliation law might frustrate the attempt to deter such arrangements.

As illustrated above, exogenously higher p_1 or p_2 (strengthening substantive law) increases t_{E2}^d, the left side of Equation (4.10), creating a disequilibrium. Given such an increase, the equilibrium condition can still hold if t_{E2}^s increases by the same magnitude, restoring the required equality. In principle, given that $\partial t_{E2}^s/\partial \omega < 0$ and $\partial t_{E2}^s/\partial \chi < 0$, both demonstrated above, this could occur with an exogenously lower q_1 or q_2. This would mean that policy makers would have strengthened the enforcement of substantive law while weakening the enforcement of spoliation law, a plausible scenario if a scarcity of law-enforcement resources, broadly defined, necessitated a tradeoff between the enforcement of the two modes of law. This result illustrates a possibility intimated in the one-criminal variant and suggested by legal scholars in several works.

Solum and Marzen (1987) noted that many prosecutors elect not to pursue spoliation cases because of a belief that doing so constitutes a "misallocation of scarce prosecutorial resources," and Sommers and Seibert (1999) attributed a similar sentiment to Canadian prosecutors. As indicated earlier, Porat and Stein (1997) argued that the two modes of law must complement each other to allow the most efficient application of both. In their words, a given case might exhibit "tension between deterrence as related to evidential damage and deterrence in connection with primary damage" (p. 53); Porat and Stein characterize the optimization of both as "patently impossible." These patterns would imply that society could promote one of the objectives only at the expense of the other, and third-party spoliation conspiracies may form more effectively as a consequence. A formal analysis of socially optimal antispoliation policy, beyond the present scope, might reveal more insights along these lines. One also sees an indication of why legal observers might advocate greater judicial discretion or alterations of standards of proof (of spoliation) as alternative means of bolstering the spoliation-conviction probability q_2; more sweeping reform of spoliation law might require more extensive reallocations of already-scarce enforcement resources. Future empirical research studying the connection between the prosecution of evidentiary violations and substantive violations might shed light on the extent and consequences of tradeoffs between the two modes of law enforcement in practice.

If sufficient enforcement resources made such tradeoffs unnecessary, allowing q_1 and q_2 to move in the same direction as p_1 and p_2, then the only way that $t_{E2}{}^s$ could otherwise increase to match an increase in $t_{E2}{}^d$ would be for the agent to have lesser career concerns: $t_{E2}{}^s$, the right side of Equation (4.10), clearly is decreasing in η, the agent's reputation-based probability of income loss due to spoliation, and in $y(t)$, the agent's potential future earnings. Given strengthened substantive law, this suggests that criminals interested in forming third-party spoliation arrangements would most readily attract agents who possess minimal expected reductions in their future income streams, such as due to lesser labor-market skills or a lesser initial reputation. By contrast, an agent who has a higher public profile, and thus relies more heavily on her reputation to generate current and future income, would less efficiently match up with a criminal in this situation.

As also illustrated above, increasing q_1 or q_2 (strengthening spoliation law) decreases $t_{E2}{}^s$ and similarly disturbs the equilibrium condition. In principle, the equilibrium condition might still hold if $t_{E2}{}^d$ increased by the same magnitude. This could occur with a higher p_1 or p_2, but this too would imply the existence of a fundamental tradeoff between the enforcement of substantive law and spoliation law. Absent such a tradeoff, lawmakers maintain p_1 and p_2, and $t_{E2}{}^d$ could increase only if the criminal's career concerns were higher, because $t_{E2}{}^d$ is clearly increasing in $a(t)$. This suggests that, given strengthened spoliation law, criminals with greater projected wealth—those likely with financially more to lose from incarceration for the primary crime—could more efficiently create third-party spoliation arrangements. This reinforces an intuition by Porat and Stein (1997) that wealthier defendants, including corporations or skilled professionals, would have a relatively greater proclivity to damage (or in this case intentionally destroy) evidence of illegalities. Future empirical research may also shed light on the specifics of principal-agent matches in actual third-party spoliation cases.

IV. EMPIRICAL POSSIBILITIES

Scholarly research on the interconnections between evidence, evidentiary rules, and criminal behavior currently suffers from a dearth of empirical studies, in great part due to the difficulty of constructing proper data sets. Indeed, recognition of this shortfall serves as partial motivation for relatively new scholarly organizations like the Society for Empirical Legal Studies (begun in 2006), which states a commitment to encouraging and developing multidisciplinary empirical and experimental scholarship on legal matters. As suggested within this chapter, many of the elements of the model developed here have the potential to motivate or function as concrete, testable hypotheses in future empirical studies of evidence-destruction behavior, such as might occur in an individual, corporate, or political setting. I want to highlight this potential further in this section.

As part of the building blocks of the analysis, we acknowledge the fundamental ambiguity of the relationship between individual spoliation behavior and the possibility of primary-crime detection, that is, the fact that $\partial p_1 / \partial t_E$ plausibly may take on any sign. This simple but important theoretical ambiguity invites empirical analysis designed to assess the extent to which spoliation ultimately increases a violator's vulnerability to detection. A researcher who had access to a sample of known illegalities that allowed observation of variation in the extent of spoliation and the incidence of detection or arrest could conceivably address the question directly. Depending on the contents of such a data set, one might further attempt to link the $\partial p_1 / \partial t_E$ relationship to exogenous factors such as the nature of criminal or police technology or expertise, the type of crime, and other factors. Because constructing case-level data sets that would enable such analysis always incurs significant, and sometimes prohibitive, time costs, experimental or computational agent-based simulative approaches may offer alternative opportunities for empirical investigation.

A more traditional opportunity for empirical analysis may exist in the context of Propositions 1 and 2, which speak generally to the relationship between elements of spoliation law and the deterrence of primary crime. The comparative-static relationships relevant to these propositions lend themselves to studies designed around a natural experiment in legal reform, such as if jurisdictions widely strengthened their spoliation laws through the adoption of a spoliation tort or by other means. As noted in Chapter 1, a natural-experiment study design, where feasible, can facilitate clean investigation not only of specific hypotheses but also of the *efficiency* of the regime change in question, that is, whether the policy alteration accomplished what policy makers set out to accomplish. Empirical researchers might also take advantage of cross-jurisdictional variation in spoliation law, such as might exist across states, provinces, or nations. The theoretical observations and discussion that surround Proposition 1 also point to the possible *encouragement* of spoliation for certain crimes. Whether researchers pursued a traditional, data-centered econometric approach or a more experimental or simulative approach, one could envision empirical studies that examined the relationship between the *severity* of crime and the incidence of spoliation, tuned analytically by the seemingly inevitable interactivity of substantive and spoliation law.

Conceptual points derived in the context of the two-person variant of the model also suggest the potential for intriguing empirical analysis, such as that surrounding Proposition 3 on the sustainability of spoliation conspiracies. Given a sufficient sample of legal cases containing incidences of spoliation, one might examine empirically the relationship between variation in spoliation law and the *nature* of spoliation (solo vs. conspiratorial). Similarly, one might examine the incidence of solo or conspiratorial spoliation as a function of primary-crime severity or centered on a natural experiment in legal reform, whether pertaining to substantive or spoliation law. Indeed, within the context of the model, the nature of C2's participation and her identity either as a fellow criminal or as a nonculpable agent suggest possible interactive or mediating effects.

Do we see, in practice, a greater preponderance of two-criminal spoliation conspiracies over third-party spoliation conspiracies, as suggested by Proposition 3? And what observable exogenous factors most strongly influence the formation of third-party conspiracies in particular? These questions also become addressable given a proper sampling of legal cases, and along the way researchers might investigate the empirical role of factors such as the toughness of spoliation and substantive law, the availability or relative scarcity of law-enforcement or other legal resources, and agent career concerns. Among other potential applications, one can envision empirical studies interested in the nature, sustainability, and dynamics of political cover-ups, wherein politicians become the primary unit of analysis.

V. CONCLUSION

Because crimes leave evidence, and evidence creates a risk of detection and eventual sanction for those crimes, criminals may have an incentive to destroy (spoliate) that evidence. Evidence destruction imposes costs on individual plaintiffs in legal matters by forcing plaintiffs to meet higher standards of proof; it imposes costs on society in the form of lost opportunities to discover truth in those matters. This chapter has developed an economic model of evidence destruction that illustrates how we might think about spoliation behavior by criminals acting alone and by criminals acting in partnerships, including third-party spoliation conspiracies. The model further illustrates how various factors exogenous to criminals' decisions, most importantly elements of substantive and spoliation law, might alternately deter or even encourage such behavior. The analysis takes motivation from an insightful, ongoing discussion among legal scholars about the conceptualization and application of evidentiary rules in general and spoliation law in particular; the present model lends formal structure to several points suggested only intuitively in this literature. The analysis also complements literature devoted to the economic analysis of avoidance of law.

As economic analysis of these issues continues, future theoretical models might study two-criminal spoliation in the context of a repeated game, to allow fuller investigation of the role of reputation, learning, and other intertemporal phenomena. One might also extend the model to involve more than two criminals, to allow study of spoliation by criminal teams or coalitions. Such considerations may carry implications for deterrence beyond those examined in this chapter, as might studies that concentrate on the formation of socially optimal spoliation policy and studies that investigate matters of evidence, spoliation, and criminal behavior empirically.

CHAPTER 5

The Recommission of Crime: Recidivism

Commit a crime and the earth is made of glass. Commit a crime, and it
seems as if a coat of snow fell on the ground, such as reveals in the
woods the track of every partridge, and fox, and squirrel.

—RALPH WALDO EMERSON

I. INTRODUCTION

Suppose someone does commit a crime. If authorities capture and convict this person, he or she will most likely incur a fine, imprisonment, or
some other sanction. Having received punishment for one crime, this offender, like every offender, faces a decision whether to commit crime
again. What factors influence how convicted criminals resolve this choice,
and how effective are specific sanctions at preventing subsequent crime?
These basic questions lie at the heart of economic analysis of the recommission of crime, recidivism, the focus of this last analytical chapter dealing with the economic behavior of criminals. Over the course of Part One,
we have examined how an offender might plan a crime, how a crime might
result in violence and other damages, and the possibility that a criminal
might destroy evidence of a crime. To conclude Part One—in essence
reaching the end of our implied "life cycle" of criminal activity—we take
some time to think about how a criminal might decide to start the cycle
of crime all over again.

Because recidivism involves the commission of illegal activity following at least one episode of official sanctioning, scholarly research on recidivism carries natural and direct relevance for public policy. Recidivism
research can reveal the circumstances that make sanctioning mechanisms
especially effective or ineffective. Scholars also recognize that repeat offenders commit a significant amount of the crime, especially property
crime, that occurs in society. Studying recidivism among prison releasees
in 1994, Langan and Levin (2002) found that about 67.5% of the 272,111

releasees they sampled (from fifteen states) were rearrested within three years; a comparable study of 1983 releasees had found a rearrest rate of 62%, obviously suggesting rising criminality among recividists over time. Fully a quarter of the sample releasees studied by Langan and Levin found themselves resentenced for a new crime. The vast majority of these recidivists were robbers, burglars, larcenists, and those involved in possessing, selling, or using illegal weapons.

Economic analysis of the effectiveness of punishment mechanisms, in the context of recidivism, began with Becker (1968), who recognized that fines and imprisonment incur differential costs for society when used as punishments for criminals. Punishment types vary in the degree to which they offer reductions of social loss, create personal restitution for victims, and deter subsequent crime. Ehrlich (1973) wrote further about these matters, casting his analysis less from the perspective of society than from the perspective of the individual criminal who might commit that further crime. Economists like Barton and Turnbull (1981) and Trumbull (1989) later observed that economic research into the subsequent commission of crime by previously convicted criminals gives us an opportunity to probe the causes of crime more deeply than we might with a random sampling of the population (although the latter practice does offer greater generalizability) and, in Trumbull's words, permits us "to estimate the effects of punishment on [known] offenders' future behavior" (p. 427).

This chapter presents a brief theoretical analysis of individual-level crime and recidivism based on the familiar Beckerian model structure seen in many studies and previously in this book. Before analytically considering the recommission of crime in this exercise, we consider the commission of some *initial* crime (and its subsequent sanctioning). A previously convicted offender then faces a marginal decision to commit (new) crime comparable to that faced by a first-time criminal, but the potential recidivist plausibly faces altered marginal benefits and marginal costs of crime owing to his identity as a known offender. We examine recidivism empirically in this chapter using a special data set that tracks criminal careers from a sampling of cases tried in U.S. federal judicial districts. The empirical analysis illustrates the application of econometric duration analysis in the study of recidivism and allows investigation of how specific crimes, sanctioning mechanisms, and even distinguishable political eras may have influenced individual-level recidivism.

II. CONCEPTUAL ELEMENTS OF CRIME AND RECIDIVISM

The analysis presented in this section demonstrates, in broad strokes, how we might conceptualize the commission and the recommission of crime using familiar economic tools, the same sort of approach seen in Chapters 2 and 4. A key objective of this discussion is to show how the basic theoretical components of a model of crime and recidivism connect to important policy-rich issues such as enforcement, sanctioning, and rehabilitation. Once we view the model structure in its basic form, we can easily envision avenues by which the model facilitates analysis of narrower or perhaps more complex phenomena and relationships. Observing how these issues become relevant within the context of a conceptual model—even one sketched in broad terms—also helps us clarify the role and contributions of scholarly literature devoted to these topics and helps set the stage for empirical analysis.

Suppose an economic agent potentially gains utility from two commodities, one emanating from time allocated to illegal activity (t_I) and the other from time allocated to legal activity, t_L. If the individual engages in illegal activity, he faces a possible utility gain $G = G(t_I)$. The agent faces a probability of apprehension and conviction, p. (I fuse these probabilities for simplicity in this exposition; a more probing model would more properly separate the probabilities of apprehension and conviction, and perhaps other actions, to clarify the role of enforcement behavior at different stages of the enforcement process.) Thus, the probability of committing the illegality successfully, safe from apprehension or conviction, is $1 - p$. If apprehended and convicted, the agent receives a sanction (utility cost) $F(t_I)$, making the net gain from illegality $G(t_I) - F(t_I)$. The agent faces no sanction if not apprehended. Pursuant to these functions, I assume, consistent with classic properties, that $\partial G/\partial t_I > 0$, $\partial p/\partial t_I > 0$, and $\partial F/\partial t_I > 0$; that is, illegal activity creates the possibility of obtaining the illegal gain, enhances the probability of sustaining a punitive sanction, and motivates the sanction itself. In the manner of Sjoquist (1973), we also can imagine that the agent receives utility from licit earnings, denoted as W and obtainable only through legal time allocation; hence, $W = W(t_L)$ and $\partial W/\partial t_L > 0$.

Given these components, we can express the agent's objective function as expected utility $Z = p(t_I)[G(t_I) - F(t_I), \ W(t_L)] + [1 - p(t_I)][G(t_I), \ W(t_L)]$. As in any time-allocation model of crime, the agent will maximize Z with respect to t_I and t_L to find the optimal levels of legal and illegal activity, respectively, subject to the normalized time constraint $t_I + t_L + t_E = 1$, the component t_E representing time devoted to leisure. I will focus on optimal t_I here. If we impose the time constraint directly, we can rewrite the objective function as $Z = p(t_I)[G(t_I) - F(t_I), \ W(1 - t_I - t_E)] + [1 - p(t_I)]$ $[G(t_I), \ W(1 - t_I - t_E)]$. The first-order condition for the selection of utility-maximizing illegal activity, $\partial Z/\partial t_I = 0$, implies, following some algebraic simplification, that $\partial G/\partial t_I = (\partial p/\partial t_I)F + (\partial F/\partial t_I)p + \partial W/\partial t_I$. Of course, this first-order condition establishes the necessary condition for the existence of an expected-utility maximizing t_I and as such indicates that this optimal level of illegality occurs when the marginal benefit of the illegality equals the marginal cost of the illegality. By implication, and expressed more formally, if we denote $t_I^* = \text{argmax}(Z)$, then logically $t_I^* > 0$ if $\partial G/\partial t_I > (\partial p/\partial t_I)F + (\partial F/\partial t_I)p + \partial W/\partial t_I$.

In this inequality expression, the term $\partial G/\partial t_I$ represents the marginal benefit of the illegality. Sjoquist (1973) long ago pointed out that illegal activity may offer psychic gains, financial gains, or both, implying that the marginal benefit of crime may take a monetary form or a more "multi-attributed" form, as characterized by Block and Heineke (1975). So, if the individual contemplates a property crime like burglary or robbery, as in Chapters 2 and 3, the gain may take the form of the monetary value obtainable from the stolen property; with a crime such as assault or rape, the gain may take the form of utility derived from the commission of the violence in general or even directed toward a specific victim. The right side of the inequality condition constitutes the marginal cost—or marginal disutility—of the illegality. The first two terms indicate how the commission of the illegality impacts the expected sanction cost pF, each component assumed to vary directly in illegal time. The last term indicates the degree to which illegal activity alters (in fact, reduces) the available income from licit activity and allows the model to recognize that the commission of crime incurs opportunity costs.

Most scholarly discussions of recidivism take place under the assumption not only that the hypothetical individual has already committed a crime but moreover that he has already incurred an official sanction for a crime. As a purely conceptual matter, we might prefer to define recidivism as the individual repetition of *illegal activity*, a result of just this sort of optimization process. But as a practical matter, we generally can observe a person's previous illegality only by way of his previous arrest or conviction record—his "rap sheet." As Kim et al. (1993) discuss, this fact explains the ambiguous empirical relationship between enforcement activity and recidivism: in practice, the recidivism we observe reflects a confounding of the individual decision to commit crime and the state's efforts to prevent it. But even as we recognize this fact, we can use the essentials of the model sketched here to explore the agent's decision to commit crime subsequent to some previous episode of illegal activity and sanctioning.

A person who has committed a crime and incurred a sanction faces the same sort of optimization problem when considering committing crime again, and indeed much does remain the same. For a given crime opportunity, the illegal activity offers a potential gain; the commission of the crime still creates an expected sanction cost; and the illegality still takes time away from licit activity. Consequently we can still characterize the illegality condition as $\partial G/\partial t_I > (\partial p/\partial t_I)F + (\partial F/\partial t_I)p + \partial W/\partial t_I$. But because this known criminal, who might now become a recidivist criminal, confronts this decision with a *history* of official sanctioning and lost licit opportunities, the marginal benefit and perhaps more importantly the marginal cost of committing a new crime may now differ from how they influenced the agent in the commission of the first crime.

To study this formally, we could readily define some or all of the components of the economic agent's expected utility function—the gain to illegality, the probability of apprehension and conviction, the sanction, the licit income loss—so that they vary in time as well as in the endogenous time-allocation behavior. We could then differentiate the illegality condition above to characterize mathematically how the passage of time, component by component, influences the offender's new decision process. But on this occasion let's think through the essential determinants and comparative statics of recidivism by focusing more on the economic intuition inside that process.

For the moment, suppose the hypothetical offender considers committing the identical crime as before: another bank robbery, another purse-snatching, another embezzlement of a company's profits. Under this assumption (relaxed later), one might reasonably imagine that the new crime offers essentially the same marginal benefit as the first crime, in which case only the marginal costs may differ. Recall that the first two terms of the marginal cost expression collectively capture how illegality impacts the apprehension/conviction probability and the sanction. Does the commission of this new crime (albeit the same *type* of crime as before) impact this probability? It does, if police engage in increased monitoring of the activities of convicted criminals, making their subsequent crimes, at the margin, more vulnerable to detection. It does, if prosecutors allocate additional resources to the conviction of repeat criminals. As noted in Chapter 4, monitoring plays a significant role in the course of law enforcement in general, as studied notably by Malik (1990), Mookherjee and Png (1992), and Jost (2001). Leung et al. (2005) and Curry and Klumpp (2009) also consider the role of discrimination in arrest and conviction, a practice that may become especially predictable where police monitor known, previously convicted criminals. Burnovski and Safra (1994) and Benson, Rasmussen, and Kim (1998) furthermore analyze the implications of increasing allocations of resources to policing and punishment.

Does the commission of a new illegality impact the magnitude of the sanction for the crime, in either absolute or marginal terms? It does, if lawmakers legislate and judges impose harsher penalties for repeat offenders, as in the three-strikes law; of course, Owens (2009) analyzed a *reduction* of penalty severity in Maryland. For some time, as chronicled in Chapter 1, economists have analyzed the concept of variable (and, in particular, *increasing*) sanctions for repeat offenders, a literature that reconsiders the role of the expected sanction in economic models of crime. Indeed, writing about a tendency of earlier theoretical modelers of crime to assume only fixed probabilities for arrest and imprisonment, Schmidt and Witte (1984, p. 172) characterized this analytical treatment as a "manifestly unreasonable state of affairs, because (at least for most crimes) the probability of arrest or conviction must rise with the number of offenses." One might still reasonably specify fixed probabilities in static models designed to explain illegal activity observed at a moment in time—I have already done so in this book—but one cannot deny the substance of this point in the analysis of repeat crime. The extensive economic literature on optimal punishment, exemplified in theoretical work by Polinsky and Rubinfeld (1991), Polinsky and Shavell (1998), Bar-Gill and Harel (2001), and Emons (2003), reflects a commitment to studying the implications of imposing incrementally harsher sanctions on repeat criminals. Empirical analysis along these lines, such as by Levitt (1998) and Wilhite and Allen (2008), also shows us that while increased penalties of this sort may concretely increase the expected cost of criminality, as suggested here, such law may not really improve the overall societal crime rate in the long run.

Does the commission of a new illegality affect the loss of licit income represented by $\partial W/\partial t_I$? If a personal history of crime and sanctioning makes the effect $\partial W/\partial t_I$ greater in absolute value, then essentially this experience would have made (subsequent) illegal activity more costly at the margin; that is to say, the criminal would have more to lose by engaging in new illegal activity. This would imply that the earlier experience, particularly the sanctioning episode, must have exerted a net rehabilitative effect on the criminal, or more precisely on the value of the criminal's human capital as potentially applied to legal work, thus discouraging recidivism. But if this experience lowers the absolute value of $\partial W/\partial t_I$, then the sanctioning process would have reduced this element of the marginal cost of a higher-order illegality. Rather than reinforcing the criminal's licit human capital skills, the sanctioning episode would have led to their degradation, thus encouraging recidivism.

The crime economist Isaac Ehrlich, whose work occupies a central place in the development of the field as a whole, has commented extensively on these exact possibilities. From an economic perspective, recidivism turns on offenders' personal preferences and opportunities—the opportunity to commit illegal activity and the opportunity to engage in legal activity. In fact, even holding personal preferences constant, we might still see variation in optimal illegal activity owing to variation in those opportunities. As Ehrlich (1973, p. 529) puts it, "Even if there were no systematic variations in preferences for crime from one period to another . . . , an offender is likely to repeat his illegitimate activity if the opportunities available to him remain unchanged." Legitimate opportunities may dry up because of either reputational effects or the effects of imprisonment (the most severe sanction type short of capital punishment) on human capital skills and employment opportunities. On this point, Ehrlich (1981, p. 315) later observed that to the extent imprisonment "result[s] in the relative depreciation of legitimate knowledge and skills, it may lead to an increase in the rate of recidivism . . . in their postrelease period." One can find additional theoretical and empirical insights along these lines in research by Grogger (1998), Borland and Hunter (2000), Baik and Kim (2001), and Gould, Weinberg, and Mustard (2002). Western (2006) also investigates the labor-market implications of incarceration in his probing sociological study of inequality in imprisonment.

By applying a relatively simple economic modeling approach, then, we can see directly how three key components of the problem potentially influence individual recidivism: enforcement, sanctioning, and rehabilitation. As indicated above, all have attracted extensive attention from researchers and all have great policy relevance. At the same time, however, because the hypothetical offender's decision process involves so many "moving parts," and not all move in the same direction, for the same reasons, or with the same pace even as time passes, theoretical modelers usually have trouble making clean predictions about recidivism, especially in relation to the effectiveness of sanctioning mechanisms. In her important empirical study of the economic model of crime, Witte (1980) chose not even to derive formal comparative statics (nor have I done so here), arguing that the ambiguities fundamental to the problem render the relevant issues largely empirical questions.

Prediction becomes even more challenging when we relax the assumption of identical crime types. While criminals do specialize—they recognize the same efficiency benefits that any worker would—they also engage in crime-switching, and one might easily imagine an escalation of crime severity. Hazelwood, Reboussin, and Warren (1989) and Funk and Kugler (2003) provide evidence of exactly this phenomenon. As discussed above, the crime and sanctioning experience may erode a criminal's legitimate human capital skills or refine his criminal human capital skills, and of course a new crime may offer an altered (and especially a greater) marginal benefit $\partial G/\partial t_I$. Just as plausibly, the repeat criminal might well *seek out* more rewarding crimes as a means of compensating for the implied greater marginal cost (associated with greater enforcement or sanctioning) described above. As in financial decision making, a criminal agent may seek greater criminal returns, perhaps leading to more severe crimes, as a hedge against a (likely accurate) perception of a greater risk—all tuned, of course, by the offender's personal preference for risk.

The broad model structure we have considered here also allows us to see how incapacitation, the removal of a known criminal from society through some sort of confinement, can reduce observable crime rates. At the same time, it highlights the importance of clearly defining our terms and our objectives when constructing models of recidivism. If an individual, confined criminal has no opportunity to commit a new crime, thus potentially contributing to a lowering of the observable crime rate, then confinement essentially reduces the marginal benefit of all available crimes to zero. Furthermore, it seems reasonable that any attempt to commit crime while under confinement would at least attract attention from authorities charged with monitoring such criminals—an apprehension probability effect—and may even attract stiffer penalties associated with the attempted or actual commission of crime while under confinement.

But the assumption of a zero marginal benefit makes sense only if we refer to crime committed in free society; crime obviously does occur inside prisons, for example, implying that some confined criminals clearly must perceive a nonzero marginal benefit for certain acts despite the likely nontrivial marginal cost. Researchers in the economics of crime generally, and understandably, focus their analysis on crime committed in free society, where the overwhelming majority of potential victims are not themselves criminals. But crimes committed in confinement also have unwilling victims who suffer harm and in any case constitute recidivism in their own right—certainly in the conceptual sense and likely in the empirical sense as well if those illegalities spur harsher punishments. Researchers interested in studying the nature of illegal activity committed inside prisons or by confined criminals generally might first think about such activity as recidivism behavior, possibly formulating hypotheses within a model structure such as that outlined here. Research of this nature has become increasingly important as government officials wrestle with how to make prisons more effective rehabilitative institutions.

III. EMPIRICAL ANALYSIS

A. Data and Methodology

Recidivism differs from most other phenomena we typically study in crime economics because it so centrally involves the passage of time—a fact that has immediate implications for the data and econometric methodology one might ideally employ to study the recommission of crime empirically. The phenomena we have studied so far in Part One lend themselves to cross-sectional empirical analysis, where data allow: we can reasonably investigate an offender's planning behaviors, the extent of violence or damages resulting from a crime, or even the act of evidence destruction without regard to how much time it takes for these phenomena to unfold. But recidivism can make sense only in the context of a duration, a length of time between one crime-and-sanction event and a subsequent crime-and-sanction event that may never happen or that we may never observe. Where feasible, a number of researchers interested in crime and recidivism have taken advantage of (typically rare) panel data sets, which by their dual cross-sectional/time-series nature permit a direct statistical control for the passage of time and its associated error structure. Studies by Greenberg and Kessler (1981), Trumbull (1989), Cornwell and Trumbull (1994), and Allen (2002, 2005) provide useful examples of this approach. In the absence of panel data sets, recidivism researchers generally have turned to econometric methodologies designed to model the determinants of durations and the time-conditional probability (the *hazard*) that the period of time between observed crimes comes to an end due to recidivism.

We can conceptualize this duration within the context of the modeling approach developed above. When we as modelers observe a period of time between crimes, or in more practical terms between arrests or sanctioning events, we can imagine that during that period of time the marginal cost of crime must have exceeded the marginal benefit of crime for the average offender, holding constant enforcement activity, such that the individual elected not to commit a new crime. Which specific elements of the marginal benefit and marginal cost proved particularly influential in shaping this underlying decision and the implied duration becomes an empirical question. One can then draw a link between these theoretical essentials and the econometric analysis of duration data.

For a sampling of known offenders, we can observe at a point in time, denoted T_K, the amount of time between a given offender's previous crime or arrest and his arrest for a subsequent crime, if the latter has occurred; in the absence of a later arrest, the individual has a right-censored duration observation. The nonnegativity and censoring of the dependent variable, the duration between arrests, render ordinary least squares analysis of this duration inappropriate. Furthermore, as Greene (2008) discusses, the primary outcome of interest in most duration studies becomes not so much the length or determinants of the duration itself but instead the probability, or hazard, that the period in question will come to an end given that it has lasted to a certain point. In the present context, we might then wonder whether the hazard of criminal recidivism increases, decreases, or even stays the same as time passes. But as suggested within the conceptual discussion, certain circumstances, some under the control of law enforcement, may plausibly reduce or increase this hazard by altering the marginal benefits and marginal costs of committing a new crime.

To estimate econometric hazard models, economic researchers have frequently applied nonparametric and semiparametric statistical approaches. These approaches have the benefit of allowing the modeler to avoid imposing a specific functional form on the probability distribution underlying the duration data and the associated hazard but typically require fairly limiting assumptions about the properties of the hazard. One such approach, the popular Cox proportional hazard (PH) model, suggested in Cox (1972), specifies that the hazard of failure (the hazard of recidivism), expressed as a function of the individual duration observation t_i, varies according to $\lambda(t_i) = \lambda_0(t_i) \exp(-X_i\beta)$, where X_i represents the vector of covariates, β the vector of estimable parameters, and λ_0 an unobserved, individual-specific baseline hazard of recidivism. In practice, the modeler estimates λ_0 using variables that control for the heterogeneity that exists within a sample of offenders. One obtains estimates of β through maximization of a likelihood function that accounts for (1) individuals who exhibit a *failure time* at time T_K (i.e., those who exhibit recidivism) and (2) individuals who remain "at risk" of failure (recidivism) at T_K and thus have right-censored durations. Kalbfleisch and Prentice (1980) and Greene (2008) provide further detail on the construction and optimization of this likelihood function as well as additional discussion of nonparametric models for duration analysis.

Despite the ease of estimation and inference associated with the Cox PH model, statistically valid application of this methodology requires that the baseline hazard not vary over time, that is, that a single hazard of failure holds for the entire observed duration. But this may not hold in practice. As an alternative, researchers more frequently turn to parametric modeling approaches that allow greater flexibility with respect to the possible behavior of the hazard of failure. This is the estimation approach taken in this chapter.

As with the PH model, this approach analytically involves construction and maximization of a likelihood function that accounts for contributions from offenders who exhibit a failure time and from those with censored duration data. The parametric approach departs by imposing a specific functional form on the probability of a failure (or, alternatively, the probability of survival). The Weibull distribution, which has a hazard function $\lambda(t) = p\delta t^{p-1}$ defined with constant δ and estimable parameter p, inherently allows for either positive duration dependence (wherein the hazard of failure increases over time, $\partial\lambda/\partial t > 0$) or negative duration dependence (in which case it decreases over time, $\partial\lambda/\partial t < 0$), conditional on the value of p. If $p = 1$, as might emerge from the estimation of a Weibull hazard model, then the hazard function collapses to $\lambda(t) = \delta$, a constant consistent with the exponential probability distribution function. In essence, within a parametric approach to estimating hazard models, we let the data determine the behavior of the hazard of failure as a result of the maximum likelihood estimation of β and the statistical parameter p.

For empirical purposes in this chapter, I use a data set emanating from criminological research by Weisburd, Waring, and Chayet (2000) that focused on the initial arrest, sanctioning, and eventual recommission of crime especially by "white-collar" criminals. (One can think of white-collar crime as nonphysical illegal activity involving concealment or guile to obtain money or property, avoid payment of money or property, or gain some other business or personal advantage, as essentially defined by Herbert Edelhertz, a former Department of Justice prosecutor. See Coleman 1998.) The researchers extracted the data from court records of U.S. federal judicial districts to determine the nature and disposition of an offender's initial offense charge, the nature and severity of any sanctions imposed for those crimes, and whether any subsequent arrest occurred. Those who show a subsequent arrest at the time of sampling (1995) exhibit recidivism; the others have censored durations between arrests.

The white-collar crime data set has limitations that prevent a more comprehensive empirical analysis of an economic model of crime and recidivism. It does not reliably specify the state in which offenses and arrests occurred, preventing an investigation of how state-level legal-wage availability or enforcement activities (as examples) influence recidivism; recall the comparable analysis undertaken in the empirical analysis of criminal planning in Chapter 2. The data set furthermore contains no information on the demographic characteristics of the offenders themselves, an artifact of the extraction of the original data solely from court records. Thus, we cannot investigate the relationship between an offender's licit human capital and the tendency for recidivism, among other questions. However, the data set does allow investigation of the role of the type of crime, the nature of sanctions, and the era in which offenders first entered the system—all variables described below. The usable sample consists of 3,283 initial offenders.

A set of twelve dummy variables captures the individual's initial charge. The variables named Fraud, Embezzlement, Tax Offense, and Antitrust indicate charges of the white-collar crimes of particular scholarly interest to Weisburd and his colleagues. (Becker 1968 referred to these as "adult crimes," as distinguished from crimes typically committed by youths, like auto thefts.) The additional eight initial crime-type variables indicate charges of forgery, driving under the influence (DUI), larceny, burglary, assault, involvement with dangerous drugs, gambling, and conspiracy. (The data set does not specify the *nature* of the alleged involvement with drugs or the nature of any conspiracy.) Of the 3,283 observations, 2,420 (74%) had at least one of these twelve charges; the remaining 863 had sundry other charges ranging from drunkenness to obstruction of justice, none of which individually constituted more than 1% of the total sample. Similar to the approach of Witte (1980), these offenses make up the reference category for the twelve initial charge variables. As an additional measure of the severity of the initial, or entry, arrest, I also incorporate the variable Number of Charges. A greater number of initial charges may connote a more serious set of initial offenses, a greater marginal benefit of crime, and possibly a greater tendency for recidivism, other things being equal.

A set of seven dummy variables captures the initial sentence, comprising the imposition of incarceration, mere time served, fines, probation, community service, monetary restitution, and payment of court costs. As noted by Becker, some of these sanctions force offenders to compensate victims and society not only for the harm they do but also for the cost of apprehending and adjudicating them. The reference group consists of those not convicted of their initial charges and who therefore incurred no initial sanction.

The white-collar crime data set also contains sufficient information to allow the construction of variables indicating the era in which the initial charges occurred. The year of the initial charge ranged from 1936 to 1990 in this data set. I incorporate a set of dummy variables to capture the period of time prior to 1960 as well as the decades of the 1960s and 1970s. The collective era of the 1980s and 1990s serves as the reference category for these variables. By virtue of the sampling procedure, the data set contains more observations of offenders whose initial offense occurred during the 1970s than in any other period of time. The question becomes whether the law-enforcement environment of the 1970s differed enough from that of the other eras to affect the results of the other variables, particularly the initial charge variables. To the extent that legal authorities target certain crimes more aggressively in some eras than in others, different crimes may offer different benefits or costs in different eras, potentially affecting the recidivism outcome.

Along similar lines, I also construct and incorporate three era dummy variables that attempt to capture part of the U.S. political landscape over the period of years covered by the data. These variables indicate whether the year of the initial charge occurred during a presidential election year, whether it occurred in the first year of a new presidential term, and whether it occurred during a Republican (as opposed to a Democratic) presidential term. In the absence of variables measuring enforcement activity at the individual or state level, these variables at least allow an indirect look at how recidivism varies across different political environments. If estimated type-of-crime effects appeared robust to the inclusion of the era or political indicator variables, we would have stronger evidence that the nature of the offense itself—not the era in which it occurred—exerts a greater influence on recidivism one way or the other. Study of these outcomes revisits in a minor way a similar analysis by Levitt (1997), discussed further by Levitt and Dubner (2005) in *Freakonomics*, that documented systematic reduction in U.S. crime related to mayoral and gubernatorial election years. To investigate these issues, we consider the results of an initial hazard model (referred to as Model 1) that omits the era variables, a second (Model 2) that incorporates them, and follow-up models that have the same essential structure as Model 2.

B. Hazard Results

Both regressor-specific and global tests of hazard proportionality due to Grambsch and Therneau (1994) conducted alongside estimation of Cox PH models of recidivism revealed compelling evidence to reject the null hypotheses of time-constant hazard rates for the white-collar crime data set. Thus, for this chapter I estimate and discuss maximum-likelihood hazard models parameterized using the Weibull distribution, which allows for a nonconstant global hazard rate, or nonzero duration dependence. See Table 5.1.

TABLE 5.1 *Hazard Results: Determinants of Recidivism*

	Model 1	Model 2	Model 3	Model 4	Model 5
Violations					
Fraud	1.282[a]	1.108	1.068	1.081	1.034
	(0.119)	(0.105)	(0.102)	(0.102)	(0.099)
Embezzlement	2.493[a]	2.066[a]	2.043[a]	2.076[a]	2.001[a]
	(0.311)	(0.262)	(0.260)	(0.263)	(0.255)
Tax Offense	1.411[a]	1.141	1.078	1.096	1.033
	(0.199)	(0.163)	(0.155)	(0.157)	(0.149)
Antitrust	2.828[a]	2.206[a]	2.137[a]	2.262[a]	2.118[b]
	(0.506)	(0.400)	(0.387)	(0.157)	(0.385)
Forgery	0.573[b]	0.554[a]	0.547[a]	0.552[a]	0.568[a]
	(0.132)	(0.128)	(0.126)	(0.127)	(0.131)
DUI	0.664	0.625[c]	0.627[c]	0.637	0.645
	(0.190)	(0.180)	(0.180)	(0.183)	(0.185)
Larceny	0.813	0.784[c]	0.791[c]	0.790[c]	0.793[c]
	(0.113)	(0.110)	(0.111)	(0.110)	(0.111)
Burglary	0.531[b]	0.570[b]	0.569[c]	0.576[b]	0.576[b]
	(0.147)	(0.158)	(0.157)	(0.159)	(0.159)
Assault	0.595[b]	0.579[b]	0.584[b]	0.560[b]	0.566[b]
	(0.147)	(0.143)	(0.144)	(0.138)	(0.140)
Dangerous Drugs	0.564[a]	0.498[a]	0.501[a]	0.504[a]	0.500[a]
	(0.122)	(0.108)	(0.109)	(0.109)	(0.109)
Gambling	1.315	1.190	1.202	1.244	1.218
	(0.326)	(0.295)	(0.298)	(0.309)	(0.302)
Conspiracy	1.947[a]	1.576[b]	1.578[b]	1.605[b]	1.562[b]
	(0.435)	(0.353)	(0.353)	(0.359)	(0.350)
Number of Charges	1.103[a]	1.060	1.065	1.063	1.061
	(0.042)	(0.043)	(0.043)	(0.043)	(0.043)
Sanctions					
Incarceration	1.254[a]	1.237[a]	1.251[a]	1.236[a]	1.237[a]
	(0.084)	(0.083)	(0.083)	(0.083)	(0.083)
Fines	1.536[a]	1.574[a]	1.606[a]	1.584[a]	1.599[a]
	(0.124)	(0.127)	(0.129)	(0.127)	(0.128)
Time Served	1.996[c]	1.739	1.868[c]	1.881[c]	1.922[c]
	(0.761)	(0.663)	(0.713)	(0.718)	(0.735)
Probation	3.289[a]	2.952[a]	2.902[a]	2.866[a]	2.801[a]
	(0.248)	(0.228)	(0.226)	(0.222)	(0.218)
Community Service	0.811	0.780	0.814	0.740	0.832
	(0.249)	(0.240)	(0.250)	(0.227)	(0.257)
Restitution	1.215[c]	1.164	1.171	1.154	1.171
	(0.145)	(0.139)	(0.140)	(0.138)	(0.140)
Court Costs	1.350	1.394[c]	1.462[b]	1.438[b]	1.443[b]
	(0.249)	(0.296)	(0.272)	(0.268)	(0.269)

(continued)

TABLE 5.1 *(Continued)*

	Model 1	Model 2	Model 3	Model 4	Model 5
Era					
Prior to 1960	—	0.575[a] (0.099)	0.572[a] (0.214)	0.532[c] (0.092)	0.521[a] (0.090)
1960s	—	0.325[a] (0.051)	0.319[a] (0.050)	0.259[a] (0.042)	0.274[a] (0.045)
1970s	—	0.945 (0.103)	0.956 (0.104)	0.905 (0.140)	0.842 (0.094)
Election Year	—	1.042 (0.073)	1.200[b] (0.094)	—	—
First Year of Term	—	—	1.396[a] (0.105)	—	1.433[a] (0.159)
Republican President	—	—	—	0.715[a] (0.048)	0.917 (0.092)
Republican President × First Year of Term	—	—	—	—	0.554[a] (0.104)
p	0.511[s] (0.014)	0.531[a] (0.028)	0.534[a] (0.028)	0.536[a] (0.015)	0.537[a] (0.015)
Likelihood ratio chi-square	810.44[a]	900.91[a]	920.17[a]	924.89[a]	937.63[a]
Number of observations	3,283	3,283	3,283	3,283	3,283

Notes: Estimated hazard ratios with standard errors in parentheses. [a]Statistically significant at 1% level; [b]statistically significant at 5% level; [c]statistically significant at 10% level.

Model 1 shows that certain offense types encourage while others discourage the recommission of crime. Among the variables that roughly capture "white-collar" crime—fraud, embezzlement, tax offenses, and antitrust violations—all exhibit estimated hazard rates significantly above 1.0, indicating that such violators exhibit greater hazards of recidivism than other violators, other things being equal. This essential conclusion matches that of Weisburd, Waring, and Chayet (1995) and provides evidence that so-called white-collar criminals show no greater reluctance to recommit crime than other offenders; white-collar crime apparently provides a sufficiently compelling marginal benefit to repetition. Individuals with an initial charge of conspiracy also show a significantly greater hazard of recidivism, suggesting that offenders who engage in plots with others to commit crimes exhibit a greater tendency to commit future crime. If such a result held widely, we might have a glimmer of empirical evidence of the theoretical finding, seen in Chapter 4, that primarily *career* criminals would have an inclination to engage in criminal conspiracies, perhaps including third-party spoliation arrangements. All other crime types that exhibit statistically significant marginal hazard rates are associated with significantly *lesser* hazards of recidivism: forgery, burglary, assault, and involvement with dangerous drugs.

Elsewhere in Model 1, offenders who initially incurred incarceration, probation, or an order to make monetary restitution as sanctions show a significantly greater hazard of recidivism compared to unconvicted offenders. By contrast, those who incurred only time served, community service, or court costs recidivated at a hazard rate not significantly different than that of the reference group. Conceivably, those who were incarcerated, incurred fines, or served probation committed more serious crimes than others and thus more likely constitute career criminals who likely have a greater incentive to commit crime again. Studying the offense variables more closely, evidence reveals that the sanction of incarceration may actually reinforce recidivism among those arrested for fraud and tax offenses. When those sentenced to incarceration are removed from the sample, the variables Fraud, Tax Offense, and Conspiracy completely lose significance in Model 1, while Embezzlement and Antitrust retain their significance. Apparently, the actions of incarcerated offenders drive the results indicating greater recidivism by convicted frauds, tax offenders, and conspirators. By contrast, convicted embezzlers and antitrust violators appear just as likely to recidivate with or without incarceration.

Model 2 controls for the era of the initial offense as a way to account for differences over time in the aggressiveness with which authorities may have pursued various types of violations. (Note that this variable does not serve as a proxy for age because, for each observation, the offender could have been *any* age at the time of the initial offense.) Results indicate that those initially arrested prior to 1960 and during the 1960s show a significantly smaller hazard of recidivism than the comparison group, but those initially arrested during the 1970s do not exhibit a hazard significantly different than that of the reference group. In principle, if a significant era effect emerged and at the same time the initial charge variables remained robust in significance, we might interpret the pattern as evidence that law enforcement in the earlier eras under analysis more effectively curtailed recidivism and 1970s law enforcement less effectively curtailed recidivism relative to the 1980s and 1990s. But the actual results support a different conclusion.

When the hazard model accounts for era, the previously significant hazard rates for fraud and tax offenses lose statistical significance, but the hazard rates for embezzlement, antitrust violations, and conspiracy remain robust and in excess of unity. This pattern suggests that the apparently increasing hazard of recidivism associated with those first two offense types reflects more the era than the offenses themselves. Violators of this type apparently typify relatively more effective enforcement and rehabilitation during that decade. But convicted embezzlers and antitrust violators appear to have a greater proclivity for recidivism independent of the era, suggesting that such violators more closely exhibit the characteristics of career criminals. All of the offense type variables associated with a significantly *lesser* hazard of recidivism in Model 1 retain their significance in Model 2, indicating that era did not affect the likelihood of recidivism among those offense types.

The behavior of the estimated offense-type hazard rates when the model controls for era raises the question of how various offense types vary across eras in this sample. Studying this, one does see a demonstratively greater representation of burglary cases prior to 1960 and during the 1960s than in the other eras. This most likely reflects the original sampling procedure, but it does not appear to affect the hazard of burglary recidivism when we control for era. Fraud and tax offenses show similar patterns, much more represented in the 1970s than in any other era. But results comparable to Model 2 emerge when we run the model confined only to 1970s cases; no offense charge variables emerge as significant when we look at cases originating outside the 1970s.

An intriguing pattern emerges when we incrementally incorporate the political-era variables, as seen in Models 3, 4, and 5. In Model 3, both the variable named Election Year and First Year of Term emerge as significantly greater than unity, indicating that those whose offenses occurred in a presidential election year or in the first year of a presidential term exhibit a greater hazard of recidivism than others. The era variables Prior to 1960 and 1960s retain their significance levels from Model 2. In Model 4, the variable Republican President replaces these initial political-era variables and emerges as significantly less than unity, suggesting that suspects initially charged in such an era exhibit lesser hazards of recidivism than those charged during a Democratic presidential term. In a final specification incorporating First Year of Term, Republican President, and the interaction of these variables, First Year of Term proves significant and greater than unity, the interaction proves significant and less than unity, and Republican President, uninteracted, proves insignificant. So, to the extent that the nature of law enforcement or crime opportunity discouraged the recommission of crime during Republican presidential administrations, the effect appears concentrated among those arrested and sanctioned in the first years of those terms. Meanwhile, presidential first years appear consistent with greater recidivism in Democratic eras but lesser recidivism in Republican eras. One should not draw sweeping conclusions from these results about the political economy of public policy as it relates to or influences recidivism, but researchers interested in these connections might use these results as food for thought or as a starting point for studies that can incorporate more detailed data about law enforcement resource allocation.

The initial sentence variables retain their essential pattern from Model 1, but the court cost sanction newly emerges as significant with a marginal hazard rate greater than unity, marking yet another form of sentencing associated with a greater hazard of recidivism. Fewer than 50 of the cases in the data set involved court costs as a sanction, preventing a more focused statistical examination of the circumstances surrounding this sanction. Each of the hazard models estimated for this chapter yield extremely significant likelihood ratio chi-square statistics, indicative of strong model fit despite the limitations of the white-collar crime data set. Perhaps more interestingly, the hazard models definitively yield significant estimates of the Weibull statistical parameter p ranging only from 0.511 to 0.537, giving strong indication of negative duration dependence within the sample under analysis. On balance, despite some evidence showing circumstances that contribute to a greater hazard of recidivism, this finding demonstrates that the individuals under analysis show an overall decreasing hazard of recidivism.

IV. CONCLUSION

In this chapter we have seen how one might use the basic structure of the economic model of crime to analyze the *initial* commission of crime and the *subsequent* commission of crime, recidivism. The essential components of the hypothetical offender's objective function within this model allow avenues for conceptualizing, at least in broad strokes, how the gains to crime as well as matters relating to enforcement, sanctioning, and rehabilitation can influence the decision to recommit crime, sometimes in ways that notoriously defy clean theoretical prediction. These elements make it easy to understand why recidivism research becomes especially relevant to public-policy concerns. Economic analysis of recidivism also reveals the central role of the passage of time: the fact that the amount of time that elapses *between* crimes (or arrests, or sanctioning episodes) becomes the central empirical outcome of interest. In the recidivism literature, this motivates the estimation of econometric duration models, such as the parametric Weibull hazard models investigated here. The essential empirical result observed in this chapter suggests that "white-collar" criminals exhibit no lesser tendency toward becoming *career* criminals as other criminals, reinforcing conclusions by previous researchers. The results also give notice that the political landscape that surrounds crime prevention may have an impact on individual recidivism, shades of Levitt's (1997) discovery that it can have an impact on crime rates overall.

Our economic analysis of the behavior of criminals thus reaches the end of the stylized life cycle of crime suggested at the beginning of Part One. At this point in that cycle, a hypothetical criminal, whether now incarcerated or still walking the streets, again has the opportunity to stop committing crime or to continue committing crime. The issues we have observed throughout Part One—ranging from the planning of what now becomes a new crime to the possibility of destroying evidence of that new crime—become relevant again, and the life cycle may well begin anew. But at the same time, the criminal confronts these decisions tempered by at least one round of experience with crime and possibly punishment.

In light of this sequencing, what comes next, analytically, in the study of criminal behavior? From a scholarly perspective, the next phase of modeling can take on a more dynamic character that reflects the repeated nature of crime as emphasized in this chapter. We can start to think about the commission and recommission of crime, and the sanctioning and re-sanctioning of criminals, as part of a larger, intertemporal system of crime and punishment that yields equilibrium or steady-state sequences of criminal activity. In that orientation, the challenge becomes to make policy that alters not just static individual decisions to commit crime—the analytical scope of Part One of this book—but indeed that alters whole *paths* of criminal behavior in a socially favorable direction. Like the incorporation of social interaction into economic models of crime, this essentially dynamic approach to crime represents one of the new frontiers in the economic analysis of crime and especially recidivism. Of course, as noted frequently to this point, many other opportunities for new economic research on criminal behavior, both theoretical and empirical, remain available to us as well.

PART TWO

Victim Behavior

CHAPTER 6

Who Are Victims? A Review

The first lines of defence against criminals are the victims themselves.

—MICHAEL BADNARIK

I. INTRODUCTION

Most of the crime we worry about in society has clear victims, individuals who suffer harm as a consequence of that crime, and so the scholarly economic analysis of crime involves studying not only the circumstances and behavior of criminals but also the circumstances and behavior of victims. Over the course of Part One, we saw how victims play key roles in various crime outcomes even as we examine behaviors and phenomena solely from the perspective of offenders. Criminals plan crimes partly due to uncertainty about how victims will respond to what they do; offenders' actions, planned or otherwise, impose costs directly on victims in the form of physical violence or other damages; the criminal destruction of evidence harms victims' ability to receive fair legal redress for the losses they incur; and recidivism just perpetuates the cycle of harm. But crime carries implications for victim behavior that range well beyond these connections. In Part Two of this book, we take a more detailed look at how individuals make economic choices in environments in which they may become or have already become victims of crime. We begin by taking a look back at earlier research in this area.

The scholarly literature on crime victims, their choices, and their circumstances occupies not just economics but other social science disciplines as well—most notably criminology, but also sociology, psychology, and public health. We observe a comparable disciplinary scope in research on criminal behavior. In general, however, economic research on victims has lagged behind economic research on criminals. This may reflect a preference by economists to focus on enforcement factors most directly under the control of policy makers and that bear directly on the decision calculus of *offenders*; it may reflect a long-standing shortage of data sets that would enable proper empirical testing of economic theory uniquely relevant to victims and their circumstances; or perhaps earlier researchers regarded studying victims as an implicit and begrudging concession to the inevitability of crime, running counter to the notion of criminal *deterrence* as a primary scholarly motivation. Regardless, researchers, starting in the 1980s, have now demonstrated a vivid recognition of the policy and practical relevance of economic analysis of crime victims, including how victim actions can, in fact, aid the deterrence of crime. At the same time, data sets on victims have become much more readily available, and the quality of their content has steadily improved from the time crime economic research began in earnest in the late 1960s and early 1970s. These developments have facilitated extraordinary research on the economics of crime victimization.

Economists working in this area have focused primarily on issues of self-protection against crime, victim resistance of offenders, various forms of recourse victims take in the aftermath of crime, and labor-market implications of crime victimization. In this chapter we review some of the most important theoretical and empirical contributions to research along these lines, much as how Chapter 1 introduced economic research on criminals. As we make our way through this literature, we will observe a number of open questions that offer opportunities for future research, some of it to be conducted within the remaining chapters of this book.

II. THEORETICAL ADVANCES

A. Self-Protection

One of the best-developed areas of economic analysis of crime victim behavior relates to an activity generally practiced before anyone ever becomes a victim: self-protection. The extensive development of this literature reflects a wider interest by economists in activities and market systems that closely resemble and surround the individual decision to self-protect. Self-protection sharply resembles self-*insurance*, and economists have long wondered how the two coexist and what the act of self-protection might imply for insurance markets generally. One can think of self-protection as a form of private law enforcement, which further raises the question of how self-protection coexists with, and affects the efficiency of, public (governmental) efforts at law enforcement. As economic thinking about these issues has evolved, so has our understanding of self-protection as a distinct economic activity and the factors influencing it. Reflecting the growth of crime economic research generally, the earliest work in this area began in the 1970s, in research that often blended economic theory with legal theory.

In one of the seminal articles in this area, Ehrlich and Becker (1972) embedded the notion of self-protection into a generalized theory of demand for insurance. Ehrlich and Becker incorporated two major elements that assisted derivation of their model and influenced later models. First, in studying self-protection, they emphasized and pursued a state-preference approach, an orientation attributed to Arrow (1963, 1964) and famously applied in the analysis of criminal behavior. Within this approach, the modeler ascribes an economic agent's preferences to states of the world. A person might envision a potential loss state in which crime victimization (e.g., property theft) occurs and a nonloss state in which it does not, each state occurring according to some probability. On the one hand, engaging in some loss-preventive activity (like self-protection) increases the likelihood of the nonloss state, but on the other hand this activity incurs costs that one must pay whether the loss state occurs or not, and of course people have constrained time and budgets to allocate to loss prevention. Given that economic agents face this conundrum, we wonder which, if any, preventive mechanisms they will choose, and how much. Second, Ehrlich and Becker clarified the meaning of and differences between market insurance, self-insurance, and self-protection and brought these concepts to the forefront of their analysis. In the present context, given that a loss may occur, any insurance reduces the *magnitude* of a loss; we can purchase that insurance in formal markets from companies willing to assume some of our risk of loss, or we can use our personal wealth to restore lost property ourselves. By comparison, self-protective actions reduce the *probability* of a loss; in locking our doors, for example, we attempt to reduce the likelihood that someone will successfully burglarize our homes and property.

All of these forms of loss prevention and reduction have prices, and Ehrlich and Becker showed that while consumers regard market- and self-insurance as substitutes, they may regard market insurance and self-protection as either substitutes or complements. In thinking about self-protection against crime, one could view *public* protection as a form of market insurance, if only to the extent that the presence and actions of police reduce the magnitude of loss from crime victimization. A greater presence of police could reduce the marginal benefit of self-protection, thus discouraging it. Alternatively, a greater police presence could connote a greater risk of victimization, in which case police protection and self-protection become complementary in the production of law enforcement and self-protection becomes *more* likely. The nature of the relationship between police presence and individual self-protection activity becomes one of the key empirical questions motivated by the Ehrlich-Becker analysis. As we shall see, empirical researchers have addressed this to some extent, and we revisit the question in Chapter 7.

Where Ehrlich and Becker concentrated on delineating differences between various generalized modes of loss-prevention activity, including modes of insurance, Landes and Posner (1975) focused more pointedly on law enforcement itself. In an extensive and sweeping article, Landes and Posner grounded their analysis in the notion that the enforcement of law takes place as the result of a market process. In the "enforcement industry," citizens demand enforcement, offenders supply the crime that generates opportunities for enforcement, and the output becomes the apprehension and punishment of those offenders. Given that this market functions as other markets do, one can imagine varying degrees of competition among those who would produce enforcement as well as the creation of externalities, given that law enforcement classically constitutes a public good. Within that not uncomplicated market setting lies a fundamental analytical tension between public and private enforcement of the law and even *among* private enforcers themselves, the very citizens who lock their doors, activate alarms, carry weapons, and walk in groups at night.

Among its many insights relevant to self-protection as an individual economic behavior, the Landes-Posner model illustrates how private enforcement can lead to "overenforcement" from a social-resource perspective. As a means of deterring crime, the state may set a relatively high "fine" (using the term generically to mean any sanction) to reduce its necessary allocation of enforcement resources (e.g., police). But the private enforcer—privy only to her own information but able to allocate her own resources, both scarce by definition—may misinterpret this as a signal of worsening crime and engage in a socially unnecessary allocation of resources toward self-protection. Through their emphasis of a market-based conceptualization of enforcement, Landes and Posner thus offer an alternative theoretical explanation for the relationship between public and private modes of protection against crime. One sees elements of the Landes-Posner model in later models of self-protection developed by Shavell (1991), Philipson and Posner (1996), and Lakdawalla and Zanjani (2005), all of which incorporate not only the private benefits but also the public benefits (positive externality effects) of self- protection activity.

Most of the modelers who have made theoretical advances in the economic analysis of self-protection following Ehrlich and Becker (1972) and Landes and Posner (1975) have studied the problem at a comparatively more micro level of analysis. This orientation actually befits a movement toward investigating the behavior empirically, starting with Komesar (1973) and Bartel (1975) and continuing through novel work by Clotfelter (1977a, 1977b). Like the earlier modelers, Clotfelter emphasized the application of the theory of demand to the issue of self-protection. In the first of two influential papers in this area, Clotfelter (1977b) illustrated how the demand for a given self-protection mode depends on its price, its productivity, the protector's risk tastes, and the price-protection relationship; furthermore, because some self-protective modes require more time resources than others (staying home at night requires a greater commitment of time than setting a burglar alarm), Clotfelter's model suggested a concrete link between self-protection behavior and the value of a person's time (among other relationships). In the second, and more broadly focused, of these papers, Clotfelter (1977a) tackled the question of substitutability between public and private goods in general, using the public-protection/private-protection issue as a motivating example and empirical object lesson. Clotfelter cast individual utility as a function of output to which both private and public goods and services contribute production, with police protection representing one possible example of the latter. A customary utility-maximization process determines the individual's optimal level of either type of good, allowing one to formalize the relationship between public and private protection.

Other modelers have placed a greater emphasis on the social context of self-protection behavior—the inherent interaction (or lack thereof) between potential crime victims and society in general, including potential offenders. These efforts echo to some extent the contemporary movement toward more socially contextual models of crime itself, outlined in Chapter 1, and indeed they inform the analysis of self-protection upcoming in Chapter 7. McDonald and Balkin (1983) questioned the informational content and thus the ultimate accuracy of traditional crime rate statistics, arguing that we should concentrate on the amount of crime that exists per unit of individual *exposure* to crime (a "real" crime rate) and that furthermore individuals choose how much optimal exposure they want anyway, suggesting a utility maximization of a type not seen in the foundational models. In their model of individual self-defense under various gun-law regimes, Mialon and Wiseman (2005) similarly recognized possible equilibria where the potential victim "lies low," that is, avoids normal social activity, which then has implications for the type of person more likely to populate the streets at night (namely, criminals) and for losses of personal freedom and positive externalities of community protection. By incorporating an element of social interaction, and even endogenizing that element, these models permit richer conceptualizations of self-protection behavior than we saw in the earliest generation of models. These works notwithstanding, analysis of the social context of crime-victim behaviors and outcomes remains an underdeveloped area of research in crime economics as a whole.

B. Victim Recourse

Economists have also significantly developed theoretical models of various crime victim behaviors that can occur in the immediate aftermath of a violation. These largely involve analysis of important life-course decisions faced by victims of domestic violence and the reporting decision made by victims of rape and other crimes—mechanisms of victim recourse. These two strands of analysis have much in common, perhaps most importantly the fact that both illustrate the vital connection between the actions taken by victims and the wider desire to deter crime. Victim recourse of the type studied in this area of economics also frequently involves a victim either seeking assistance from or providing information to someone in a position to make the victimization cease (a social-support service, a domestic violence shelter) or otherwise remove the offender from society altogether (a police investigator, a prosecutor). Either mechanism reduces a criminal opportunity and may deter future crimes.

Economic theory relating to domestic violence evolved out of interest in the scarce-resource allocation that takes place within the confines of a household. Because households traditionally have two primary decision makers (husband and wife)—who may possess different household and market skills, who face constraints of time and budget, and who have regular contact with one another—family decision making lends itself readily to applications of bargaining theory and other modeling approaches that speak to power, the issuance of threats, compromises, and equilibrium intrahousehold distributions of welfare among husbands, wives, and children. Manser and Brown (1980) and McElroy and Horney (1981) provide significant foundational analysis in this context; Pollak (1994) provides an illuminating exposition of the role of power in models of this type.

Employing a noncooperative game theoretic approach to family decision making, Tauchen, Witte, and Long (1991) presented the seminal economic model of domestic violence, incorporating, inter alia, the notion that one party (the male aggressor) gains utility in part from the commission of violence and that he uses violence as a source of controlling the actions of the other (the female victim). Such an environment carries implications for the nature of resource allocation within a family structure characterized by coercive decision making. Because Tauchen, Witte, and Long imagine that *both* parties make decisions in this model, the hypothetical wife, although a victim, has opportunities to leave the relationship and incur costs in the form of lost income and household stability, or stay and incur the risk of continued abuse; indeed a key result of their analysis demonstrates how an abuse victim might have a greater incentive to continue the relationship given greater family income. But more generally, the Tauchen-Witte-Long analysis makes it clear that we might posit reasonable, rigorous models involving victims of crime making economic decisions autonomously, much as Becker, Ehrlich, and others posited for criminals.

Theoretical (and empirical) research appearing since Tauchen, Witte, and Long (1991) in some ways reinforces and in some ways refines their analysis—the way of all scholarship, of course—often revealing subtler implications. In a series of papers in this area, the applied game theorists Amy Farmer and Jill Tiefenthaler, building on the earlier application of bargaining models, cast greater attention on the abuse victim's "threat point," the value of the victim's alternatives outside the abusive relationship in question. In a noncooperative bargaining context, formal protective services become reasonable threat points for abuse victims: given opportunities to obtain assistance in the wake of their experiences, more women may more likely leave abusive relationships. But this possibility fails to explain repeat use of such services by individual victims, why a victim would use such a service only to return to the abusive relationship. To Farmer and Tiefenthaler (1996), this suggested the possibility that abuse victims employ such services partly to signal (to their abusers) an intention to leave. Victims who have legitimate threat points leave, while other victims use services as a bluff in an effort to curtail the abuse, which empirically does sometimes occur. By incorporating the notion of signaling as part of the victim's strategic toolkit, Farmer and Tiefenthaler suggest how domestic violence victims may have a slightly altered motive than emphasized in the earlier model and thus refine the conclusion that the violence ends only when the relationship ends. Farmer and Tiefenthaler (1997) later present a somewhat more expanded version of the model, focusing on the role of women's income and other postmarital wealth as sources of the victim threat point. In that article and in Farmer and Tiefenthaler (2003), they demonstrate empirically how greater income opportunities for women reduce the incidence of domestic violence, a finding further reinforced by Bowlus and Seitz (2006).

More recent developments of theoretical models of crime victim behavior along these lines have taken a more dynamic approach, emphasizing the role of time and generations in explaining the actions of victims. The model developed and tested by Bowlus and Seitz (2006) reflects this approach, as does an earlier model developed by Pollak (2004). Pollak's intergenerational model rests on novel but realistic assumptions about marriage markets and individual family backgrounds. Male violence depends on whether a husband grew up in a violent home, a wife's acceptance of violence (in relationships) depends on whether she grew up in a violent home, and those who grew up in violent homes tend to marry each other. Imagining that important life events (marriages, births, signals of violence, divorce, and actual violence) follow a time line, Pollak then derives steady-state percentages of the population engaged in violence (say) from one hypothetical time period to the next. This facilitates intuitive comparative statics of variation in the equilibrium level of violence as a function of family background and illustrates how violence can be self-perpetuating. The model also shows how an individual victim's background in a nonviolent family setting can make her more likely to divorce an abusive husband. In essence, the model allows not just personal violence but also personal *empowerment* to transfer through generations.

Pollak's model facilitates these conclusions relying on heuristics and evolutionary rules rather than individual optimization, much in the spirit of the models of crime developed by Glaeser, Sacerdote, and Scheinkman (1996) and Glaeser and Sacerdote (1999), reviewed in Chapter 1. While the model cannot speak to matters of social policy as directly as the models rooted in individual optimization and bargaining theory—a fact Pollak acknowledges—it does demonstrate how a *culture* of domestic violence, and therefore a culture of a type of crime victimization and victim behavior, can develop. In this way the model serves as an effective complement to the analysis of street crime culture developed by Silverman (2004). Breaking that cycle of victimization becomes the central challenge for policy and procedure.

If we think about domestic violence, also known as family violence, as a unique crime type—distinguishable from simple harassment or assault that could occur on the street, inflicted by strangers—then a victim's primary recourse, as we have seen, may take the form of assistance-seeking, divorce, or employment. But in the absence of familiarity or an existing relationship between criminal and victim, these forms of recourse become less relevant analytically. For traditional street crimes and property crimes, the victim's most important immediate recourse instead may become *reporting*, the transmission of information about the crime to others, especially police authorities in a position to transform that information into apprehension (if not eventual punishment) of the offender. Economists have developed theoretical models of crime reporting to a lesser extent than models of domestic violence victim behavior, but the models that exist do help us further clarify our thinking about this part of the connection between crime, victimization, and deterrence.

In their theoretical and empirical analysis of burglary and its deterrence, Goldberg and Nold (1980) became two of the first economists to incorporate the possibility of victim reporting into an economic model of crime. Recall that elements of their analysis informed aspects of the study of criminal planning and crime outcomes presented in Chapters 2 and 3. In the Goldberg-Nold model, households (potential victims of burglary) could benefit from reporting because it increased the likelihood of recovering their property, illustrating in essence how reporting can become an important part of the market-insurance process. The primary cost of reporting in the model took the form of opportunity time costs, associated with personal visits to police that victims would have to make. But the possibility of victim reporting increased the risk of committing the crime, thus potentially enhancing deterrence. While Goldberg and Nold did not theoretically model reporting as a matter of concentration, their analysis brought to light questions about reporting and its determinants; it also provided a starting point for thinking about the *under*reporting of some crime, a notorious impediment to enforcement, information gathering, and ultimately deterrence.

Among violent crimes, comprising rape and sexual assault, burglary and robbery, and simple and aggravated assault, Rennison (2001) noted that rates of reporting tend to hover around 40–50%, but within that category of crimes rape victims report at the lowest rates. In Allen (2007), motivated by the chronic underreporting of this crime, I modeled individual victim reporting as a problem of information revelation, where information becomes a scarce resource usable in the acquisition of social support and legal justice—both assumed to map directly into the victim's utility function. This approach allows one to explore more fully what we mean by the benefits and costs of reporting, especially realizing that victims who report certain crimes—notably domestic violence and rape—not only incur expenditures of time but also potentially incur social costs in the form of recrimination and shame, a syndrome discussed and documented copiously by criminologists and psychologists. These costs make up part of the "price" of reporting if we think about the decision to reveal information about the crime as an exercise in consumer demand for support and justice. This conceptual approach also helps us frame why some choose not to report. A victim feeling that her victimization is wholly a personal, private matter or fearing reprisal from her attacker, as examples, reflects reporting costs that have decidedly social origins.

The model presented in Allen (2009) analyzes reporting by domestic violence victims, emphasizing among other things that the information provided by victims to *researchers* (not just to police) helps those victims create ("purchase") social awareness of the crime, which then assists in the creation of legal justice for future victims. The modeling of victim reporting as an economic behavior, which we revisit in Chapter 9, helps us understand crime victims' objectives and constraints, vital as the literature moves toward a more generalized economic model of crime victim behavior.

C. Other Actions, Other Outcomes

People do more than just self-protect against crime and react in the immediate aftermath of crime, and they certainly care about more than this, but economic theory has seldom ranged beyond these considerations. One can view this book as an effort toward further development of economic analysis of crime victim behavior, by presenting new research and by demonstrating the potential for further research. The models and studies that do exist—focused primarily on victim resistance and labor-market behavior—give us a useful starting point and definitely spark the desire to learn more.

Scholars study victim resistance because victims actually do engage in resistance, and in any case, resistance represents another possible avenue by which victims might take greater control of the criminal situations they encounter, potentially lessening the severity of crime. Bureau of Justice Statistics (BJS) figures published in 2007 document a wide variety of resistance measures that crime victims take in the moment of their victimizations, ranging from the issuance of verbal warnings, threats, and alarms, to physically attacking their offenders, to running away and hiding from their offenders. More than half of all victims of crimes of violence engaged in one of these active forms of resistance; of those who resisted at all, 65% indicated it helped the situation (in their view) and only 5% indicated it hurt the situation. (For more, study the BJS's summary of *Criminal Victimization in the United States* online at bjs.ojp.usdoj.gov.)

Learning about conditions under which resistance—or perhaps specific types of resistance—would logically occur and when it either defuses or escalates a criminal encounter becomes critical for researchers interested in this behavior. As an economic choice, resistance resembles self-protection in that both involve the victim's adopting some sort of self-defense activity (indeed, the BJS calls *resistance* measures *self-protective* measures), but resistance takes place during, rather than before, the commission of a crime. As such, certain issues related to the individual victim's physical ability to defend herself and implications of the activity for postcrime violence become more centrally relevant than in the study of self-protection or other precrime activities.

The model presented by Cook (1986) demonstrates the application of microeconomic analytical tools to the study of resistance and shows the potential for devising further applications in new models. Cook recognized that because resistance makes sense when criminals and victims directly interact with one another, one could employ a game theoretic approach to formalize actions by criminals (physical attack or mere threats), reactions by victims (resistance or compliance), and plausible equilibrium *sets* of criminal and victim behaviors resulting from this interaction. Domestic violence modelers recognize the same analytical potential, of course. Because the criminal (the "robber" in Cook's application) and the victim make decisions sequentially, the equilibria unfold according to a series of conditional probabilities. By studying these probabilities, as Cook did, one can compare the likelihood of certain sequences of events (e.g., attack-comply-attack vs. attack-resist-attack), consider exogenous factors that might alter the likelihood of a given outcome, and use the equilibria supported by the model to guide empirical analysis of the issue. We have seen minimal study of victim resistance by economists since the work of Cook (1986). Most of what we know about resistance comes from empirical studies in criminology that have no grounding in economic theory. In Chapter 8, we build on the work of Cook and that of criminologists to present a new theoretical and empirical analysis of resistance that reveals various other elements of crimes and victims that can shape resistance outcomes.

Crime victims, we know, experience the consequences of crime directly, in the form of physical injury, emotional trauma, and lost property. Any or all of these outcomes might conceivably interfere with a crime victim's everyday decision making, including their labor-market behavior. BJS data from 2007 indicate that, among crime victimizations resulting in lost work time, the highest percentages of those incidents involved completed violence, stolen property (especially motor vehicle thefts), and some sort of assault. Beyond the direct losses of well-being and security that come from crime victimization, crime may disrupt a person's willingness or ability to earn income from working, leading to lost access to wealth for the individual and lost productivity for society. Cohen (2005) presents a rich discussion and quantification of exactly these sorts of victimization costs. Economic research on the labor-market implications of crime victimization, though somewhat rare, again highlights the possibilities for learning more.

Perhaps the most intriguing paper pursuant to this general research question, Hamermesh (1999b), comes at the issue more from the perspective of workers than from the perspective of crime victims as such—a useful lesson as we think about developing new studies of the connection between crime victimization and work. In complementary research, Hamermesh (1999a) had observed an appreciable decline in evening and night work from the 1970s into the 1990s, and he raised the possibility that actual or perceived crime might help to explain this trend; in essence, crime might be influencing not just work itself but indeed the *timing* of work. To lend structure to this possibility, Hamermesh devised a job-matching model in which hypothetical workers maximize utility specified as a function of leisure at specific times of day and hypothetical employers can earn profit by producing at specific times of day; in equilibrium, workers sort to employers according to each of their preferences for work and production at specific hours, and as an artifact we observe a distribution of work occurring across the hours of the day. Greater crime, or more precisely a greater *fear* of crime, magnifies the value workers place on leisure, which may necessitate employers' offering different wages for night jobs (which present the greater danger of victimization); Hamermesh models this using insights from McDonald and Balkin (1983), whose theoretical analysis of exposure to crime helps us view the economics of victims in a more social context. To the extent that less work overall occurs at night, crime would have altered the timing of work.

Hamermesh's model strikes a chord analytically in large part because of its grounding in traditional (albeit modified) labor-supply theory. In a similar spirit, and in an effort to make a further contribution to economic research on crime victimization and labor-market outcomes, Chapter 10 will present a new application of labor-supply theory in a more direct analysis of postvictimization employment outcomes. The analysis in that chapter will illustrate fairly intuitive determinants of the postvictimization decision to work as well as subtler conditions under which key comparative-static relationships hold.

III. EMPIRICAL ADVANCES

A. Self-Protection

Ehrlich and Becker (1972) presented no empirical analysis to accompany their theoretical model of self-protection and insurance, but empirical analysis by other researchers soon followed. Komesar (1973) conceptualized crime prevention within the context of household production theory, a foreshadowing of the approach eventually adopted by domestic violence researchers, arguing that a person's experience with or fear of crime forces a reallocation of household resources (including time) toward *recovery* from crime or *prevention* of crime (household burglary in particular). This approach led to the natural formation of empirical questions about the efficacy of crime prevention (household insurance in his study) on the incidence of crime. Using mid-1960s data from the National Opinion Research Center and probit methodology, Komesar found, among other things, a greater probability of burglary among uninsured households. This finding lent support to Komesar's hypothesis that households more vulnerable to burglary may find insurance prohibitively costly to obtain, leading them to substitute less effective self-insurance and making them all the more vulnerable—another cycle of victimization. But Komesar recognized that this result could have plausible alternative explanations, and in any case the empirical analysis did not centrally address self-protection as a distinct economic choice.

Building on Komesar's work, and motivated partly by the increasing crime rates that had become prevalent in the early 1970s, Bartel (1975) undertook a more pointed investigation of self-protection behavior, concentrating on how *firms* make this choice. Conceptually, Bartel employed the state-preference approach introduced by Ehrlich and Becker (1972) and further incorporated the notion that entrepreneurs might elect to protect their firms (against crime) themselves, or alternatively hire guards, watchmen, or protective services to do this. Of course, decision makers in firms, like decision makers in households, make these choices against a backdrop in which police also offer protection. Using data from the 1968 Survey of Crime against Business, Bartel estimated logit models to study determinants of the use of a guard or a protective service. Among other findings, she found empirical evidence that firms respond more dramatically to a greater probability of a loss than to a greater anticipated size of loss (a result hinting at the disparate crime-deterrence effects of certainty versus severity of punishment researchers would later discover) and that firms did not appear to use insurance as a substitute for private protection. Higher crime *rates* may thus have a greater influence on self-protection than does greater proficiency among offenders, and economic agents may use various modes of crime prevention as complements.

Among other reasons, Bartel's empirical analysis of self-protection by firms proved illuminating because it recognized that economic agents indeed tend to have a variety of ways to protect themselves against crime, but it still begged the question as it pertained to people. Clotfelter (1977b) made significant strides toward filling this gap. Using data gathered through a 1971 survey of households in and around Washington, D.C., Clotfelter endeavored to estimate determinants not just of the use of self-protection in general but of the use of specific measures of self-protection: the installation of extra locks, the use of a watchdog, staying home at night, and others. By incorporating data that ascertained a wide variety of possible self-protective measures, Clotfelter could confront directly the fact that different measures carry different "prices," some primarily in the form of out-of-pocket expenses and others involving primarily time, or opportunity, costs. Among other results, Clotfelter found that low-income households more prevalently stayed home as a precaution against crime, a predictable outcome if we assume that poorer households incur relatively lower opportunity costs of time use than high-income households. By the same logic, one might predict that more affluent households, which presumably possess more valuable time and incur higher opportunity costs of staying home, would adopt more price-intensive self-protective measures, like home burglar alarms. Philipson and Posner (1996) show empirical evidence of exactly this relationship.

Opportunities for further empirical research on self-protection exist. Previous researchers have not universally employed individual-level data to investigate hypotheses emanating from theoretical models of self-protection, nor have they accounted econometrically for the fact that individuals may select any of several self-protective measures at the same time. Depending on the nature of the research question, one might employ multinomial logit or probit analysis or even a simultaneous-equations approach such as that seen in Chapter 2. In light of these opportunities, Chapter 7 will present a new study of self-protection that examines generalized and mode-specific self-protective behavior among a subpopulation of individuals whose safety and security from crime has become of increasing public concern: university students. As we shall see, the results of our analysis of self-protection carry implications for the economics of crime and victimization as well as the economics of education.

B. Victim Recourse and Labor-Market Outcomes

Before it became an established part of the landscape of economic research, empirical analysis of domestic violence outcomes underwent significant development in other social sciences—especially sociology, criminology, and psychology—an evolution seen in many areas of the scholarly analysis of crime and victimization. Papers by Gelles (1976) and Strube and Barbour (1983) serve as valuable starting points in the study of a now vast literature. In their pioneering economic analysis of domestic violence, Tauchen, Witte, and Long (1991) sought to determine the extent to which real families and the victims of abuse living inside them functioned and behaved in accordance with their theoretical model of coercive household resource allocation. They employed a sample of 125 known victims of physical partner abuse in Santa Barbara County, California, and a bounded influence regression technique that controlled for the statistical impact of outliers (the data set contained within its relatively small sample a nontrivial number of victims of extraordinarily frequent abuse). Among their results, incidences of violence appeared positively related to the husband's income but negatively related to the wife's income, at least for low- and middle-income couples; among more affluent couples, both partners' incomes appeared associated with lesser violence. In addition, Tauchen, Witte, and Long observed significantly less violence among couples where the victim had safe places to stay (i.e., with family, with friends, or in affordable lodging). While Tauchen, Witte, and Long used a less than ideal data set (besides containing a limited number of observations, it contained only known victims and no nonvictims, although the authors adjust for this econometrically) and did not specifically model actual decisions victims made—actual recourses they took—their empirical analysis clarified the sorts of research questions empirical researchers would eventually develop much further.

Subsequent to the Tauchen-Witte-Long study, empirical researchers have gradually incorporated larger, more statistically representative, and more geographically diverse samples. In testing hypotheses emanating

from their game theoretic analysis of domestic violence, Farmer and Tiefenthaler (1997) made use of data on samples of victims from two different communities, Omaha and Charlotte, and found reinforcing evidence
that higher incomes among women tend to reduce domestic violence.
Although this study did not analyze the specific link between abuse victimization and victims' labor-market behavior, it did suggest the possibility of
a systematic relationship. Using a much larger, statistically representative
sample from the National Crime Victimization Survey (NCVS), a data set
also employed in Chapters 8, 9, and 10 of this book, Farmer and Tiefenthaler (2003) drew a similar conclusion about the role of human capital
development and the economic well-being of women in explaining the
overall downward trend in domestic violence during the 1990s. Using
data from Canada, Bowlus and Seitz (2006) demonstrate a similar empirical link between women's employment prior to marriage, the incidence
of abuse, and the use of *divorce* as recourse. By contrast to this strand of
the literature, economists have not extensively investigated the empirical
impact of the presence or quality of social-support services in shaping
domestic-violence (victim) outcomes or, more directly, the individual decision to use such services where they exist. Within a model designed to
explain domestic violence as an outcome, both the violence itself and the
use of services (for their own benefit, for signaling purposes, or otherwise)
become endogenous, as seen within the various theoretical models reviewed earlier. Researchers certainly have the tools to deal with this econometrically, but the problem remains the unavailability of proper data.

Where better data exist, empirical researchers interested in domestic
violence outcomes have frequently made use of data sets that feature
samples of crime victims, as apparent from the above. Victim-based data
sets have also aided the development of research on victim reporting of
crime. As discussed in Chapter 1, the earliest individual-level data sets
used in empirical analysis of the economic model of crime, a type of data
rarely encountered in any case, tended to specify the criminal as the unit
of analysis. Although the existence of a crime implies the existence of at
least one victim, one obviously could not infer much about crime victim
behavior from variables constructed from the perspective of offenders.
As victim-based data sets have become more readily available and have

improved over time (often facilitated by research funded by the National Institute of Justice), they have provided incrementally more valuable information about crime victims and the circumstances of their crimes and lives. Scholarly researchers have correspondingly investigated more refined questions and employed more sophisticated econometric techniques that enable us to think more critically about the crime victimization experience.

In their study of burglary reporting and deterrence, Goldberg and Nold (1980) used victimization data (the National Crime Panel) that revealed, among other things, a roughly 50% reporting rate among burglaries. Their ability to observe a selection of households that had not reported their victimizations enabled them to estimate a rudimentary but reasonable logit model of reporting along the way to estimating models of victimization and deterrence. Among other findings, older victims, victims with larger amounts of loot stolen and property damage, and those present when the burglary occurred all appeared significantly more likely to report. In Allen (2007), I used victim data from the National Crime Survey (also used by Cook 1986, later renamed the National Crime Victimization Survey) to study determinants of the decision to report and not report rape, focusing on the role of social support availability and evidentiary indicators of the likelihood of investigative pursuit and offender apprehension. In results comparable in nature to some of Goldberg and Nold's, empirical evidence showed that, at the margin, more severe crimes—those involving injuries, a property theft, and weapon use—significantly encouraged reporting. The NCS victim data also permitted multinomial logit estimation of reasons for not reporting. We will see this technique later within the new studies of self-protection and reporting in Chapters 7 and 9. In Allen (2009), NCVS data allowed an examination of domestic violence victims' simultaneous selection of parameters of victim-researcher interviews and the revelation of information using multivariate probit analysis and simulated maximum likelihood estimation.

Empirical economic research that demonstrates a connection between crime victimization and labor-market participation or earnings, as seen in the domestic violence literature, hints at the more direct question of how victimization impacts labor-market outcomes themselves. The few economists who have wrestled with this sort of question have, quite refreshingly, synthesized data sets one might not immediately think of when considering data relevant to crime economic research. To examine how people time their work hours, and what influences this timing, Hamermesh (1999a) started with labor-market supplements to the monthly Current Population Survey, long compiled by the Bureau of Labor Statistics, and linked those individual-level data to municipality-level Uniform Crime Report (UCR) data compiled by the FBI. This exercise facilitated Hamermesh's discovery that higher homicide rates motivate a move away from night-time work and toward daytime work, consistent with a prediction of his theoretical model. Silverman and Mitchell (2004) similarly wondered whether higher local crime rates led older workers to retire earlier than they would have otherwise. To find out, they linked individual-level longitudinal data from the nationally representative Health and Retirement Study to UCR data—much as Hamermesh had done—to facilitate the estimation of logit models of early retirement. This exercise enabled them to observe, among other results, that primarily *expected* murder rates (those occurring in accordance with an estimated linear five-year crime rate trend) altered people's retirement plans, at least among those in good health; higher expected *and* unexpected murder rates appeared to spur early retirement by those in poor health.

The Hamermesh and Silverman-Mitchell studies, interesting enough on their own terms, suggest additional ways economic research on crime victims can progress. Their blending of labor economics and crime economics—an approach that obviously has precedent in Becker (1968), who relied heavily on principles of time allocation—contributes to the body of knowledge in both disciplines. Their creative linkages of different types of data indicate how researchers interested in the crime victim experience, even obliquely, can sometimes overcome data limitations—which is critical, given that the singularly perfect economic data set does not exist.

CHAPTER 7

Self-Protection Against Crime Victimization

No realistic, sane person goes around Chicago without protection.

—SAUL BELLOW

I. INTRODUCTION

In Part One we examined offender behaviors and some of the consequences of those behaviors over what amounts to a "life cycle," or logical sequencing, of crime. In Part Two we take a comparable approach, examining what one could interpret as a life cycle of crime *victimization*. Over the remaining chapters of this book, we will use economic analysis to investigate the decision by victims to resist a criminal offender, report their victimizations to police (and the consequences of that reporting), and participate in the labor market subsequent to victimization. But our work actually starts with the realization that individual-level crime victimization is not inevitable. Every person understands that crime victimization could occur, and many of us engage in various forms of self-protection behavior as a means of preventing it, obviously to varying degrees of effectiveness. Just as potential criminals plan their crimes, potential victims plan for the possibility of crime happening to them. So, before we think about the economic choices that people make once they have truly become victims of crime, we should first examine the decision to self-protect. Who chooses to self-protect, what modes of self-protection do they choose, and why?

As noted in Chapter 6, economists have investigated self-protection fairly extensively, in large part because the behavior has immediate implications for overarching issues relating to the demand for insurance and the role and effectiveness of public police protection, the latter carrying important implications for social resource allocation. The earliest, seminal discussions of these issues by Ehrlich and Becker (1972), Bartel (1975), and Landes and Posner (1975) recognized that the private enforcement of crime, of which individual self-protection represents one component, constituted, in the words of Landes and Posner, "a pervasive feature of the existing social and economic system" (p. 1). That is to say, we have always had private protection, and it has always coexisted with public, or societal, forms of protection against all sorts of harm, crime included. But the two forms of protection occur not without some tension, especially given that the same individuals who might engage in private protection also cast votes that help determine the level of public protection, and a key question remains whether private self-protection functions in practice as a complement or as a substitute for formal police protection. We will address this question at an individual level of analysis in this chapter. Economists have similarly considered how, at an individual level, self-protection (which reduces the *probability* of a loss from crime victimization) coexists with self-insurance (which reduces or restores the *magnitude* of an actual loss from crime).

The fact that individual self-protection behavior might plausibly increase or decrease in the presence of other forms of crime protection—whether emanating exogenously from the state or endogenously from our own behavior—reflects a fundamental uncertainty that exists when an economic agent makes the self-protection decision. The state-preference approach to the analysis of self-protection, self-insurance, and related behaviors, particularly as espoused in the important papers of Ehrlich and Becker (1972) and Bartel (1975), incorporates the probabilistic nature of these choices and indeed underlies most economic models of victim and offender behavior to the present day. While self-protection (or comparable behavior) reduces the probability of encountering the loss state, it also creates a nontrivial cost that the individual must incur in either state. The simultaneous existence of a marginal benefit and marginal cost of self-protection thus establishes the possibility of an equilibrium, nonzero level of self-protection and, by implication, an individual equilibrium *tolerance* of crime, as Ehrlich (1996) characterized it. Various personal and environmental factors, some of which we also encounter in the study of *offender* behavior, influence the probability and potential magnitude of a loss, the individual utility obtainable in either state, and other key outcomes. The entire process leads to observable variation in the extent to which individuals engage in self-protection and the manner in which they self-protect, and we can demonstrate these connections both theoretically and empirically.

To illustrate how one might apply a state-preference approach in the analysis of self-protection, I will first develop a simple but useful economic model of this behavior. The model will show how the essential elements within a state-preference approach influence the determination of optimal self-protection by a hypothetical economic agent, and it will facilitate straightforward derivation of comparative-static results that function as empirically testable hypotheses. The relative simplicity of the model's structure will also make it easy to see how one might modify its properties or its orientation to address other types of behavior in future research. To study the self-protection decision empirically, I will use an extraordinary data set that ascertains, among other information, the extent and nature of self-protection within a large sample of U.S. university students. The empirical analysis will thus demonstrate how the predictions of the theoretical model translate to practical measurement using econometric tools (dichotomous and multinomial logit) and more specifically how economic agents make self-protection decisions within an empirical setting that carries increasing policy relevance and has not been studied heretofore in the self-protection literature: college campuses.

II. A SIMPLE MODEL OF SELF-PROTECTION

A. Basic Setup

In this section I develop an economic model that takes a state-preference approach patterned along the lines of classic models advanced by Ehrlich and Becker (1972) and Bartel (1975). Suppose a hypothetical economic agent may encounter two possible states: a loss state in which crime victimization occurs and a nonloss state in which it does not. Denote as p the probability that crime victimization occurs, so that $1-p$ represents the probability of nonvictimization. Suppose this probability is increasing in activities that expose the agent to the risk of victimization (henceforth: social exposure activities), denoted r, and decreasing in self-protection activity, denoted as s. Writing the victimization probability as the function $p = p(r, s)$, these properties imply that $\partial p / \partial r > 0$ and $\partial p / \partial s < 0$.

The latter property of this probability function reflects the assumption, originally seen in Ehrlich and Becker (1972), that self-protection, by definition, reduces the probability of a loss. Later we will consider how this probability varies in factors exogenous to the agent, such as the overall crime rate. In her analysis of firms' demand for self-protection, Bartel (1975) imagined location as a key exogenous determinant of this probability; some neighborhoods pose a greater danger of crime victimization than others. More generally, modeling the probability of victimization, or the probability of the loss state, as a function of variables under the control of the decision maker represents one of the key features of the state-preference approach and how it departed from earlier treatments of economic behavior undertaken in a hazardous or risky environment. Ehrlich and Becker (1972) in essence rejected the common assumption to that point of a loss probability independent of the economic agent's actions. While we as individual decision makers cannot do anything about whether criminals exist in society or the area where we live, at least in the short run, we *can* influence the likelihood that we personally will become victims of crime. Preventing our own victimization loss, as distinguished from preventing such a loss to others in society, represents our most direct objective anyway; benefits that spill over to others become positive externalities.

Social exposure activities yield utility at the same time that they contribute to the risk of victimization, and so we can write utility as $U = U(r)$. McDonald and Balkin (1983) incorporate this fact as a key element in their analysis of individual self-protection in urban environments: the demand for self-protection naturally coexists with a demand for utility-generating activities that expose a person to crime. Because the agent engages in social exposure activities in either the loss or the nonloss state, the agent receives utility in either state. Suppose self-protection activity, even as it dampens the probability of victimization, incurs a cost $c = c(s)$ such that $c(0) = 0$ and $\partial c / \partial s > 0$: an agent does not necessarily engage in self-protection, but self-protection incurs nonzero costs if adopted. In the loss state, denote the loss as $k = k(r)$ such that $\partial k / \partial r > 0$; that is, the loss magnitude varies directly with the quantity of activities that expose the agent to risk. As with the loss functions conceptualized by Ehrlich and

Becker (1972) and Bartel (1975), the loss function conceptualized here casts the loss as a function of the agent's own behavior. However, in the interest of studying self-protection behavior as a matter of concentration, I do not cast the loss as a (decreasing) function of self-*insurance* behavior in the manner of the earlier treatments. The present treatment of the loss function actually hews more closely to that of McDonald and Balkin (1983), who emphasized the role of social exposure to crime in their analysis of self-protection. As discussed more fully below, the potential magnitude of a loss will depend exogenously on the type of crime the agent might encounter.

As in the seminal state-preference models, as well as the more recent analysis of self-protection by Lakdawalla and Zanjani (2005), the hypothetical agent's objective function takes an expected utility form, $Z = p(r, s)$ $[U(r) - c(s) - k(r)] + [1 - p(r, s)][U(r) - c(s)]$, and the hypothetical agent will seek the level of self-protection, s^*, that maximizes Z. One can readily interpret s^* as the "private demand" for self-protection, as characterized by many authors. As seen in other chapters, the use of a generalized utility function prevents us from expressing the optimal level of self-protection in a closed form algebraically. However, we can characterize, through comparative-static analysis, how that optimal self-protection changes given variation in key exogenous factors relevant to the individual. Pursuant to this analysis, note that the first-order condition for maximization of Z with respect to s is $Z_s = \partial Z/\partial s = (\partial p/\partial s)[U(r) - c(s) - k(r)] - p(r, s)$ $(\partial c/\partial s) - (\partial p/\partial s)[U(r) - c(s)] - [1 - p(r, s)](\partial c/\partial s) = 0$, which allows derivation of comparative statics.

One should note that a modeler could take a more holistic approach to this optimization problem by deriving the agent's expected-utility maximizing social exposure as well, allowing a formalized analysis of determinants of social exposure activity and its implied opposite, social *avoidance* activity. After all, in their investigation of the costs of gun crime borne by victims, Cook and Ludwig (2000) relate how some residents of a violent neighborhood in New York would veritably "hibernate" inside their homes to prevent victimization; people might go years without ever seeing their neighbors. However, for this chapter, I concentrate on how variation in factors affecting the probability of victimization, social exposure and risk, and the loss potentially incurred in the event of victimization affect the self-protection decision. As we see later, these factors take intriguing empirical forms when we investigate self-protection by university students.

B. Comparative Statics

1. Probability of Victimization Let $p = p(r, s; \varphi)$ such that $\varphi > 0$ captures exogenous factors that increase the probability of victimization (that is, $\partial p / \partial \varphi > 0$). As examples, φ might represent the percentage of criminal offenders that exist in a society or the measurable crime rate in a locality; such factors directly and unambiguously would increase the likelihood of crime victimization separate from actions the economic agent might take. With this in mind, I assume that $\partial^2 p / \partial r \partial \varphi > 0$, meaning that greater victimization-risk factors reinforce (exacerbate) the extent to which the agent's social exposure activity creates a risk of victimization. By contrast, given the definition of φ, one must assume that $\partial^2 p / \partial s \partial \varphi < 0$, indicating that greater victimization-risk factors *dampen* the extent to which self-protection activity reduces the probability of victimization.

Exogenous variation in the probability of victimization thus affects equilibrium self-protection according to the derivative $\partial s^* / \partial \varphi$. To study this derivative, we must differentiate Z_s with respect to φ, which yields (after simplification) $\partial^2 Z / \partial s \partial \varphi = -(\partial^2 p / \partial s \partial \varphi) k(r)$. Given that $s^* = \text{argmax}(Z)$, the sign of this expression will yield the sign of $\partial s^* / \partial \varphi$. Here, $\partial p / \partial s < 0$ (self-protection reduces the probability of victimization), and $\partial^2 p / \partial s \partial \varphi < 0$, as noted above. Because the agent faces a nonzero loss in the event of victimization, $k > 0$ as well, rendering $\partial s^* / \partial \varphi > 0$. This formalizes the hypothesis that exogenous circumstances that heighten the probability of victimization, such as a greater overall crime rate, encourage individual self-protection. Ehrlich (1996) provides an additional discussion of the economic intuition behind this relationship.

This comparative static also helps us see the conceptually ambiguous relationship between the presence of police—or more generally the protective actions of the state—and the individual self-protection decision. A factor such as the degree of criminality in a city clearly implies a greater risk of victimization (a greater value for φ) and thus unambiguously encourages self-protection. But a greater per capita presence of police may imply either a higher or a lower value for φ. If more police implies a higher φ, then essentially the greater police presence reflects a decision by policy makers to deploy more police as a reaction to crime, not an uncommon phenomenon. The individual would respond by taking the greater police presence as a signal of greater victimization risk and thus increase self-protection, all in accordance with $\partial s^*/\partial\varphi > 0$. (In a model aimed at explaining more aggregated patterns, one might even assume a degree of endogeneity of societal police presence, reflecting voting by individuals in that society; within such an approach, one might predict the outcome $\partial s^*/\partial\varphi > 0$ most definitively for those who voted for the greater deployment of police.) But if more police implies a lesser φ, then the greater police presence reflects a dominant deterrent effect, as suggested by Landes and Posner (1975), and signals a lesser probability of victimization. The greater presence of police would discourage self-protection, still in accordance with $\partial s^*/\partial\varphi > 0$.

The latter possibility, also demonstrated by Ehrlich and Becker (1972), resembles, but does not exactly mirror, the moral hazard outcome discussed by many authors in the self-protection literature, including Ehrlich and Becker themselves. Strictly speaking, moral hazard as applied to the present context would constitute a reduction in individual self-protection—a private action that increases the likelihood of the loss state—as a reaction to greater publicly provided insurance. But police systematically provide protection against the probability of a loss (crime victimization), not recovery of utility or property resulting from that loss, the role of insurance. The theoretically ambiguous relationship between self-protection behavior and the presence of police more accurately reflects the fact that individuals might plausibly regard private (or self-) protection and public protection as either complements or substitutes in the generation of utility. If individuals view these essentially as complements, we expect greater self-protection given a greater presence of police, other things being equal; if they view them as substitutes, we expect individual self-protection to slacken in response to greater police presence. As Philipson and Posner (1996) discuss at length, either outcome may carry not only implications for the individual but also important social implications: an overallocation of social resources to crime prevention on one hand, a shortage of positive externalities associated with private protection on the other. In the empirical sections of this chapter, we will investigate, among other things, how university students make self-protection choices in reaction to a greater presence of campus police.

2. *Social Exposure*   Normal social activities at once generate utility and expose an individual to the risk of crime victimization. Consider how variation in such activities affects equilibrium self-protection, or $\partial s^*/\partial r$. Studying $Z_{sr} = \partial^2 Z/\partial s \partial r$, we have, following simplification, $Z_{sr} = -(\partial p/\partial s)$ $(\partial U/\partial r)(\partial k/\partial r + 1) - \partial^2 p/\partial s \partial r[U(r) - c(s)]$, the sign of which will yield that of $\partial s^*/\partial r$.

Inside Z_{sr}, the effect $\partial p/\partial s < 0$ and all other components are positive, leaving the first term positive. In the second term, one can assume that $U(r) - c(s) > 0$ by recognizing that the agent will not engage in self-protection to such an extent as to create net disutility from social activities and self-protection. This leaves the sign of Z_{sr} and thus $\partial s^*/\partial r$ dependent on the sign of the second derivative $\partial^2 p/\partial s \partial r$. Suppose $\partial^2 p/\partial s \partial r < 0$, which would mean that utility-generating social exposure activities dampen or undermine the effect by which self-protective activity reduces the risk of victimization. This possibility would ensure that $\partial s^*/\partial r > 0$, that is, that greater social exposure activity would motivate greater self-protection activity. This might prevail among socially isolated individuals—those who have limited opportunity to rely on other people (e.g., members of their social network) or institutions (e.g., high-security living quarters) as complements to their personal self-protection actions. Alternatively, suppose $\partial^2 p/\partial s \partial r > 0$, meaning that social exposure activity reinforces or complements the risk reduction facilitated by self-protection activity. In this latter case, $\partial s^*/\partial r$ may take on any sign, including the possibility that greater social exposure activity reduces self-protection. This case seems the more plausible of the two if social exposure activities tend to occur in the company of other people, whose presence would indeed seem likely to reinforce the self-protective activity of the individual under analysis. One might expect that people who engage in more socially exposing (but utility-generating) activities may favor especially *social* forms of self-protective measures. We can probe this hypothesis empirically by examining the selection of specific modes of self-protection, some of which carry more social content than others.

3. Exogenous Loss Factors We can write the victimization loss function more expansively as $k = k(r; \lambda)$ so that $\partial k/\partial \lambda > 0$ and $\partial^2 k/\partial r \partial \lambda > 0$, these properties indicating that the exogenous factor λ increases the magnitude of the loss and reinforces, by assumption, the effect whereby greater social exposure *creates* a greater potential loss from victimization. As more severe crimes impose qualitatively and quantitatively greater losses, λ may capture the type of crime potentially sustained by the agent. Differentiating the first-order condition with respect to λ yields $\partial^2 Z/\partial s \partial \lambda = -(\partial p/\partial s)$ $(\partial k/\partial \lambda) > 0$, indicating rather intuitively that a greater potential loss encourages self-protection, that is, $\partial s^*/\partial \lambda > 0$. Along the lines of how we define the loss function and its properties in the present model, Komesar (1973), emphasizing a household-production/time-allocation approach to the analysis of self-protection, imagined that more severe losses from more severe crimes implied larger transaction costs (borne by households) of dealing with market insurance as a precaution against crime victimization. To the extent that this would encourage self-protection as an alternative, the outcome would conform to this comparative static. Because k represents only a possible loss, we investigate the loss hypothesis empirically by examining how individuals feel about the potential for certain types of crime victimization and how those opinions translate to self-protection behavior. If successive crime victimizations generate greater marginal disutility for victims, this comparative-static result may also suggest that victims of previous crimes, and more severe crimes, may engage in more self-protection currently.

III. DATA AND EMPIRICAL METHODOLOGY

To investigate these self-protection hypotheses empirically, I use a data set originally compiled by Fisher, Sloan, and Cullen (2001) for their study *Understanding Crime Victimization among College Students in the United States, 1993–1994* (henceforth referred to as the college crime data set). The data set contains a significant amount of information useful for economists and other social scientists interested in analyzing aspects of the crime victimization experience generally and for those with a specific interest in studying victims and potential victims on university campuses. Most importantly for this chapter, the data set contains information on the extent to which the students who make up the sample respondents— over 3,000 total respondents resident at twelve U.S. universities— engaged in self-protection activities as a means of preventing crime victimization and the specific self-protective measures they adopted. Variables along these lines, incorporated alongside variables that account for the essential elements of the theoretical model, will allow us to investigate how individuals make the self-protection decision. When we observe this activity, we essentially are taking a snapshot of how these university students have adopted self-protection as an implied equilibrium outcome; future researchers should take similar snapshots in other empirical environments as well.

The theoretical model connects to the econometric methodology in a familiar way. From the perspective of theory, the hypothetical agent i engages in a utility-maximizing level of self-protection, s_i^*. This self-protection level conceivably varies according to a simple regression relationship, but in practice self-protection reflects a discrete choice, and so we observe self-protection as a dichotomous variable indicating whether the person self-protected or did not. Assuming the logistic cumulative distribution function for the error structure in the latent regression, one estimates the parameter vector β using maximum-likelihood logit analysis. In modeling econometrically an individual's choice among self-protective modes, we use multinomial logit (MNL) analysis. In the MNL setting, the probability that the ith agent selects self-protection category j is $\text{Prob}(y_i=j)=\text{Prob}[\exp(\beta_j'X_i)/\Sigma_k\exp(\beta_j'X_i)]$ for categories $j=\{1, 2, 3, \ldots, k\}$, and the probability of selecting the referent category (e.g., no self-protection) is $\text{Prob}(y_i=j)=[1+\Sigma_k\exp(\beta_j'X_i)]^{-1}$. We again estimate β using the method of maximum likelihood.

As part of a lengthy, varied questionnaire administered to university students enrolled at the twelve campuses in question (unnamed to protect confidentiality) during academic year 1993–1994, college crime data surveyors provided respondents the opportunity to indicate the frequency with which they practiced any of twelve specified modes of self-protection against crime victimization while on campus. Respondents may have indicated that they "always," "frequently," "sometimes," or "never" engaged in these actions. Some of the self-protective measures did not apply to all students; for example, the securing of a bicycle or automobile on campus would not apply to students who did not use these modes of transportation on campus. Of the twelve self-protective measures suggested within the survey, six had a nontrivial number of students (at least 100 students of the usable sample of 3,266) who indicated that they *always* engaged in that measure. These include locking one's room when leaving it (but staying in one's residential building), avoiding specific areas of campus at night, walking with someone to that person's destination at night, holding one's keys in a defensive manner, asking someone to watch any unattended property, and carrying a (nonfirearm) weapon such as mace, pepper spray, or a knife.

Clotfelter (1977b) and McDonald and Balkin (1983) have studied these sorts of self-protection measures as well, using data sets of a similar scope as the college crime data set. As in Clotfelter's study, this chapter concentrates on the adoption of self-protection measures that incur only opportunity costs, not monetary costs. For dichotomous logit purposes, the variable called Self-Protection equals 1 if a student respondent indicated that he or she *always* practiced at least one of the six measures specified above and equals 0 otherwise. Within the sample of 3,266, 57.2% indicated always using at least one of these measures. For multinomial logit purposes, I define a six-level categorical variable that accounts for the selection of each one of these self-protective actions. The respondents cited always locking their rooms most often (22.7%) and always walking with someone else on campus least often (3.3%). To the extent that the adoption of various self-protective measures reflects personal equilibrium outcomes, these figures give us some idea of the level of self-protection deemed optimal by the individuals under analysis. The 42.8% of the sample who did not *always* practice any of these measures (which includes those who *never* practiced any of them) make up the referent category.

The central explanatory variables incorporated for this study correspond to the three essential elements of the theoretical model, as highlighted in the discussion of comparative statics: the likelihood of victimization, social exposure activities, and potential loss magnitude. The logit models will also incorporate controls for individual demographic characteristics and certain physical characteristics of the campus itself.

Among the controls for victimization likelihood, the variable Full-Time Police measures the number of full-time, nonvolunteer police officers employed by the university in question; on average, 18.5 full-time police officers were used among the respondent campuses. The dummy variable Security Guards equals 1 if a university used professional security guards rather than police officers to patrol the campus (the data set does not indicate exactly how many security guards a given campus used); approximately 9% of the students in the sample were enrolled at schools that deployed security guards in this way. To obtain this information, campus crime data surveyors gathered information about campus police and security guard employment (as well as other information relating to campus security measures) with the aid of a supplemental questionnaire answered by security administrators at the respondent universities. On a university campus, police and guards represent *public* sources of protection comparable to city or state police officers in broader society. The comparative-static prediction $\partial s^*/\partial \varphi < 0$ suggests that, other things being equal, a greater presence of police and guards would generally discourage student self-protection activity if students generally regard police presence as indicative of a safer campus.

The variable City Crime Rate represents the rate of crime per 100,000 units of population in the city or county in which the university is located. To the extent that crime in the broader community can spill over onto a university campus, one expects, and the model suggests, that a greater such crime rate would motivate greater use of self-protection by students. The variable Total Undergraduates, capturing the total number of undergraduate students enrolled during the 1993–1994 academic year, controls for the fact that more populous university campuses likely employ more police and have a greater number of potential offenders, as in a larger city. This variable has a mean of approximately 9,500 and ranges from a minimum of 1,212 to a maximum of 22,892 undergraduates, indicative of the wide variety of schools contained within the primary sample. A university campus constitutes a self-contained community, and so issues of population size, population density, and overall criminality plausibly become as relevant to self-protection on campus as they do to self-protection in cities and towns. Clotfelter (1977a) observed that greater population density in a community may actually reduce the efficiency of police, potentially exacerbating the problem of crime in a given community. Wilhite (2006), studying private and public protection computationally, discovered that as population increased, community quality of life declined, crime increased, and private self-protection increased.

To capture the potential magnitude of a loss from crime victimization, the empirical models will incorporate variables that ascertain student respondents' opinions as to the seriousness of specific crimes on or near campus and whether respondents had sustained specific crimes previously as students at their current universities. The opinion variables, comparable to those incorporated by McDonald and Balkin (1983), ascertain whether students consider violent crime (e.g., robbery, rape, assault, and murder) or property theft as "very serious" problems on or near campus. The reference group for these variables consists of those who regard them as less serious, including those who regard them as no problem at all at their schools. The previous-victimization variables incorporated here ascertain whether students had previously sustained a theft, an assault, a sexual assault (which includes rape), or a physical attack without a weapon. Within the sample, 27.3% had previously sustained a theft, the most common previous victimization; no more than about 3% had sustained any type of assault or unweaponed attack. The degree-of-seriousness and previous-victimization variables specify varying degrees of severity of crimes—whether in perception or in the reality of having sustained them—allowing at least indirect measures of the potential loss from victimization.

To measure student respondents' social exposure, I make use of ten variables that capture aspects of students' lifestyles. A critical assumption of the theoretical model holds that social activities that generate utility for an economic agent also expose the agent to the risk of crime victimization. As seen earlier, greater social exposure activities theoretically may encourage or discourage self-protection, depending on the extent to which social activity reinforces or undermines the tendency for self-protection to prevent victimization. Furthermore, this outcome may well depend on the social context of the self-protection and of the social exposure activity. To capture social exposure activities for the present analysis, I incorporate variables that ascertain students' average amount spent weekly on entertainment (about $35 on average), the frequency per month with which they attend on-campus sporting events and other entertainment such as movies, concerts, and plays (about 1 per month on average), the average number of nights (defined as 6:00 PM to midnight) per week they spend "out partying" (about 1 on average, but modally 0), and the average number of days and nights spent on campus since the beginning of the academic year (August–September 1993). Social exposure variables also include students' assessments of the likelihood, on a scale of 1 (definitely not likely) to 10 (definitely likely), that they would regularly consume three or more alcoholic beverages or regularly take recreational drugs during the next year; the average respondent reported a 4 for the likelihood of heavy drinking but only 1 for the likelihood of recreational drug use. Finally, the social exposure variables capture whether a respondent lives on campus (such as in a dorm, fraternity house, or sorority house) and whether the respondent held a job during the academic year.

The controls for student demographic characteristics account for the respondents' class rank, chronological age as of 1993–1994, gender, and race. I use separate controls for class rank and age because a sample of university students may contain student respondents of nontraditional age, implying a less than obvious correlation between class rank and chronological age. Although 20.8% of the sample held the rank of freshman, the average age of the sample was twenty-four years. Female students slightly outnumber male students in the sample, as women account for 56% of the respondents; the race dummy variables account for black students (12% of the sample), Hispanic students (9%), and Asian students (8%). The controls for campus characteristics include the variable Acreage, measured in hundreds of acres, and a dummy indicating whether the campus has a fenced boundary. The average respondent campus took up approximately 400 acres of space, and only about a quarter of the campuses indicated having a fenced boundary.

IV. LOGIT RESULTS

A. *Dichotomous Logit Results: The Decision to Self-Protect*

A simple dichotomous logit model of the self-protection decision gives us an indication of what influences self-protection in general; see Table 7.1. The variables Full-Time Police, Security Guards, and City Crime Rate represent the most direct measures of exogenous victimization probability. In this model, greater numbers of police and guards significantly reduce the probability of self-protection for the student respondents under analysis, consistent with the prediction that $\partial s^*/\partial \varphi > 0$ and the notion that students regard campuses with more police as safer. A positive significant coefficient estimate for City Crime Rate also indicates that higher crime rates in the city as a whole appear to encourage self-protection activity, as hypothesized. Bartel (1975) similarly found that a higher community crime rate significantly increased the likelihood that firms would use self-protective services. Individual students also show a greater probability of self-protection when surrounded by a larger number of total undergraduates, consistent with hypotheses and previous research pertaining to the population/self-protection relationship.

Among the various measures of social exposure activity, Nights Partying, Heavy Drinking Likelihood, and Drugs Likelihood emerge as significantly negative, consistent with the prediction $\partial s^*/\partial r < 0$. This also gives indirect evidence that campus leisure activities, which expose an agent to victimization risk, generally reinforce the loss-probability reduction facilitated by self-protection. That is, social-exposure activities do not appear to *dampen* the effect of self-protection. The MNL model, described below, will reveal how the various social activities modeled here impact specific types of self-protection, including those with relatively greater social content. Respondents who had been employed during the school year also show a significantly lesser tendency to engage in self-protection. To the extent that employment activity, like leisure activity, requires social exposure to crime victimization, this outcome also supports the hypothesis $\partial s^*/\partial r < 0$.

TABLE 7.1 *Dichotomous Logit Results: The Decision to Self-Protect (Dependent Variable: Self-Protection)*

	β̂	SE	p
Intercept	−0.848	0.354	0.02
Victimization Likelihood			
Full-Time Police	−0.020	0.008	0.01
Security Guards	−0.836	0.207	0.00
City Crime Rate	0.072	0.013	0.00
Total Undergraduates	0.078	0.017	0.00
Potential Loss Magnitude			
Violent Crime Very Serious on Campus	0.272	0.177	0.12
Violent Crime Very Serious Near Campus	0.272	0.125	0.03
Theft Very Serious on Campus	0.168	0.162	0.30
Theft Very Serious Near Campus	0.285	0.126	0.02
Previous Victim of Theft	−0.005	0.090	0.96
Previous Victim of Assault	0.150	0.228	0.51
Previous Victim of Sexual Assault	0.260	0.211	0.22
Previous Victim of Unweaponed Attack	0.171	0.446	0.70
Social Exposure			
Entertainment Spending	−0.003	0.014	0.82
Sporting Events	−0.021	0.028	0.46
Movies, Concerts, Plays	0.009	0.032	0.78
Nights Partying	−0.061	0.036	0.09
Heavy Drinking Likelihood	−0.026	0.013	0.04
Drugs Likelihood	−0.054	0.022	0.02
Live off Campus	0.253	0.126	0.04
Days on Campus	−0.005	0.033	0.89
Nights on Campus	0.047	0.026	0.07
Employed	−0.162	0.080	0.04
Student Characteristics			
Freshman	−0.127	0.103	0.22
Age	0.007	0.007	0.34
Female	0.743	0.081	0.00
Black	0.076	0.127	0.55
Asian	−0.016	0.149	0.91
Hispanic	0.376	0.142	0.01
Campus Characteristics			
Acreage	−0.095	0.016	0.00
Fenced Boundary	0.503	0.147	0.00
Likelihood ratio chi-square (H_0: $\beta = 0$)	380.00		0.00
Sample size		3,266	

Note: SE = Standard Error.

Among the variables that relate to potential loss magnitude, student respondents who had previously been victims of crime show no significant tendency to self-protect or to avoid self-protection. However, independent of this experience, those who viewed violent crime as very serious *near* campus and those who viewed theft as very serious *near* campus show a significantly greater use of self-protection, other things being equal. To some extent, these variables may represent alternative measures of the probability of victimization, at least as indirectly assessed by respondents themselves. But they have value as measures of potential loss magnitude in that they indicate specific *types* of crime that students regard as particularly serious, which is important because more serious crimes imply more severe utility losses. The self-protection response to perceived crime problems *near* campus rather than *on* campus appears consistent with the City Crime Rate result discussed above.

One might speculate that these self-protective reactions to the broader crime rate and to perceived degrees of crime seriousness near campus primarily reflect the experiences and opinions of off-campus residents. To probe this, I estimated the dichotomous logit model incorporating as additional regressors interactions of Live Off Campus with the variables City Crime Rate and the four indicators of (respondent-assessed) seriousness of violent crime and theft on or near campus. These interactions proved mostly statistically insignificant, indicating that the primary logit results do not simply reflect *where* the respondents resided as students. However, the interaction of Live Off Campus with the indicator of very serious theft near campus did emerge as significantly positive in this follow-up model, evidence that the assessment of theft near campus as very serious primarily motivated self-protection activity by students living off campus.

Among the controls for respondent demographics and the university environment, the dichotomous logit model shows that female students self-protect more prevalently than males do and that Hispanic students self-protect more prevalently than white students do. The other student race variables prove statistically insignificant in this model. The student respondents appear less likely to self-protect on physically larger campuses but appear more likely to self-protect on campuses that have fenced boundaries. According to these variables, we would expect to see the most self-protection by students at somewhat smaller, densely populated universities that have fenced boundaries. We will consider the role of the university's physical environment further in the discussion of the multinomial logit results.

B. Multinomial Logit Results: Modes of Self-Protection

Table 7.2 displays results from a multinomial logit model estimated for the six-category dependent variable described in Section III. First consider how the measures of victimization probability affect the selection of various self-protection modes. Full-Time Police exerts a significantly negative impact for each category except for category 1 (locking up), where it is statistically insignificant. Vollaard and Koning (2009) recently discovered a comparable pattern, using Dutch crime victimization data, indicating that a greater presence of police significantly reduced "victim precaution" activities such as the avoidance of unsafe places. We also see that the presence of security guards, which some campuses under analysis appear to use as substitutes for full-time police, exerts a significantly negative effect for all categories at or better than the 10% level of significance and strongest for category 6 (asking property watch) and category 7 (carrying a weapon). So, a greater presence of police and guards appears to reduce the diligence with which these respondents adopt virtually all of the personal self-protection measures we can model here. But diligence locking up appears unaffected by the presence of police and guards. Elsewhere, City Crime Rate exerts a predicted positive effect on some, but not all, of these self-protective measures. A higher crime rate significantly encourages categories 1 (locking up), 5 (carrying keys defensively), and 6 (asking watch), but it does not appear to encourage respondents to avoid places on campus at night, walk with others at night, or carry a weapon. These findings may indicate that a greater crime rate in the surrounding community translates primarily as a perceived greater risk of property theft onto the nearby college campus. A larger number of undergraduates significantly encourages all of the self-protection methods other than diligent room lockup. This provides further evidence that

TABLE 7.2   *Multinomial Logit Results: Modes of Self-Protection (Dependent Variable: Self-Protection Categories)*

	Dependent Variable Categories					
	(1)	(2)	(3)	(4)	(5)	(6)
Intercept	−1.175[a]	−4.066[a]	−7.298[a]	−4.941[a]	−3.656[a]	−2.095[a]
	(0.433)	(0.933)	(1.110)	(0.831)	(0.566)	(0.610)
Victimization Likelihood						
Full-Time Police	−0.00	−0.036[c]	−0.054[b]	−0.055[a]	−0.034[a]	−0.036[a]
	(0.009)	(0.021)	(0.024)	(0.019)	(0.012)	(0.013)
Security Guards	−0.469[c]	−1.021[c]	−1.095[b]	−0.806[b]	−1.406[a]	−1.050[a]
	(0.263)	(0.563)	(0.545)	(0.420)	(0.351)	(0.317)
City Crime Rate	0.065[a]	0.054	0.011	0.102[a]	0.114[a]	0.033
	(0.016)	(0.037)	(0.042)	(0.034)	(0.021)	(0.022)
Total Undergraduates	0.22	0.093[b]	0.201[a]	0.154[a]	0.126[a]	0.119[a]
	(0.21)	(0.47)	(0.054)	(0.043)	(0.028)	(0.030)
Potential Loss Magnitude						
Violent Crime Very Serious on Campus	0.186	0.444	0.414	0.489	0.237	0.319
	(0.227)	(0.413)	(0.400)	(0.357)	(0.262)	(0.265)
Violent Crime Very Serious Near Campus	0.152	0.435	0.405	0.162	0.311[c]	0.477[a]
	(0.159)	(0.315)	(0.327)	(0.280)	(0.192)	(0.192)
Theft Very Serious on Campus	−0.111	−0.686	0.714[b]	0.376	0.384[c]	0.428[c]
	(0.216)	(0.505)	(0.350)	(0.323)	(0.225)	(0.237)
Theft Very Serious Near Campus	0.125	0.327	0.411	0.714[a]	0.332[c]	0.346[c]
	(0.161)	(0.325)	(0.327)	(0.274)	(0.332)	(0.194)
Previous Victim of Theft	−0.076	0.117	0.033	−0.022	−0.028	0.169
	(0.111)	(0.245)	(0.264)	(0.231)	(0.147)	(0.153)
Previous Victim of Assault	−0.218	0.466	−0.127	0.538	0.606[c]	0.124
	(0.314)	(0.543)	(0.702)	(0.496)	(0.327)	(0.372)
Previous Victim of Sexual Assault	−0.042	1.042[a]	0.210	−0.003	−0.486	0.700[a]
	(0.317)	(0.400)	(0.494)	(0.455)	(0.394)	(0.280)
Previous Victim of Unweaponed Attack	0.095	−28.98	1.644[c]	0.791	0.121	0.429
	(0.576)	(195)	(0.935)	(0.934)	(0.709)	(0.692)
Social Exposure						
Entertainment Spending	−0.011	−0.105[b]	0.005	−0.019	0.027	0.010
	(0.017)	(0.051)	(0.042)	(0.035)	(0.021)	(0.024)
Sporting Events	−0.061[c]	−0.224[a]	0.230[a]	−0.014	0.066	−0.034
	(0.036)	(0.090)	(0.075)	(0.073)	(0.045)	(0.049)
Movies, Concerts, Plays	0.007	−0.158[c]	−0.015	0.050	0.044	0.002
	(0.040)	(0.093)	(0.090)	(0.078)	(0.052)	(0.054)
Nights Partying	−0.036	−0.025	−0.161	−0.098	−0.034	−0.123[b]
	(0.045)	(0.102)	(0.113)	(0.094)	(0.058)	(0.064)
Heavy Drinking Likelihood	−0.033[b]	−0.066[c]	−0.058	0.016	−0.011	−0.015
	(0.016)	(0.037)	(0.040)	(0.031)	(0.021)	(0.022)

(*continued*)

TABLE 7.2 *(Continued)*

	Dependent Variable Categories					
	(1)	(2)	(3)	(4)	(5)	(6)
Drugs Likelihood	−0.062[b]	0.025	−0.052	−0.002	−0.044	−0.108[b]
	(0.028)	(0.059)	(0.089)	(0.059)	(0.039)	(0.047)
Live off Campus	0.285[c]	0.157	0.384	−0.243	0.295	0.341
	(0.157)	(0.349)	(0.367)	(0.322)	(0.204)	(0.217)
Days on Campus	0.029	0.023	−0.035	−0.190[a]	0.017	−0.018
	(0.041)	(0.088)	(0.086)	(0.066)	(0.052)	(0.054)
Nights on Campus	0.011	0.123[c]	0.192[a]	0.093	0.049	0.051
	(0.032)	(0.070)	(0.071)	(0.061)	(0.040)	(0.043)
Employed	−0.181[c]	−0.285	−0.120	−0.023	−0.139	−0.153
	(0.098)	(0.213)	(0.222)	(0.193)	(0.126)	(0.134)
Student Characteristics						
Freshman	−0.130	−0.248	0.349	−0.334	−0.147	−0.114
	(0.133)	(0.296)	(0.273)	(0.270)	(0.174)	(0.174)
Age	0.014	0.023	0.014	0.028[b]	0.008	−0.030[b]
	(0.009)	(0.018)	(0.018)	(0.014)	(0.011)	(0.013)
Female	−0.304[a]	1.119[a]	3.576[a]	2.572[a]	1.142[a]	1.868[a]
	(0.102)	(0.247)	(0.523)	(0.308)	(0.135)	(0.166)
Black	0.009	−0.264	0.760[a]	0.042	0.356[b]	−0.168
	(0.159)	(0.390)	(0.297)	(0.282)	(0.185)	(0.204)
Asian	0.060	0.873[a]	0.042	−0.740	0.085	−0.838[a]
	(0.176)	(0.320)	(0.429)	(0.541)	(0.235)	(0.324)
Hispanic	0.187	0.134	0.561	1.088[a]	0.637[a]	0.207
	(0.174)	(0.421)	(0.396)	(0.290)	(0.204)	(0.249)
Campus Characteristics						
Acreage	−0.047[b]	−0.043	−0.135[a]	−0.137[a]	−0.137[a]	−0.154[a]
	(0.021)	(0.043)	(0.047)	(0.042)	(0.029)	(0.028)
Fenced Boundary	0.192	0.600[c]	1.315[a]	0.908[a]	0.627[a]	0.821[a]
	(0.185)	(0.374)	(0.381)	(0.316)	(0.230)	(0.225)
Likelihood ratio chi-square (H_0: $\beta = 0$)	1089.94[a]					
Sample size	3,266					

Notes: [a]Statistically significant at 1% level; [b]statistically significant at 5% level; [c]statistically significant at 10% level.

more heavily populated campuses put students on greater alert for crime victimization.

With respect to social exposure activity, the dichotomous logit model suggested, with varying degrees of statistical significance, that respondents who partied more frequently, who had a tendency to drink heavily and take recreational drugs, and who held jobs during the school year all showed a significantly lesser likelihood of engaging in diligent self-protection compared to those who did not exhibit these activities and tendencies. The question now becomes how these social exposure activities affect the selection of specific modes of self-protection.

Examining the results in the MNL setting, one can first observe that none of the social exposure activities significantly influences category 6 (asking watch). Apparently this self-protective activity has a more systematic association with issues of loss probability, previous victimization, and demographics, as discussed further below. Where statistically significant, most of the social exposure factors *discourage* the consistent use of the highlighted self-protection measures. The category 1 equation reveals that respondents who attend sporting events more often, who foresee especially heavy drinking and drug use, and who have been employed show a lesser probability of diligent lockup. Frequent sports attenders and heavy drinkers also show fewer tendencies to avoid places at night. However, more frequent sports attenders do show a significantly greater probability of walking with someone preventively, consistent with the nature of sporting events as largely social activities. Those who attend parties more frequently and who project future frequent drug use show a significantly lesser probability of carrying a weapon at all times, but those who spend more nights per week on campus show the opposite. Those who spend more time at night on campus may differ from partiers or others engaged in exceedingly risky activity.

An earlier, brief look at the respondent-opinion variables (relating to crime severity on or near campus) gave an indication of how perceptions of greater risk of theft influence the various self-protection choices. Let us look more closely at these variables now, as well as the variables capturing respondents' previous crime victimization.

Perceptions of the seriousness of violent crime or theft exert no significant impact on the lockup decision or on avoiding campus places at night. In essence, these results indicate that the students under analysis would do these things with their current frequency, net of the costs, no matter how serious they considered these crimes on or near campus. We see some significance in relation to categories 4, 5, 6, and 7. As observed earlier, perception of very serious theft *on* campus motivates always walking with others at night, and perception of very serious theft *near* campus motivates always carrying keys defensively. Both perceptions appear to motivate diligently asking others to watch unattended property (significant at 8% and 7% levels), and always carrying a defensive weapon. The only self-protection category influenced significantly by perception of very serious violent crime is category 7 (carrying a weapon), positive at the 1% level.

The dichotomous logit model showed no significant influence of previous crime victimization. One might conclude that previous crime victimization simply does not influence the self-protection decision at hand, but, alternatively, previous crime victims may significantly favor some measures and significantly reject other measures, potentially leaving their net effect hidden when estimated in a dichotomous logit setting. By statistically separating the self-protective measures, MNL analysis can help us reveal these patterns, if they exist.

As it happens, the previous-victimization variables exert no significant effect in categories 1 and 5, indicating that the students under analysis tend to lock up and carry keys defensively with their preferred level of diligence regardless of their previous victimization. But previous victimization does appear significant in explaining the other self-protection measures. Previous sexual assault victims show a significant probability of selecting categories 2 and 7, avoiding places at night and carrying defensive (nonfirearm) weapons at all times. Victims of other crimes show different self-protective tendencies. Previous victims of nonweaponed attacks show a significant probability of selecting category 4, diligently walking with others at night; previous victims of assault show a significant tendency toward category 6, asking others to watch unattended property. Curiously, previous victims of *theft* do not exhibit this particular tendency, but this may only mean that such victims seldom or never leave property unattended at all. Of the four previous crime types represented among these variables—the only ones available in the college crime data set—arguably sexual assault (which includes rape) carries the greatest severity. Previous sexual assault victimization also represents the only one of the four types of victimization studied here that influences more than one of the highlighted self-protection categories. To the extent that previous victimization translates to a greater perceived loss from any subsequent victimization, this provides some evidence that a greater potential victimization loss magnitude more strongly motivates self-protective activity.

Of the demographic and campus-environment factors in the MNL model, only Freshman fails to achieve significance for any category, indicating that freshmen and upperclassmen exhibit no particular differences in their tendencies to adopt specific self-protection measures. Not surprisingly, especially in light of the dichotomous logit results, female students adopt virtually every self-protective measure more prevalently than males. The MNL model does show a curious negative sign in relation to category 1, indicating that males always lock up more prevalently than females do. But this may partly reflect the types of crime typically sustained by males and females and the places where males and females in the sample tended to reside as students.

Probing these gender differences more closely, *t*-tests reveal that males had previously sustained crimes in general significantly more frequently than females, especially the crime of property theft. Although previous theft victimization does not itself significantly influence the selection of any of the self-protective categories studied here, theft clearly represents the type of crime that would sensibly motivate diligent locking of doors. By contrast, and not surprisingly, females more frequently had previously sustained a sexual assault. If many or most sexual assaults sustained by female college students occur away from the security of their primary living quarters, this particular victimization experience might not motivate especially diligent locking of residential doors. Indeed, as observed within the MNL results, this experience appears to motivate more *externally directed* forms of self-protection: the social avoidance of potentially dangerous places and the use of defensive weapons.

For living quarters, additional *t*-tests do reveal differences between the male and female students under analysis. Females, compared to males, less frequently belonged to a Greek social organization (a fraternity or sorority). Consistent with this, among on-campus residents, a greater percentage of females than males live in dorms and a greater percentage of males live in fraternity houses. Because dorms generally lie under university control and typically involve shared rooms, they may feature a greater degree of official security and may even present greater opportunities for students to rely on roommates or floor mates to handle routine security measures, leading to less diligent locking up among (disproportionately female) residents.

While class rank appears statistically insignificant as a determinant of self-protection choices, age itself does appear significant, older students showing a significantly greater tendency for category 5 (carrying keys defensively) and for not carrying a defensive weapon. Relative to white students, black and Hispanic students show significant tendencies to select category 6 (asking watch), but they diverge in other categories. Relative to whites, blacks more likely walk with others on campus, but Hispanics more likely carry keys defensively on campus. Asian students show a significant tendency to avoid places at night and are significantly less likely than whites to carry weapons. The lesser tendency for Hispanic students in the sample to adopt more socially oriented self-protective measures may reflect less-developed social networks and other differences compared to both white and black students. Indeed, relative to white students, Hispanic students more frequently reside off campus, less frequently belong to fraternities and sororities, and less frequently attend sporting events—characteristics suggestive of lesser on-campus social-network development but also true of black students. However, while a significantly greater proportion of Hispanic students are male, a significantly greater proportion of black students are female. The self-protection patterns observed along blacks and Hispanics may track more closely to the experiences and choices of gender groups than racial groups.

Among the measures of campus physical environment, the variable Acreage emerges as significantly negative in all but category 2, consistent with dichotomous logit evidence that students at especially larger campuses do not engage in individual self-protection behavior as prevalently as students at smaller campuses, other things being equal. Although students on smaller campuses appear more likely to lock up without fail, diligently walk with others, ask others to watch unattended property, and carry defensive weapons, campus size appears unrelated to the nighttime avoidance decision. Quite possibly, smaller campuses, given their lesser overall physical area, simply have fewer dangerous places one should avoid at night. Univariate statistical evidence suggests that larger campuses have a greater police presence (both overall and on a per-student basis) and that these universities more frequently had (when surveyed) recently hired *more* police officers. In light of the empirical finding that a greater presence of police generally discourages individual self-protection, the MNL result pertaining to campus acreage may indicate how students regard more spacious (and therefore less population dense) campuses as generally safer.

Students who attend schools that have fenced boundaries show significant tendencies toward self-protection generally (as discovered in the dichotomous logit model) and for self-protection categories 3, 4, 5, and 6. This result merits further scrutiny from future researchers interested not only in the economics of crime and victimization but also in how economic agents choose and react to their physical surroundings, including university campuses. For present purposes, this individual-level result would seem to reflect a significant university-level commitment to campus crime prevention and security, as indicated by the mere presence of a fenced boundary. In the present sample, university campuses that have fenced boundaries also have significantly smaller enrollments (although not significantly smaller acreages) than those without. Predictably, in light of their comparatively smaller enrollments, fenced-boundary campuses employ significantly fewer full-time police officers than unfenced campuses, but they employ significantly more police officers on a *per-student* basis. The greater tendency toward self-protection for individual students at these campuses becomes quite consistent with the overall commitment to campus safety demonstrated by these universities and by the students' decision to attend them. These possibilities raise important questions for future researchers in both the economics of crime and the economics of education. What motivates students to attend universities that display a greater commitment to campus crime prevention, and how does this decision shape future decisions, including those they may encounter as victims of crime?

V. CONCLUSION

The scholarly analysis of self-protection behavior interests economists because it pushes a number of familiar but important conceptual buttons: the dual use of public and private forms of protection, decision-making under uncertainty, and opportunity costs that have lifestyle implications—to name a few. This chapter presents a simple economic model of self-protection that touches on these elements and tests its hypotheses empirically using data on university students, whose social exposure and self-protective actions may provide a window to comparable actions taken within the larger society. That the students under analysis make decisions in a manner consistent with the predictions of the theoretical model, developed within the classic state-preference orientation, reinforces this approach as a way of thinking about self-protection as an economic behavior. The specific empirical results furthermore give us an idea of how university students make decisions in the presence of campus police, other students, and the threat of crime that exists on campus and that seeps in from society outside the campus. Future research undertaken along the lines of this chapter, using the essential theoretical approach seen here, can yield insights that matter to decisions and phenomena that take place within educational institutions as well as to self-protective activities that take place in cities and towns. Future researchers should also think further about how people choose self-protection alongside ordinary social activity; the optimal level of self-protection, and the implied optimal *tolerance* for crime, could ebb and flow depending on how much social activity a person wants to engage in and the direct and opportunity costs of that activity.

Of course, crime victimization can occur despite the best efforts of individuals to prevent it, which means that much of our economic analysis of crime victim behavior indeed pertains to the aftermath of that victimization. Possibly the scariest crimes of all involve direct contact between criminals and victims: robbery, assault, abduction, rape. This fact becomes all the more prominent as we move forward in our consideration of the behaviors of victims. Given that person-on-person crimes do occur and that we wish to explore the idea of the crime victim as an economic agent even in explosive circumstances where instinct would seemingly trump economic rationality (households plagued by domestic violence, stores and city streets made dangerous by robbers and muggers), we definitely want to learn something about how crime victims react in the very moment of crimes. So, in Chapter 8, we turn our attention to victim resistance. If we can demonstrate that crime victims make resistance decisions in a manner consistent with an economic model devised using reasonable assumptions, we can lend further support to the notion of using economic analysis to study the actions of crime victims, demonstrate another avenue toward reducing the consequences of crime, and learn more about the relationship between crime and violence.

CHAPTER 8

The Decision to Resist

Resistance at all cost is the most senseless act there is.

—FRIEDRICH DURRENMATT

I. INTRODUCTION

Victims suffer the material, physical, and emotional consequences of crime in varying degrees depending on the type of crime. In this chapter we investigate the motivations and outcomes of an activity that has the potential to either increase or reduce the severity of these outcomes in person-on-person crimes: resistance. Studying victim resistance using economic tools carries practical relevance because it helps us clarify circumstances under which victim resistance might offer an avenue toward making crime less harmful. What we learn can inform the advice given to potential crime victims as to whether and how to offer resistance. It carries analytical relevance because scholarly study of victim resistance has only sparsely appeared in economics and could benefit from further theoretical development and empirical sophistication. It also helps us gain a clearer understanding of the relationship between crime and violent injury. In this way, our analysis of resistance here can lend perspective to some of the results observed in Chapter 3, where we studied the incidence of violence and damages resulting from crime.

Scholars in economics, criminology, and psychology have frequently raised the possibility of connections between victim resistance and the nature or severity of a crime's consequences. Ullman and Knight (1992, p. 32), commenting on the resistance decision of rape victims, observed, "The attitudes and behaviors that the survivor [of a rape] exhibits during the course of the assault can influence the severity of the [crime's] psychological consequences." In another study, Ullman (1998) similarly noted that victims of completed rape experience more psychological trauma than experienced even by victims of *attempted* rape. Green and Pomeroy

(2007) also noted that differences in psychological symptomology depend greatly on the extent of violence involved in a criminal episode. These observations suggest that resistance, although risky, can reduce the severity of the consequences of crime, including in ways economists usually do not measure.

In his important early economic analysis of victim resistance in the context of robbery, Cook (1986) recognized that robbery has elements of a property crime and of a crime of violence: robberies not only impose property losses but also frequently involve significant injuries and even losses of life. Cook also recognized that the surprise, unprovoked nature of most robberies creates significant degrees of fear among actual and potential victims. Along similar lines, Powdthavee (2005) noted that crime victims suffer not only from financial loss but also from psychological trauma, experiences that adversely affect their quality of life. Robst and Smith (2008) analyze this connection as it pertains to long-term consequences of childhood sexual abuse. Scholars in criminology and psychology have emphasized and empirically documented a number of other emotional consequences of crime victimization as well.

Cook's analysis provides a valuable starting point for developing economic models of victim resistance that we can investigate empirically. Cook envisioned a sequential process whereby offenders attack and victims offer physical resistance by turn; the resulting series of actions and reactions yields several possible equilibrium sequences that vary by the degree of associated violence and resistance. (We will adopt a comparable analytic framework in this chapter.) Due to data limitations, Cook could investigate only two of these outcomes empirically, and in fact his empirical analysis excluded cases involving unarmed robberies, robberies by youths, and robberies by women. The confinement of the empirical analysis only to robberies— and then only to some robberies—calls into question what we can infer more broadly about the determinants of violence and resistance in criminal encounters. But Cook's study still shows us how we can learn more about victim resistance when our empirical analysis takes motivation from concrete theoretical predictions.

The most notable and extensive scholarly analysis of victim resistance has appeared in criminological studies, such as by Ullman (1998), Kleck and DeLone (1993), Kleck and Gertz (1995), and Tark and Kleck (2004). Kleck and Gertz (1995) point out that a key motivation of criminological study of resistance lies in the desire to improve upon an earlier tendency for scholars to ignore victim behavior in studies of crime and to view criminal encounters essentially as "mutual-combat" situations. The historic emphasis on criminal behavior and lack of emphasis on victim behavior in economics also appears to have played out in criminology. But as Kleck and Gertz and other authors in criminology make clear, victims resist for entirely legitimate purposes like injury and property loss avoidance; in other words, criminologists need not view victim resistance as any more impulsive or any less rational or logical as criminal behavior itself, a view that obviously accords with the economic approach.

The primary strength of the criminological studies lies in their use of novel data sets and creative explanatory variables. Their primary weakness lies in their empirical execution. The criminological studies have generally shown minimal recognition of econometric methods that would allow more comprehensive investigation of hypotheses; perhaps more fundamentally, the hypotheses generally investigated in them tend to have little or no grounding in a formalized theory of crime victim behavior. In this chapter we take a new look at victim resistance and offender violence within the confines of an economic model, building on the insights of previous researchers in economics and other disciplines.

II. A MODEL OF VICTIM RESISTANCE

A. Definitions and Assumptions

The analysis of victim resistance presented in this section takes the form of three sequential games, comparable to Cook's (1986) approach. Many of the elements of the model developed here furthermore incorporate insights from previous empirical studies of resistance and criminal violence seen in criminology and psychology. Game 1 relates to physical resistance, Game 2 to verbal resistance, and Game 3 to victim flight, whereby the victim potentially runs away from ("flees") an offender. For analytical and expositional purposes, I will use the term *fight* to refer to all physical resistance by a victim, including the (empirically rare) use of a weapon, and the term *yell* to refer to verbal resistance. As illustrated below, the three forms of resistance studied here potentially impact different components of a hypothetical offender's payoffs; this consequently influences the type of resistance a victim selects (if any) in equilibrium, the offender's subsequent reaction, and the observable artifacts of an encounter at its conclusion. Studying the three forms of resistance also allows us to analyze how crime victims select among several different resistance *strategies*, as Ullman and Knight (1992) aptly characterize them, rather than just physical resistance, the narrower focus of Cook (1986) and others.

For each variant of the model, an offender (masculine) interacts with a victim (feminine). Let u denote the utility the offender gains from some primary crime (e.g., rape or robbery) and g the secondary utility the offender obtains from *assault*, defined here as physical violence inflicted ancillary to the primary crime. Denote Δg as the utility the offender obtains from any additional, postresistance assault. That an offender may gain utility from a primary assault and from a secondary assault reflects the offender's essential "viciousness," such as emphasized in many previous studies and further probed recently by Foreman-Peck and Moore (2010). Cook (1986) noted that most gun robbery victims in his study offered no resistance and that most who sustained injuries had not resisted, suggesting intriguingly that much robbery violence was "gratuitous rather than being necessary to complete the robbery successfully" (p. 412). Kleck and DeLone (1993) similarly note the role of using violence as a means of intimidation, and Hazelwood, Reboussin, and Warren (1989) document how the commission of ancillary violence creates measurable physical pleasure for some offenders (rapists in their study). In a study of victims' resistance to rape, Ullman (1998) further commented on the likelihood that offenders use two types of violence: that "primarily instrumental in completing the rape" and that used to inflict "violence for its own sake."

Let p_g denote the probability that the offender engages in this ancillary violence in reaction to resistance; this probability, which becomes particularly relevant in the model when assault occurs *after* some resistance, allows for the possibility (noted also by Cook 1986) that the offender does *not* escalate the use of force. That is, we do not assume that resistance guarantees provocation. Define p_i as the probability that the offender will sustain an injury due to victim resistance, and let i denote the extent of any injury inflicted on the offender (realized as a utility loss); the offender's expected injury loss thus becomes $p_i i$. This theoretical construct reflects the possibility, explored by Kleck and DeLone (1993) and Tark and Kleck (2004), that when an offender and a victim encounter one another, the victim may well have a willingness and a capability not only for eventually reporting the crime (our topic in Chapter 9), to the offender's detriment, but also, and more immediately, for self-defense, which has direct consequences for offender costs.

Whether the offender engages in assault or not, he faces a sanction f associated with the commission of the primary crime; an offender who assaults further faces an added sanction $\Delta f > 0$ associated with ancillary violence perpetrated in the commission of the primary crime. As discussed in Chapter 2, many jurisdictions codify malice laws, extra sanctions for "special circumstances" in certain crimes. An offender who snatches a woman's purse faces a sanction for the larceny; if the offender knocks the victim unconscious in the process, the offender may face an extended sanction depending on the jurisdiction. Define p_f as the probability that the offender incurs any sanction, which allows for the fact that police do not detect all crime or apprehend all known offenders. Finally, $-v$ represents the victim's utility loss from sustaining the primary crime, as in the form of psychological trauma (see Powdthavee 2005; Green and Pomeroy 2007). For simplicity, I assume that the offender's utility gain from assault equals the disutility the victim sustains from that assault, so that $|g| = |v|$.

Consider the sequence of actions that unfolds in each variant of the resistance model. In all three variants, either the offender or the victim may move first following the offender's commission of the primary crime, taken as given. (In conceding the commission of the primary crime analytically, I do not model the possibility that the hypothetical victim resists preemptive to a given crime victimization, as if sensing an imminent vulnerability to the crime. However, as we shall see, the model does allow for a victim to resist preemptive to an ancillary *assault*.) In Game 1, if the offender moves first, the offender either assaults the victim or does not. Given offender assault, the victim either fights (physically resists) or does not. Not fighting ends the encounter; fighting may end the encounter or provoke further assault. Given initial offender nonassault, the victim still either fights or does not, and fighting again either ends the encounter or provokes a postresistance assault by the offender. In the alternative sequence, the *victim* moves first following commission of the crime and either fights or does not; given the victim's decision, the offender then either assaults or does not. Game 2 unfolds with a comparable sequence of actions, differing only by the victim's resisting *verbally*, such as through shouting to attract the attention of others. Game 3 involves an initial postcrime offender assault or nonassault, followed by the victim fleeing or not fleeing the offender. In the alternative sequence, the victim moves first, making the flight decision following the primary crime but prior to the offender's assault decision.

In Game 1, if the sequence {no assault, fight, no assault} prevails, the offender receives payoff $u - p_i i - p_f f$. That is, the offender gains utility from the commission of the primary crime but loses utility due to the expected injury (due to the victim's physical resistance) and the expected sanction. If the sequence {no assault, no fight} prevails, the offender receives $u - p_f f$, indicating that in the absence of resistance, the offender incurs only the expected sanction cost. If {assault, fight, assault} prevails, the offender receives $u + g + \Delta g - p_i i - p_f (f + \Delta f)$. The offender gains utility from the commission of the primary crime and assault as well as an increase in g associated with responding to resistance with additional violence. The offender still faces the expected injury cost and the expected sanction cost, the factor Δf reflecting the added sanction for the "special circumstance" of ancillary violence. The expected-injury factor $(p_i i)$ and the retaliation factor (Δg) disappear if the victim does not fight. The victim suffers the utility loss $-v$ associated with the primary crime and from ancillary violence but gains utility by injuring the offender and by enhancing the likelihood of sanctioning. Game 2 differs from Game 1 in that verbal resistance creates no risk of injury to the offender and immediately impacts p_f due to the possibility that yelling attracts the attention of police or bystanders who might notify police.

In relation to Game 3, I analyze only the situation where the offender moves first. Thus, after the crime has occurred, the offender has either assaulted or not, at which point the victim's decision to flee becomes relevant.

Flight affects the likelihood that the offender will have an *opportunity* to inflict either an initial assault (loss g) or a secondary assault (loss Δg) on the victim because it creates a new problem for the offender: a search (or pursuit) decision. To model pursuit, I make the injury-loss factors dependent on probabilities of "successful" search, that is, pursuit that allows the offender to assault the victim despite victim flight. Finally, as in the verbal-resistance variant, because the decision to flee may attract attention from bystanders in the area of the incident, the variable Δp_f becomes relevant as well. Table 8.1 summarizes the offender's and the victim's expected payoffs for each variant of the resistance model when the offender

TABLE 8.1 *Summary of Offender and Victim Resistance Payoffs, Offender Moves First*

	Game 1 (Physical Resistance)	
Sequence of Actions	Offender Payoff	Victim Payoff
Assault, fight, assault	$u+g+\Delta g-p_i i-p_f(f+\Delta f)$	$-v-g-\Delta g+p_i i+p_f(f+\Delta f)$
Assault, fight, no assault	$u+g-p_i i-p_f(f+\Delta f)$	$-v-g+p_i i+p_f(f+\Delta f)$
Assault, no fight	$u+g-p_f(f+\Delta f)$	$-v-g+p_i i+p_f(f+\Delta f)$
No assault, fight, assault	$u+g-p_i i+p_f(f+\Delta f)$	$-v-g+p_i i+p_f(f+\Delta f)$
No assault, fight, no assault	$u-p_i i-p_f f$	$-v+p_i i+p_f f$
No assault, no fight	$u-p_f f$	$-v+p_f f$

	Game 2 (Verbal Resistance)	
Sequence of Actions	Offender Payoff	Victim Payoff
Assault, yell, assault	$u+g+\Delta g-(p_f+\Delta p_f)(f+\Delta f)$	$-v-g-\Delta g+(p_f+\Delta p_f)(f+\Delta f)$
Assault, yell, no assault	$u+g-(p_f+\Delta p_f)(f+\Delta f)$	$-v-g+(p_f+\Delta p_f)(f+\Delta f)$
Assault, no yell	$u+g-p_f(f+\Delta f)$	$-v-g+p_f(f+\Delta f)$
No assault, yell, assault	$u+g-(p_f+\Delta p_f)(f+\Delta f)$	$-v-g+(p_f+\Delta p_f)(f+\Delta f)$
No assault, yell, no assault	$u-(p_f+\Delta p_f)f$	$-v+(p_f+\Delta p_f)f$
No assault, no yell	$u-p_f f$	$-v+p_f f$

	Game 3 (Flight)	
Sequence of Actions	Offender Payoff	Victim Payoff
Assault, flee, assault	$u+g+\Delta g-c+p_f(f+\Delta f)$	$-v-g-p_g\Delta g+(p_f+\Delta p_f)(f+\Delta f)$
Assault, no flee, no assault	$u+g+p_f(f+\Delta f)$	$-v-g+p_f(f+\Delta f)$
No assault, flee, assault	$u+g-c-p_f(f+\Delta f)$	$-v-p_g g+p_f f$
No assault, no flee, no assault	$u-p_f f$	$-v+p_f f$

moves first, a more common circumstance than resistance that precedes offender violence.

Given the model structure, and partly motivated by previous research on resistance, we address three sets of questions. (1) Under what conditions do victims choose physical resistance, verbal resistance, or flight over nonresistance? (2) Under what conditions does resistance either *provoke* or *prevent* assault? (3) How might victim resistance decisions, however resolved, vary by the type or circumstances of the crime?

B. Resistance and Resistance Types

We can now study the determinants of a victim's decision to resist in the three ways highlighted above and consider how exogenous factors might influence these choices. It turns out that many of the results depend not only on characteristics of the offender and the victim but also on the physical environment in which the crime takes place.

1. Physical Resistance Suppose the offender moves first and assaults. Making use of the expected payoffs as summarized in Table 8.1, victim indifference between fighting and not fighting implies that $p_g[(-v-g-\Delta g+p_i i +p_f(f+\Delta f)] + (1-p_g)[-v-g+p_i i+p_f(f+\Delta f)] = -v-g+p_i i+p_f(f+\Delta f)$. This condition simplifies to $p_i i-p_g\Delta g=0$, the left side representing the victim's net expected payoff from fighting, denoted V(fight|assault). Clearly, ∂V(fight|assault)$/\partial p_i>0$ and ∂V(fight|assault)$/\partial i>0$, indicating collectively that the incentive to fight increases if the victim has greater confidence in her ability to inflict an injury loss. One can also observe that ∂V(fight|assault)$/\partial p_g<0$ and ∂V(fight|assault)$/\partial\Delta g<0$, indicating that the victim's incentive to fight decreases with the degree of offender viciousness, as captured by the probability of assault p_g and the magnitude of the postresistance violence Δg. In essence, the incentive to fight declines with a greater expected victim injury loss $p_g\Delta g$, other things being equal.

Suppose the offender moves first but does not assault. Victim indifference between fighting and not fighting implies that $p_g[-v-g+p_i i+ p_f(f+\Delta f)] + (1-p_g)(-v+p_i i+p_f f) = -v+p_f f$, which simplifies to $p_i i+p_f\Delta f- p_g g=0$. Comparable to the above, the left side represents V(fight|no assault). The relationships observed in the offender-assaults case hold here.

But in addition we can observe that $\partial V(\text{fight}|\text{no assault})/\partial p_f > 0$ and $\partial V(\text{fight}|\text{assault})/\partial \Delta f > 0$, suggesting that the incentive to fight is increasing in the probability of detection and the extent of additional sanctioning for extra violence. If more severe crimes attract greater attention from police and stronger codified sanctions, a victim's incentive to engage in physical resistance may increase with the severity of the crime, other things being equal. This result points up the value of using data covering a *variety* of types of crime when analyzing victim resistance empirically.

The analysis and conclusions become simpler when the victim moves first. In the context of Game 1, the victim moving first implies that, as an immediate reaction to the commission of the primary crime, the victim makes a decision to fight (or not) preemptive to any possible assault by the offender. Victim indifference between fighting and not fighting in this circumstance implies equality between the victim's expected utility from these actions, the implicit payoffs contingent on the probability of subsequent assault (p_g) and nonassault $(1 - p_g)$. Following simplification, this condition collapses to $p_i i = 0$. Thus, for the victim to have an incentive to fight (vs. not fight), when moving first, $p_i i$ must be positive, implying that $p_i > 0$ and $i > 0$ simultaneously. Similar to the case where the offender moves first, *preemptive* physical resistance requires the victim to have complete confidence in her ability to inflict nontrivial injury on the offender. Short of this, including the possibility of victim incapacitation due to injury, or a victim at a significant age disadvantage to the offender (either very much younger or very much older), or a victim outnumbered by multiple offenders, the victim will have no particular incentive not to comply with the offender. In these cases, likely the victim has no chance to inflict injury, $p_i = 0$, or can inflict no substantive injury, $i = 0$, or both.

2. *Verbal Resistance*   Empirical analysis by Cook (1986) indicated that victims who offered physical resistance to robbery showed the highest chance of attack and serious injury, raising the possibility that victims might resist in other, less physical ways, such as through yelling for help. To consider this form of resistance analytically, pursuant to Game 2, suppose the offender moves first and assaults. Victim indifference between

yelling and not yelling at this point implies that $p_g[-v-g-\Delta g+(p_f+\Delta p_f)$ $(f+\Delta f)]+(1-p_g)[-v-g+(p_f+\Delta p_f(f+\Delta f)]=-v-g+p_f(f+\Delta f)$, or $\Delta p_f(f+\Delta f)-$ $p_g\Delta g=0$, the left side of this expression representing V(yell|assault). Observe that ∂V(yell|assault)$/\partial f=\partial V$(yell)$/\partial\Delta f=\Delta p_f>0$, indicating that the victim's incentive to yell is increasing in the primary-crime sanction (f) and the added sanction for ancillary violence (Δf) so long as $\Delta p_f>0$, that is, when verbal resistance actually does increase the probability of detection. In addition, observe that ∂V(yell|assault)$/\partial p_g<0$ and ∂V(yell|assault)$/\partial\Delta g<0$, indicating that the incentive to yell decreases with the probability of (further) assault and with the extra injury loss Δg, each of which relates to the offender's viciousness. In short, the victim has a lesser incentive to yell given a higher expected extra injury loss. If the offender moves first but does not assault, then victim indifference similarly implies, after simplification, that $\Delta p_f(p_g\Delta f+f)+p_g(p_f\Delta f-g)=0$. We still observe that ∂V(yell|no assault)$/\partial f>0$ and ∂V(yell|no assault)$/\partial\Delta f>0$, as above. (The component Δg becomes irrelevant in this sequence because of the offender's initial nonassault.) The analysis reveals again that the victim's incentive to engage in verbal resistance likely depends on the nature and type of crime involved, a possibility undeveloped in earlier analyses that focused on a single crime type.

Additional study of the comparative statics related to the incentive to yell illustrates that victims may have a greater incentive to engage in verbal resistance as a reaction to assault than to do so preemptive to an assault. Verbal resistance directly impacts p_f, the probability of offender detection. Observe that variation in Δp_f, the degree to which yelling alters the probability of detection, affects V(yell|assault) according to the derivative ∂V(yell|assault)$/\partial\Delta p_f=f+\Delta f$ and that it affects ∂V(yell|no assault) according to ∂V(yell|no assault)$/\partial\Delta p_f=f+p_g\Delta f$. Because $p_g\leq1$, ∂V (yell|assault)$/\partial\Delta p_f\geq\partial V$(yell|no assault)$/\partial\Delta p_f$. (In practice, we may in fact see $p_g<1$, which would imply a *strict* inequality of these effects.) Intuitively, a victim who has sustained the primary crime but has not sustained an assault more likely hesitates to yell, uncertain whether yelling will then provoke an assault; a victim who has already sustained an assault has less uncertainty about the offender's type (his tendency to assault) and so has less reluctance to yell. The model thus provides an economic explanation for offenders' greater tendency to move first in person-on-person crimes involving offender violence and victim resistance.

The analysis above highlights the importance of the variable Δp_f, positive variation in which increases the incentive to yell reactively or preemptively. The observations surrounding that analysis raise the question, "When would yelling most effectively increase the probability of detection?" It seems reasonable that this would occur in the presence of bystanders rather than in isolation, or in the presence of individuals the victim knows rather than in the presence of strangers. The effectiveness of yelling may also depend on whether the incident occurs indoors or outdoors and on the time of day. Put another way, the answer to this question likely depends to some extent on the observable empirical environment in which the person-on-person crime takes place. Previous authors, such as Kleck and Sayles (1990) and Kleck and DeLone (1993), have occasionally suggested how these sorts of environmental aspects of crimes might influence victim resistance, although the stated hypotheses generally have had little grounding in formal theory. The verbal-resistance variant of the current model illustrates an analytical linkage between resistance and aspects of the physical environment of a crime that we can test empirically.

Let us also briefly consider the implications of the victim's having the opportunity to move first—to yell or not yell subsequent to the primary crime but preemptive to any assault. One can readily observe that the victim's decision in this circumstance will depend on the victim's judgment of any possible injury loss associated with possible assault compared to any restitutive gain associated with attracting attention. As noted by Hazelwood, Reboussin, and Warren (1989) and Kleck and Sayles (1990), resistance understandably can lengthen the duration of an attack and expose the offender to a greater probability of detection by onlookers or police. If the victim moves first and yells, indifference between the outcomes {yell, no assault} and {yell, assault} would imply that $p_g[-v - g + (p_f + \Delta p_f)(f + \Delta f)] = (1 - p_g)[-v + (p_f + \Delta p_f)f]$. Suppose the victim, having no information about the offender's capacity for violence, carries a passive conjecture about the likelihood of assault, so that $p_g = 0.5$; then, this expression reduces to $(p_f + \Delta p_f)\Delta f = g$. If the victim moves first but does not yell—the victim acknowledging the possibility of offender assault but offering no preemptive verbal resistance—indifference between {no yell, assault} and {no yell, no assault} would imply that $p_g[-v-g+p_f(f+\Delta f)] = (1-p_g)$ $(-v+p_f f)$, which under passive conjectures simplifies to $p_f \Delta f = g$. In either case, the victim will prefer not to yell if the injury loss g fails to exceed the expected restitutive gain associated with eventual sanctioning for the assault.

Other things being equal, then, we would not expect preemptive verbal resistance in crimes carrying minimal likelihood of offender detection (e.g., crimes occurring in socially isolated environments or crimes by random strangers) or for which the law specifies minimal added sanctioning for ancillary violence. By the same token, preemptive verbal resistance would seem more predictable in crimes where the victim perceives a minimal injury loss g from ancillary assault, such as in the absence of a firearm or other weapon or given a relatively nonthreatening offender. The possibility that the victim might preemptively resist motivates an additional question as to whether yelling or silence actually pays off. To address this question, we must study the *offender's* payoffs and decisions—upcoming as part of the second set of analytical questions.

3. *Victim Flight*   Where feasible, running away from an offender, as Cook (1986) noted in the wake of his empirical findings, represents another potentially less injurious alternative to physical resistance. In the present context of Game 3, when the offender moves first and assaults, the victim must decide whether to flee or stay. Victim indifference between these actions implies that $q[-v-g-p_g\Delta g+(p_f+\Delta p_f)(f+\Delta f)] = (1-q)[-v-g+p_f(f+\Delta f)$, or more simply that $-q\Delta g +\Delta p_f(f+\Delta f) = 0$, where q represents the probability of successful pursuit; denote the left side of this expression as V(flee|assault). If the offender does not assault, victim indifference implies $-qg = 0$; denote the left side of this expression as V(flee|no assault). The first case carries the greater information and relevance. If V(flee|assault) > 0, then the victim has a greater incentive to flee than to stay. Observe that ∂V(flee|assault)$/\partial q < 0$, indicating that the victim's incentive to flee decreases with a higher probability of successful pursuit: the less likely the offender will catch the victim, the greater the incentive to flee, and vice

versa. Conceivably, the age of the victim, the age difference between criminal and victim, the presence of a firearm, the relative openness or confinement of the crime venue, the victim's gender (or perhaps criminal-victim
gender differences), or the degree of any injury to the victim could impact
this probability and thus the decision to flee. We can observe many of
these factors empirically, as described in Section III. Also note that
V(flee|assault) is increasing in the enforcement variables Δp_f, f, and Δf. In
Game 3, fleeing allows for $\Delta p_f > 0$ because of the possibility of attracting
attention from others in the moment of the crime; this of course may
hold in a more crowded social environment, for example. The effect of f
and Δf suggests that the incentive to flee increases with the severity of the
crime, other things being equal.

C. Provocation or Prevention?

Scholarly consideration of victim resistance inevitably arrives at the question of whether resistance provokes offender assault or prevents it. Kleck
and DeLone (1993) have thoughtfully observed that even as resistance
delays a criminal's actions, injures the criminal, or otherwise raises the
cost of committing the crime, resistance still might provoke the criminal
to further offenses potentially worse than the primary crime. Although
Kleck and Gertz (1995) and other studies find little or no empirical evidence that resistance does provoke criminals to attack, neither researchers nor policy advisors can take this outcome for granted.

To study the question of whether resistance provokes or prevents assault in the present setting, we concentrate on the three variants of the
model in the context of the victim moving first. The provocation of offender assault by victim resistance implies that, following resistance, the
offender has a greater incentive to assault than not to assault.

In Game 1, if the victim moves first and fights, then offender indifference between assault and nonassault implies, after simplification, that
$g = p_f \Delta f$. If the victim moves first but does not fight, offender indifference
again implies that $g = p_f \Delta f$. With respect to physical resistance, whether
the victim fights or not, the offender thus has a net incentive to assault if
the offender gains more utility from the assault than disutility from the
extra expected sanction $p_f \Delta f$. Physical resistance has no assumed effect

on p_f, and so the social environment exerts no analytically systematic effect on the decision to assault, regardless of the victim's decision to fight. Holding constant the criminal's viciousness, which determines the magnitude of g, greater enforcement activity can increase the incentive not to assault. Specifically, a higher p_f or Δf (for example, a greater police presence, or a more severe codified penalty for assault committed during a personal crime) increases the incentive not to assault, present on the right side of each indifference condition. If a higher p_f, f, or Δf signifies greater severity of the crime at the margin, ancillary assault may become less likely for the most severe crimes but more likely (not surprisingly) among the most vicious criminals. But if the most vicious criminals tend to commit the most severe crimes, at least by these measures, then this distinction becomes moot. Given that social environment becomes a nonfactor in the physical-resistance game, physical resistance seems equally effective (or ineffective, depending on your point of view) in a populated or isolated social environment, but *verbal* resistance reinforces the incentive not to assault in a more populated environment, where either p_f or Δf likely would have a greater magnitude.

In Game 2, if the victim moves first and yells, then offender indifference between assault and not assault implies that $g = (p_f + \Delta p_f)\Delta f$. If the victim moves first but does not yell, offender indifference implies that $g = p_f \Delta f$. Similar implications then emerge as seen in the context of victim decisions: greater enforcement activities and a more socially isolated environment (the latter reduces Δp_f) tend to encourage assault, other things being equal. Victim yelling can prevent assault more effectively than silence because yelling imposes the extra cost $\Delta p_f \Delta f$ on the offender. So long as $\Delta p_f > 0$ and $\Delta f > 0$, the assault condition $g > (p_f + \Delta p_f)\Delta f$ holds less readily. By not yelling, the victim relies solely on the criminal's having relatively minimal viciousness and on the enforcement activity embodied in $p_f \Delta f$. In a socially isolated setting, where Δp_f approaches zero, yelling and silence yield the same assault outcome.

We can also probe the implications of victim flight for the offender's pursuit decision, pursuant to Game 3. Assuming an initial assault, offender indifference between pursuit and nonpursuit implies that $q[u + g + \Delta g - c + p_f(f + \Delta f)] = (1 - q)[u + g - c + p_f(f + \Delta f)]$, or more simply that

$q(\Delta g - c) + (1 - q)(-c) = 0$; denote the left side of this expression as u(pursuit), the offender's net payoff from pursuit of a victim who has fled. Straightforward derivatives show the relationship of this payoff to key variables. First, ∂u(pursuit)$/\partial q > 0$, indicating that the incentive to pursue increases with the probability of successful pursuit. Crimes involving younger offenders, advantageously aged offenders, or a relatively confined physical environment may exhibit comparatively higher q, contributing to a greater likelihood of attack following victim flight. Also observe that ∂u(pursuit)$/\partial c < 0$, indicating that the incentive to pursue decreases with the cost of pursuit. Finally, observe that ∂u(pursuit)$/\partial \Delta g > 0$, indicating that the incentive to pursue increases with the offender's viciousness. Absent direct data on offender personality, often incorporated by psychologists but relatively rare in economics, we may see relevant variation in Δg by the type of crime, the severity of any injury, or the offender's history of violence or other crimes. These latter variables appear more prevalently in data sets typically used by economists.

III. EMPIRICAL ANALYSIS

A. Data and Methodology

Empirical analysis of the determinants of offender assault, victim resistance, and victims' selections from among multiple types of resistance requires data on a sample of known victims of person-on-person crimes and the circumstances of those crimes. Data from the 2004 National Crime Victimization Survey (NCVS) contain this information and other information useful for control purposes for 1,115 individuals who sustained such victimizations in the United States during 2004.

The theoretical model developed above suggests that we might empirically model the determinants of victims' decision to resist at all, their decision to resist in specific ways, and the decision by offenders to engage in ancillary assault of their victims. The NCVS contains information on whether a given victim offered resistance of any kind and, if so, in what way. For empirical purposes, I define physical resistance as having occurred where victims indicated that they attacked their offender using "physical force," with or without a weapon. The variable Victim Fought equals 1 if this occurred and 0 otherwise. I define verbal resistance as having occurred where victims indicated using actions such as shouting at the offender, turning on lights, screaming from pain, or generally making attempts to attract attention. The variable Victim Yelled equals 1 if this occurred and 0 otherwise. I define victim flight as having occurred where victims indicated that they ran away from, hid from, or locked a door in response to an offender. The variable Victim Fled equals 1 if this occurred and 0 otherwise. In the sample used for empirical analysis, 7.4% of victims offered physical resistance, 15.7% offered verbal resistance, and 13.3% fled their assailants. The variable Offender Attacked, capturing the instance of ancillary assault, equals 1 if such attack occurred and 0 if it did not. An offender attack occurred in 42.4% of the sample cases.

Dichotomous and multinomial logit analysis will enable testing of the hypotheses emanating from the model and relating to the selection of physical resistance, ancillary offender assault, and the three resistance choices as a group. As discussed earlier, a key question about victim resistance to crime concerns whether resistance provokes ancillary assault or prevents it. Authors such as Ullman and Knight (1992), Kleck and Gertz (1995), and Kleck and DeLone (1993) have commented on the notorious absence of dependable data on the *sequencing* of offender attacks and victim resistance, a limitation that has prevented scholars from fully investigating this question empirically.

For the present study, the NCVS data set permits an analysis of the timing of resistance and assault only in the context of physical resistance; future researchers might endeavor to obtain data on the sequencing of offender attack and nonphysical forms of resistance. A set of NCVS items ascertains whether any physical resistance preceded or followed any offender attack, but such items do not exist in relation to verbal resistance and flight. As part of the logit analysis of offender assault, we will investigate whether physical resistance appears to have significantly provoked this assault. The NCVS thus reflects this common data limitation but also represents an improvement compared to data sets that offer no information at all about timing. For multinomial logit analysis, the categorical dependent variable will capture whether the crime victims under analysis engaged in the three types of resistance. The comparison category will capture victims who did not resist at all. The MNL model will allow us to see how victims of person-on-person crime make their resistance choices recognizing that a given victim might resist in any of these ways in a given incident. While economists, criminologists, and other researchers have acknowledged this fact in conceptual discussions of victim resistance, the literature contains no direct statistical exploration of victim resistance choices in this manner.

The dichotomous and multinomial logit models will incorporate regressors capturing characteristics of the victim and characteristics of the offender or incident. The victim characteristics include the victim's age at the time of the incident, the number of children in the victim's household, and dummy variables indicating whether the victim was educated beyond high school, married, a home owner, employed at the time of the incident, and an urban dweller. Reflecting U.S. Census classification criteria, urban areas in the NCVS constitute areas of 2,500 or more inhabitants incorporated as cities, boroughs, villages, and towns. The models also will incorporate a measure of the number of residential moves the victim made in the preceding five years. The population density of a victim's place of residence and the frequency with which a victim has recently relocated capture aspects of a respondent victim's social network (a potentially valuable source of social support) in the absence of NCVS variables that specifically ascertain this information. As noted in Chapter 6, the impact of social network structure or quality on postcrime victimization outcomes remains an underdeveloped area of economic research; however, in other disciplines Cazenave and Straus (1990) and Green and Pomeroy (2007) provide useful, motivating discussions of the relationship between social support and the consequences of crime victimization. Individuals with better-developed social networks also may have greater potential gains to verbal resistance.

The offender and incident characteristics capture whether all or most of the offenders were strangers to the victim and whether others were present at the scene of the incident. In a previous study of reporting by rape victims (Allen 2007), I found that victims were significantly more likely to report stranger rapists than acquaintance rapists. Victims of acquaintance rape who did not report significantly cited fear of reprisal as a reason for staying silent, suggesting that familiar offenders may possess a greater tendency toward violence than strangers possess. If so, one might expect generally lesser tendencies toward offender assault and possibly greater tendencies toward physical resistance when victims encountered unfamiliar offenders in the present sample. The presence of others at the crime has implications for the potential returns to assault *and* resistance.

The models will also incorporate variables indicating whether the offender acted alone and whether the lone or youngest offender was relatively young (i.e., between ages twelve and twenty-nine, as judged by the victim), as well as separate variables indicating whether the victim was older or younger than the offender. Hazelwood, Reboussin, and Warren (1989) and Funk and Kugler (2003) show that criminal offenders tend to increase their violence over time, which, other things being equal, may have implications for the viciousness of relatively older offenders and the tendency for victims to offer resistance. Along similar lines, we will incorporate variables that capture specific *combinations* of offender and victim gender and race. Regarding gender, the models will incorporate the following dummy variables: Male Offender, Female Victim; Male Offender, Male Victim; and Female Offender, Male Victim (cases involving a female offender and victim make up the reference category). Regarding race, the models will incorporate Black Offender, White Victim; White Offender, Black Victim; and Black Offender, Black Victim (cases involving a white offender and victim make up the reference category). I pattern these variables after innovative variables similarly incorporated by Kleck and DeLone (1993). Given the clear importance of one-on-one interaction between offender and victim in the context of resistance and ancillary assault, as highlighted in the conceptual model, these variables provide information about the nature of the crime beyond what we can learn from single dummy variables capturing offender and victim gender and race.

Additional dummy variables capture whether the offender had a weapon, whether a property theft occurred, the type of crime, and whether the offender appeared under the influence of drugs (as judged by the victim). The crime-type dummy variables specifically capture incidents of rape/sexual assault, robbery, and simple and aggravated assault, with purse-snatching/pickpocketing and mere attempts and threats of criminal activity making up the reference category. This study thus uses a wider sampling of person-on-person crimes than that employed by Cook (1986), who examined only robberies by adult males, and Kleck and Sayles (1990), who examined only stranger rapes. The variables Night and Outdoors capture aspects of the physical environment of the crime.

B. Dichotomous Logit Results: Physical Resistance

Table 8.2 displays results from two dichotomous logit models of the victim's decision to resist physically. In Model 1, a baseline specification incorporating no interaction variables, we see evidence of a significant, positive association between each highlighted crime type (rape/sexual assault, robbery, and simple/aggravated assault) and the probability of physical resistance, indicating a greater tendency for physical resistance to those crimes than the less severe reference offenses, as predicted by the theoretical model. The highlighted crimes obviously involve more aggressive offender activity than those in the omitted category and so not surprisingly involve the most aggressive resistance. The variable Offender Attacked also emerges as significantly positive, indicating a direct relationship between offender assault (using terminology from the conceptual model) and a victim resisting physically. However, this result does not imply that physical resistance significantly *provoked* offender assault; we will study the timing of physical resistance and offender attack in a later set of models.

Model 1 also indicates that victims exhibited a greater tendency to fight back against lone offenders, against relatively young offenders, and in nontheft cases. Crime victims may perceive a higher expected injury inflicted for a lone offender, given the implied absence of criminal allies, creating a greater incentive to fight. In the sample, cases involving thefts of property more frequently involved an offender using a weapon than did not (48.9% vs. 23.1%), consistent with commercial robbery patterns observed in Chapter 2; this possibly created a disincentive to fight, as suggested by Cook (1986) and Kleck and DeLone (1993). Victims may regard younger offenders as less physically threatening or as more vulnerable to

TABLE 8.2 *Dichotomous Logit Results: Physical Resistance*

	Model 1	Model 2
Intercept	−6.546[a]	−6.894[a]
	(1.202)	(1.377)
Offender and Incident Characteristics		
Offender Attacked	1.118[a]	1.097[a]
	(0.341)	(0.344)
Rape/Sexual Assault	1.854[c]	1.873[c]
	(1.078)	(1.080)
Robbery	3.758[a]	3.837[a]
	(0.861)	(0.864)
Assault	2.306[a]	2.339[a]
	(0.780)	(0.781)
Others Present	0.170	0.201
	(0.319)	(0.324)
Night	0.264	0.615
	(0.272)	(0.748)
Outdoors	0.270	1.124
	(0.277)	(0.699)
All or Most Strangers	0.396	0.426
	(0.275)	(0.699)
Lone Offender	0.881[b]	1.222
	(0.402)	(0.882)
Lone Offender × MSA Central	—	1.238[c]
		(0.728)
Lone Offender × Night	—	−0.422
		(0.801)
Lone Offender × Outdoors	—	−1.004
		(0.762)
Theft Occurred	−1.321[b]	−1.344[b]
	(0.588)	(0.593)
Offender Had Weapon	−0.210	−0.231
	(0.319)	(0.319)
Offender Using Drugs	−0.520	−0.511
	(0.645)	(0.649)
Male Offender, Female Victim	−0.676	−0.726[c]
	(0.426)	(0.428)
Male Offender, Male Victim	−0.044	−0.088
	(0.389)	(0.392)
Female Offender, Male Victim	−1.556[c]	−1.625[b]
	(0.826)	(0.832)
Black Offender, White Victim	−0.517	−0.577
	(0.539)	(0.542)
White Offender, Black Victim	−0.297	−0.106
	(1.157)	(1.174)

(continued)

TABLE 8.2 *(Continued)*

	Model 1	Model 2
Black Offender, Black Victim	0.575 (0.411)	0.570 (0.413)
Lone/Youngest 12–29 Years of Age	0.740[b] (0.384)	0.777[b] (0.386)
Victim Older	−0.206 (0.380)	−0.261 (0.385)
Victim Younger	−0.031 (0.371)	−0.026 (0.371)
Victim Characteristics		
Age	−0.007 (0.016)	−0.006 (0.016)
College	−0.205 (0.265)	−0.242 (0.265)
Married	−0.781[b] (0.378)	−0.806[b] (0.382)
Home Owner	−0.122 (0.281)	−0.142 (0.284)
Children under 12	0.062 (0.141)	0.072 (0.142)
MSA Central	−0.127 (0.269)	−1.189[c] (0.678)
Employed at Victimization	0.553[c] (0.308)	0.551[c] (0.309)
Recent Moves	0.070[c] (0.041)	0.070[c] (0.041)
Chi-square (H_0: $\beta = 0$)	131.40[a]	135.57[a]
Sample size	1,115	

Notes: Standard errors appear in parentheses. [a]Statistically significant at or better than 1% level; [b]Statistically significant at or better than 5% level; [c]Statistically significant at or better than 10% level.

resistance than older offenders. Univariate statistical evidence reveals that younger offenders more frequently used weapons as part of their crimes, but we see no significant difference in weapon use by virtue of whether the victim was older or younger than the oldest offender.

The significantly negative effect estimated for the variable Female Offender, Male Victim ($p = 0.06$), combined with the insignificance of the other gender-combination variables, indicates significantly less physical resistance in this circumstance than in the reference category, female-on-female crimes. Essentially this means that, statistically, female victims more likely fought back against female offenders than male victims fought back against female offenders and that otherwise no significant difference exists along gender lines. A univariate statistical probe of the various offender and incident characteristics among the various offender-victim gender combinations reveals a telling profile of the nature of incidents involving female offenders and male victims. Among the four gender combinations, female-on-male crime most prevalently constituted simple or aggravated assaults occurring indoors, at night, without a theft, in cases where the victims had a strong suspicion of offender drug use. The offender used a weapon in 27.1% of female-on-male crimes, second only to the rate seen among male-on-male crimes; Kleck and Gertz (1995) colorfully (if somewhat indelicately) characterize male-on-male crime types as "mutual combat" situations, especially when both the offender and the victim use firearms. Female-on-male crimes also showed the greatest average number of victim injuries among the combinations, perhaps reflective of the assaults that occurred prevalently in those situations. Female assailants may well have resorted to using weapons in committing crimes against male victims as a way to compensate against lesser physical strength and indeed to discourage physical victim resistance.

In Model 1, married victims show a significantly lesser likelihood of physical resistance than single victims. Married victims may feel a greater aversion to the risk of injury associated with resistance, given relatively older age and the presence of an immediate family, but their nonresistance might also reflect the nature of the crimes they sustain. While we cannot statistically confirm greater aversion to the risk of injury associated with physical resistance, we can probe the other factors. On average, the married victims under analysis were 41.58 years old, while single victims were on average 33.18 years old, a statistically significant difference; recall the possibility from theory that older victims may not physically resist as readily as younger victims, other things being equal. Married victims also had an average of 0.812 children under age twelve compared to 0.394 children among single victims, evidence of larger immediate families among married victims. Marital status may shape the physical resistance decision in a way that mere victim age (statistically insignificant) does not because it naturally incorporates the influence of both age and family concerns. When probing victim marital status and the type of crime sustained, the most notable finding indicates that single victims more likely experience rape or sexual assault than married victims; no significant variation in victimization frequency emerges in the other crime types by marital status. To the extent that victims, regardless of their family status, aggressively resist rape and sexual assault, the greater resistance seen among single victims might reflect this pattern.

Does the positive influence of a lone offender on physical resistance vary by the physical environment of the crime? To address this, Model 2 incorporates interactions of Lone Offender with the indicators of social environment in the model. In Model 1, the social environment variables emerged as statistically insignificant. In Model 2, only the interaction between Lone Offender and Metropolitan Statistical Area (MSA) Central emerges as significant (positively), while MSA Central (uninteracted) takes on a significantly negative coefficient ($p = 0.08$). However, the uninteracted Lone Offender loses significance in this specification. These results indicate that the positive impact of Lone Offender on physical resistance suggested in Model 1 does not hold across all social environments but holds principally in crimes taking place in the central, large city. In other words, to the extent that victims physically resist solo offenders (more prevalently than multiple offenders), they do so in more densely populated rather than more isolated areas, the former likely presenting a relatively higher probability of detection.

The significance of MSA Central alone and interacted in Model 2 permits a richer interpretation, moreover, of this aspect of the crime's social environment. Making use of the coefficient estimates, the effect on the probability of physical resistance of victimization in a central city is $-1.18958 + 1.237705 \times$ Lone Offender. When Lone Offender $= 0$, central cities obviously *discourage* physical resistance against multiple offenders. When Lone Offender $= 1$, the net effect is $+0.048125$, indicating that central cities encourage physical resistance when a single offender is involved.

C. Dichotomous Logit Results: Offender Assault

Table 8.3 displays results from dichotomous logit models of offender assault: the offender's decision to attack physically. Because the NCVS does

TABLE 8.3   *Dichotomous Logit Results: Offender Attacked*

	Model 1	Model 2	Model 3
Intercept	−0.249	−0.151	−0.147
	(0.492)	(0.503)	(0.503)
Offender and Incident Characteristics			
Rape/Sexual Assault	1.128[a]	1.167[a]	1.166[a]
	(0.397)	(0.399)	(0.400)
Robbery	0.647[a]	0.517[b]	0.518[b]
	(0.227)	(0.233)	(0.233)
Victim Resisted	0.382[a]	0.204	0.203
	(0.145)	(0.148)	(0.148)
Victim Resisted × Physical Resistance	—	1.751[a]	1.852[a]
		(0.299)	(0.315)
Victim Resisted × Physical Resistance × Victim Resisted First	—	—	−1.326
			(1.004)
Others Present	0.380[b]	0.385[a]	0.390[a]
	(0.149)	(0.152)	(0.152)
Night	0.395[a]	0.367[a]	0.368[a]
	(0.136)	(0.139)	(0.139)
Outdoors	−0.588[a]	−0.637[a]	−0.636[a]
	(0.141)	(0.144)	(0.144)
All or Most Strangers	−0.390[a]	−0.424[a]	−0.436[a]
	(0.146)	(0.150)	(0.150)
Lone Offender	−0.068	−0.151	−0.147
	(0.205)	(0.210)	(0.210)
Offender Had Weapon	−0.271[c]	−0.247	−0.254
	(0.161)	(0.165)	(0.165)
Offender Using Drugs	0.163	0.189	0.186
	(0.252)	(0.253)	(0.253)
Male Offender, Female Victim	0.362[c]	0.430[b]	0.430[b]
	(0.212)	(0.217)	(0.217)
Male Offender, Male Victim	0.078	0.075	0.074
	(0.206)	(0.211)	(0.211)
Female Offender, Male Victim	1.400[a]	1.480[a]	1.477[a]
	(0.333)	(0.337)	(0.337)
Black Offender, White Victim	0.003	0.032	0.029
	(0.261)	(0.265)	(0.265)
White Offender, Black Victim	0.448	0.422	0.417
	(0.598)	(0.609)	(0.610)
Black Offender, Black Victim	−0.519[b]	−0.561[b]	−0.557[b]
	(0.251)	(0.261)	(0.261)
Lone/Youngest 12–29 Years of Age	0.214	0.112	0.099
	(0.205)	(0.211)	(0.212)
Victim Older	−0.439[b]	−0.378[c]	−0.357[c]
	(0.206)	(0.211)	(0.212)

(*continued*)

TABLE 8.3 *(continued)*

	Model 1	Model 2	Model 3
Victim Younger	−0.202	−0.190	−0.179
	(0.203)	(0.209)	(0.209)
Victim Characteristics			
Age	−0.003	−0.003	−0.003
	(0.007)	(0.007)	(0.007)
College	−0.389[a]	−0.366[a]	−0.378[a]
	(0.139)	(0.143)	(0.143)
Married	−0.274[c]	−0.219	−0.218
	(0.164)	(0.166)	(0.166)
Home Owner	−0.166	−0.144	−0.146
	(0.152)	(0.156)	(0.156)
Children under 12	−0.021	−0.021	−0.018
	(0.076)	(0.078)	(0.077)
MSA Central	−0.143	−0.130	−0.124
	(0.140)	(0.143)	(0.143)
Employed at Victimization	−0.151	−0.192	−0.187
	(0.147)	(0.150)	(0.150)
Recent Moves	0.035	0.027	0.026
	(0.030)	(0.030)	(0.030)
Chi-square (H$_0$: $\beta = 0$)	147.72[a]	188.93[a]	190.51[a]
Sample size	1,115	1,115	1,115

Notes: Standard errors appear in parentheses. [a]Statistically significant at or better than 1% level; [b]Statistically significant at or better than 5% level; [c]Statistically significant at or better than 10% level.

contain reliable data on the timing of *physical* resistance and offender assault, these models allow us to investigate whether victim resistance appears to provoke such attack. Although we cannot conduct similar analysis of the consequences of verbal resistance and flight, we neverthe-less can study the most aggressive form of resistance discussed in this chapter and in the extant resistance literature, possibly shedding light on the connection between personal resistance and violence generally.

In the offender-assault models, we focus most of our attention on the incremental incorporation of resistance and timing variables as determi-nants of offender assault. The positive, significant coefficient estimated for Victim Resisted in Model 1 clearly indicates a direct relationship be-tween resistance and assault that in essence mirrors the effect seen in the physical resistance logit models (Table 8.2). Of course, this result raises the question of whether this pertains to *any* resistance or just physical resistance. To address this, Model 2 incorporates the interaction of Victim Resisted and Physical Resistance alongside Victim Resisted (uninteracted), and the interaction emerges as positive and significant. Model 2 thus shows that resistance, broadly defined, exerts no significant effect on ancillary assault; only when we specify *physical* resistance (as opposed to verbal resistance or flight) does the positive, significant coefficient emerge.

Model 3 finally adds a three-way interaction to capture the instance of physical resistance that took place *before* the offender assaulted the victim, as ascertained through direct NCVS survey items. Not surprisingly, the offender, rather than the victim, moved first in the majority of these incidents, as suggested by the theoretical model. In principle, positive significance of the three-way interaction would provide evidence that victim (physical) resistance provoked offender violence, while negative significance would provide evidence that physical resistance prevented it. But the variable emerges as statistically insignificant even as Victim Resisted × Physical Resistance retains the significantly positive coefficient evident in Model 2. These models yield no evidence that victim resistance—at least physical resistance, the type most presume would incite the most violent offender reaction—provokes assault, consistent with findings by Kleck and Sayles (1990) and Kleck and Gertz (1995).

If a similar pattern plays out in the context of commercial robbery and the consequences of that crime for physical violence, then we would have evidence that innate offender viciousness or aggressiveness, rather than ill-advised victim resistance, represents the more definitive source of crime-related victim injury—a possibility suggested in Chapter 3 on this subject and developed further within the theoretical analysis of this chapter. If one looks closer, the three-way interaction takes on a *negative* coefficient and achieves statistical significance at $p = 0.187$, not exceedingly far from a traditionally acceptable level of significance. This result provides at least a glimmer of empirical evidence that physical resistance might even serve to prevent offender assault rather than provoke it.

To consider other determinants of offender assault, let us return to Model 1, which incorporates the same variables as used in the physical resistance logit model. The crime type variables all emerge as positive and significant, indicating that ancillary assault more likely happens with rape/ sexual assault and robbery than in the less aggressive omitted categories. This result provides additional evidence, albeit indirect, of the positive relationship between offender viciousness and the incidence of offender attack, as strongly emerges theoretically. Others Present also emerges as positive and significant, indicating that offenders more likely attack victims in this circumstance. It seems reasonable that a greater presence of others at an incident would increase the probability of detection p_f, other things being equal. Indeed, for the victims under analysis, 18.9% of the incidents that occurred with others present had resulted in an arrest or charging of a suspect at the time of sampling, compared to an 11.7% arrest rate for those victimized with no others present—a statistically significant difference. The logit result does not align with the theoretical prediction of an inverse relationship between p_f and the incentive to assault, but it does align with the accompanying hypothesis that greater offender viciousness encourages assault. That is, offenders may engage in assault with others present as an intimidation mechanism, to discourage the intervention of bystanders. Absent other information, one might speculate that especially lone offenders would engage in assault, but Lone Offender itself is insignificant in these models.

Among the indicators of the social environment of the crime, Night is positive and significant and Outdoors is negative and significant as determinants of offender assault. Nighttime may shield an assailant from identification, it may offer a sparser crowd, or it may facilitate certain types of crime more than others—any of these might plausibly encourage ancillary assault by suppressing the probability of detection. If one studies these possibilities further, in the NCVS sample, rape and sexual assault and simple/ aggravated assault occur significantly more often at night than during the day, while statistically robbery occurs just as often during the day as during the night. However, nighttime appears not to come with a larger crowd, of either nonvictims or other victims. Outdoor locations facilitate victim flight and increase the possibility of witnesses and attention from police, perhaps discouraging attack. If one probes location further, rape/sexual assault and simple/aggravated assault occur most prevalently indoors, while robbery occurs most prevalently outdoors. Ultimately, then, the significantly greater prevalence of offender assault indoors may reflect that the most violent primary crimes under analysis, likely committed by the most vicious offenders, occur indoors. Offender Had Weapon emerges as significantly negative ($p = 0.09$) only in Model 1, suggesting that weapon use may act as a substitute for ancillary assault. However, this variable, only mildly significant in Model 1, loses significance in the subsequent models that incorporate interactions.

Among the gender-match variables, Male Offender, Female Victim and Female Offender, Male Victim emerge as consistently positive and significant. This indicates that where offender assault occurs, it predominantly involves males assaulting females and females assaulting males. When victims were older than their offenders, attacks less likely occurred, perhaps because offenders felt less physically threatened by older victims.

D. Multinomial Logit Results: Types of Resistance

Examining the MNL results (Table 8.4), one can observe that marital status matters only in the selection of physical resistance, where married victims appear significantly less likely than single victims to resist physically. We have previously observed the relatively older average age and relatively larger average family size prevalent among the married, and other univariate evidence shows greater average wealth among married victims as well. Green and Pomeroy (2007) raise the question of whether crime victims with greater financial resources receive more social support in the aftermath of their victimization. Do wealthier victims *resist* differently too? Using home ownership as a measure of wealth, not surprisingly we see more prevalent home ownership among married victims than among single victims. When we incorporate an interaction variable of Married and Home Owner into the MNL model, Married remains negative and significant ($p = 0.09$), but neither Home Owner nor the interaction emerges as significant in any MNL equation. The reluctance of married victims to resist physically does not appear related to their wealth, by this measure.

As suggested within the theoretical analysis of flight, victims choose flight as a form of resistance significantly in relatively more open venues, that is, when crimes occur at night and outdoors, relative to nonresistance or the making of mere threats toward offenders (the reference categories).

TABLE 8.4   *Multinomial Logit Results: Victim Resistance Choices*

	Victim Fought (1)	Victim Yelled (2)	Victim Fled (3)
Intercept	−5.842[a]	−2.668[a]	−2.629[a]
	(1.265)	(0.737)	(0.737)
Offender and Incident Characteristics			
Offender Attacked	0.966[a]	−0.108	−0.758[a]
	(0.373)	(0.252)	(0.257)
Rape/Sexual Assault	2.627[b]	1.406[a]	1.841[a]
	(1.108)	(0.522)	(0.480)
Robbery/Attempted Robbery	4.228[a]	1.629[a]	1.692[a]
	(0.903)	(0.478)	(0.465)
Simple/Aggravated Assault	2.397[a]	0.677[b]	0.948[a]
	(0.794)	(0.279)	(0.264)
Others Present	0.001	0.644[a]	−0.537[a]
	(0.352)	(0.233)	(0.208)
Night	0.382	0.034	0.406[b]
	(0.299)	(0.201)	(0.203)
Outdoors	0.477	0.091	0.785[a]
	(0.300)	(0.209)	(0.205)
All or Most Strangers	0.516[c]	−0.013	0.270
	(0.298)	(0.214)	(0.216)
Lone Offender	0.799[c]	−0.450	0.584[c]
	(0.431)	(0.287)	(0.317)
Theft Occurred	−1.804[a]	−1.188[b]	−1.680[a]
	(0.660)	(0.511)	(0.531)
Offender Had Weapon	−0.515	−0.132	0.269
	(0.359)	(0.238)	(0.230)
Offender Using Drugs	−0.439	−0.491	−0.309
	(0.655)	(0.426)	(0.397)
Male Offender, Female Victim	−0.951[b]	0.810[a]	0.056
	(0.477)	(0.323)	(0.291)
Male Offender, Male Victim	−0.151	0.042	−0.730[b]
	(0.413)	(0.322)	(0.297)
Female Offender, Male Victim	−1.721[b]	−0.720	−1.532[b]
	(0.839)	(0.605)	(0.661)
Black Offender, White Victim	−1.115[c]	0.063	−0.650
	(0.673)	(0.372)	(0.441)
Black Offender, Black Victim	0.843[c]	0.378	−0.395
	(0.450)	(0.339)	(0.379)
White Offender, Black Victim	−0.248	0.243	−0.831
	(1.204)	(0.822)	(1.108)
Lone/Youngest 12–29 Years of Age	0.681	−0.206	0.038
	(0.426)	(0.305)	(0.299)
Victim Older	−0.248	0.190	−0.466
	(0.413)	(0.300)	(0.326)

TABLE 8.4   *(Continued)*

	Victim Fought (1)	Victim Yelled (2)	Victim Fled (3)
Victim Younger	−0.166 (0.411)	−0.047 (0.303)	0.547[c] (0.290)
Victim Characteristics			
Age	−0.014 (0.017)	−0.007 (0.011)	−0.001 (0.011)
College	−0.151 (0.290)	0.111 (0.205)	0.157 (0.207)
Home Owner	−0.041 (0.305)	−0.080 (0.223)	−0.107 (0.225)
Children under 12	−0.108 (0.183)	0.126 (0.099)	0.051 (0.110)
MSA Central	−0.250 (0.296)	0.119 (0.203)	0.203 (0.205)
Employed at Victimization	0.512 (0.337)	0.408[c] (0.226)	0.018 (0.212)
Recent Moves	0.093[b] (0.044)	−0.008 (0.044)	0.003 (0.043)
Chi-square (H_0: $\beta = 0$)		283.25 ($p = 0.00$)	
Sample size		1,115	

Notes: Standard errors appear in parentheses. [a]Statistically significant at or better than 1% level; [b]Statistically significant at or better than 5% level; [c]Statistically significant at or better than 10% level.

(The variables Night and Outdoors narrowly miss positive significance in the physical resistance equation.) Fleeing an offender at night may be particularly effective to the extent that darkness increases an offender's pursuit cost or reduces the likelihood of successful pursuit. An indoor venue for the primary crime may constrain the victim's physical ability to flee, making flight from an outdoor venue relatively more likely. When others were present at the incident, the probability of verbal resistance increased and the probability of flight decreased, consistent with the theoretical model. Others present at a crime scene obviously may hear and/or respond to a victim's verbalization. The same circumstance may offer no particular gain to fleeing: victimized among bystanders, one may not need to flee to attract attention; one may simply yell.

When a victim faces a lone offender, the probability of physical resistance and flight increases, but this factor exerts no significant influence on verbal resistance. Victims may perceive a lower probability of successful pursuit by an offender acting alone, thus encouraging flight. Victims likely also regard fighting back against multiple offenders as particularly futile, and a lone offender may be less vicious or menacing. Lone offenders, not having strength in numbers, may also seek out more isolated environments, making verbal resistance a less attractive option. Consistent with this, univariate statistical analysis does indicate that lone offenders less frequently chose central cities than other locations and that they less frequently committed their crimes outdoors. Studying the impact of Lone Offender in different social environments in MNL models that incorporate interactions (not shown), we see evidence that victims generally resist lone offenders (via fighting and fleeing) outside central cities and that victims tend not to resist multiple offenders in central cities.

With respect to offender and victim gender, the most compelling evidence to this point has suggested that female victims significantly choose verbal resistance against a male offender. Female victims in these situations may regard physical resistance as particularly ineffective. We also see evidence that male victims significantly choose compliance or other verbalizations over flight. Male victims may not fear postresistance violence, they may not believe attention caused by running from a female assailant would significantly alter the probability of detection p_f, or they may fear successful pursuit. The only strongly significant effect relevant to offender and victim race shows that black-on-black crime involves the greatest probability of resistance (physically), relative to white-on-white crime. Black offenders in the sample more frequently used weapons in general and guns in particular (although not knives) compared to other offenders. Conceivably, the black victims in the sample also disproportionately had firearms or other weapons, but in the sample only ten total victims of personal crimes attacked or threatened their offenders with firearms. The very rare occurrence of armed resistance, consistent with other studies that used archival crime-victimization data, prevents confident inference along these lines. Overall, however, the MNL result likely reflects the prevalence of black-on-black violent crime in general, which of course includes physical resistance by black victims.

As suggested at the outset of this chapter, crime victims make the resistance decision partly as a means of reducing the likelihood or severity of physical injury resulting from crime. In the wake of the MNL results, we can gain some indication of the "net effect" of resistance and of the various forms of resistance by taking a brief look at injury outcomes among the sample victims. First consider that 39.7% of the victims who engaged in no resistance at all sustained a bodily injury as a result of their victimizations; these victims suffered an average of 0.29 total injuries, and 11.4% received medical care for those injuries. Although we see no evidence that physical resistance *provokes* offender attack, victims who physically resisted do exhibit greater tendencies for injury and greater injury severity than their relevant comparison groups. Victims who fought back sustained injuries 78.9% of the time, suffered 0.55 injuries on average, and received medical care 23.9% of the time—all significantly greater than the tendencies exhibited by nonresisters. These results should not surprise anyone, because person-on-person crimes involving physical resistance create injuries as a natural by-product; resistance does not have to provoke offender attack to result in victim injuries. By contrast, however, victims who yelled or ran away exhibit injury tendencies very comparable to, and in some cases less severe than, those of nonresisters; indeed, those who fled their offenders exhibit a lesser tendency for injury, a lesser average number of injuries, and a lesser tendency to receive medical care. These patterns reinforce Cook's (1986) suggestion (untestable in his seminal article) that nonphysical forms of resistance can certainly lead to favorable, or at least not unfavorable, outcomes for victims.

IV. CONCLUSION

Among the various forms of recourse generally available to victims of crime, the scholarly study of resistance has undergone fairly minimal development in the economics literature; most of that development has taken place in criminology. Cook's (1986) analysis of the role of resistance in robbery outcomes represents the most fully realized effort at devising an economic model of resistance to crime. In this chapter we build on Cook's essential modeling approach—conceptualization of criminal-victim interaction as a sequential game, with resistance specified as a primary victim strategy—to illustrate how victims might choose from among various forms of resistance (not just physical resistance, the narrower earlier focus) and how different types of crime and physical environments of crime influence the resistance decision. Data from the NCVS allow us to demonstrate how these and other elements affect the resistance decision of actual victims, in ways predicted by the model. The results reinforce the notion that crime victims resist criminals in a manner consistent with economic logic.

While the empirical results show a significant correlation between (physical) resistance and the commission of ancillary violence by offenders, we see no evidence that physical resistance, presumably the most provocative type, actually incites offender attacks of this nature. This finding accords with comparable findings reported in criminological studies. The violence associated with crime more compellingly reflects certain observable circumstances of the primary crimes (e.g., their essential severity, nighttime, and random assailants) and by implication the less observable taste for violence present in varying degrees across the distribution of criminals. Along the way, our investigation highlights the fact that economic research on resistance (and perhaps on all types of crime victim behavior) could benefit from data that indeed speak to the actual history of or taste for violence among offenders (Foreman-Peck and Moore 2010 have broken exciting ground in this regard) and more detailed data on the timing or sequence of events that occur in criminal encounters. Do yelling and victim flight provoke or prevent ancillary criminal violence? What effect *do* they have on the outcomes of crime? These remain open questions for future research in crime economics, and we have an essential model structure to help us articulate them.

As we know from our review of economic research on crime victims in Chapter 6, the reporting of crime to police represents another important recourse potentially available to victims, and we have seen the development of scholarly analysis of the reporting decision. This research has helped us understand how reporting affects criminal activity and why some victims choose not to report. Resistance, by definition, occurs during the commission of a crime, while reporting could only happen afterward. As we traverse further along our stylized life cycle of crime victimization to consider victim behaviors that take place in the *aftermath* of victimization, we can now think about the decision to report in our present context and in so doing consider certain issues not previously studied in the reporting literature. This exercise will occupy our attention in Chapter 9.

CHAPTER 9

The Decision to Report

By not coming forward, you make yourself a victim forever.
—KELLY McGILLIS

I. INTRODUCTION

Within the context of the economic model of crime, and in practice, victim reporting becomes a critical step in the enforcement process. Reporting helps establish and solidify the link between crime and punishment demonstrated explicitly in the models of Becker (1968), Ehrlich (1973), and scholars beyond. As Goldberg and Nold (1980) recognized in their study of residential burglary, reporting creates a nontrivial probability of victim-specific enforcement that aids in establishing a disincentive for individuals to commit crime. In short, reporting aids deterrence. That said, many crimes go underreported, some notoriously so.

Although economists and other social scientists continue to study determinants of crime reporting, and by implication reasons for underreporting, researchers have not systematically connected reporting to what happens in the immediate aftermath of crime: the investigation. To what extent do police pursue the cases that victims report? Is it particularly important that victims themselves report, or can witnesses serve as substitutes? Are the answers to these questions sensitive to the nature of the crime and its evidence or to demographic characteristics of victims? Questions like these speak to the net "returns to reporting" and the immediate efficiency with which victim reporting compels police to allocate scarce investigative resources toward restitution.

To address these questions in this chapter, I first develop a conceptual model of victim reporting and police investigation, constructed in the manner of a sequential game. The model allows us to identify five possible equilibrium outcomes related to reporting and investigation. Because reporting a crime constitutes the provision of information about the crime to police, the model recognizes that either victims themselves or witnesses (where available) may provide this information. When the actual victim reports, investigative pursuit may or may not occur. If a victim does not report, a witness might report instead, and again investigative pursuit may or may not happen. In the default outcome, no one reports the crime and no one investigates the crime, implying pure costs for the victim and society. The model illustrates the generalized factors that affect the reporting decision itself and contribute to any given reporting-investigation equilibrium outcome. In so doing, it allows us to address whether reporting by the actual victims or by witnesses exerts differential impacts on investigative pursuit and, if so, under what circumstances.

As in the analysis of victim resistance in Chapter 8, I use data from the 2004 National Crime Victimization survey (NCVS) for empirical investigation. Dichotomous logit models will reveal determinants of victims' decision to report crimes, in the manner of Allen (2007, 2009). Multinomial logit models will allow further examination of the determinants of specific reporting-investigation equilibrium outcomes, as derived in the theory section. Because the empirical results appear sensitive to victim sex and victim race, we probe these demographic factors more deeply in extended gender-separated and race-separated logit models of both types. Overall, the results show evidence of differential returns to reporting for some victims, but some of this variation seems to reflect fundamental differences in the nature of crime victimization along demographic lines. Results also suggest that minority crime victims may receive lesser returns to reporting than white victims receive, partly because of greater social isolation that constrains the benefits of witness corroboration.

II. CONCEPTUAL FOUNDATION
A. Reporting and Investigation

Suppose a hypothetical crime victim (feminine for expository convenience) gains utility U from social support s, which I will assume to be increasing in the information revelation of the victim (θ) and of others (Γ), so that $s = s(\theta, \Gamma)$. As Hobfoll et al. (1990), Giles-Sims (1998), Green and Pomeroy

(2007), and others have discussed, social support, such as that emanating from family, friends, or public services, can help individuals recover from depression, anger, anxiety, and other psychological trauma associated with crime victimization. Information revelation, by the victim or by others, also allows the victim to obtain legal restitution r, additionally a positive function of investigative activity z; hence, $r = r(\theta, \Gamma, z)$. In this formulation, $\theta = 0$ if the victim does not report and $\theta = 1$ if she does report; similarly, $\Gamma = 0$ if no one else reports and $\Gamma = 1$ if someone else does report. With probability p, the victim will incur the reporting cost c, such as in the form of utility lost from other activities (an opportunity cost) or social stigma; thus, pc represents the victim's expected reporting cost. In this model, the hypothetical investigator (masculine) gains utility from the victim's restitution, subject to the investigative activity z, but also incurs investigative costs kz if he engages in investigative activity.

The commission, reporting, and investigation of a crime unfold as a sequence of events. In the simple parlance of game theory, Nature determines the occurrence and type of crime, after which the victim faces the reporting decision. Incorporating the components defined above, we can express victim net utility as $U_V = U_V[s(\theta, \Gamma) - pc(\theta) + r(\theta, \Gamma, z)]$ and investigator net utility as $U_I = U_I[r(\theta, \Gamma, z) - kz]$. As a practical matter, the probability (p) of incurring a reporting cost varies with the type of crime: some crimes involve more time-consuming victim-police interaction than others, and some crimes carry a greater threat of social recrimination or stigma than others. For example, someone who has sustained both a property loss and a physical injury may require more time to provide information than a victim without these circumstances; a victim of domestic violence or rape may face a greater social stigma than a victim of a car-jacking or burglary.

Going further, Iyengar (2009) recently has linked the emergence of mandatory arrest laws for intimate partner violence to an increase in intimate-partner homicides, an outcome explainable in part by the fact that such laws, as many victims perceive them, enhance the possibility of offender reprisal and thus reduce the incentive to report. Similarly, Owens and Matsudaira (2010) investigate the possibility that rape victims face an additional reporting cost when police jurisdictions indicate they will charge them for collecting medical evidence ("rape kits") in their cases; such a shifting of costs from investigators to victims again reduces the incentive to report, as they demonstrate empirically. Besides illustrating the fundamental role of the cost of reporting in the present context, this research reminds us of the frequently tight connection between the actions of victims and those of investigators.

In the present model, the victim does not know whether reporting will lead to investigative pursuit, defined here as police allocation of time and other resources in the interest of restitution. She therefore must assign conditional probabilities to the possible reporting and investigative outcomes. Define $\rho \equiv \text{Prob(pursue|report)}$, $1 - \rho \equiv \text{Prob(not pursue|report)}$, $\rho' \equiv \text{Prob(pursue|not report)}$, and $1 - \rho' \equiv \text{Prob(not pursue|not report)}$. In light of these contingencies, the victim will receive separate expected payoffs from reporting and not reporting; the fact that witnesses may exist, directly affecting Γ, makes it possible for the victim personally not to report and yet receive a nonzero payoff.

For the victim, indifference between reporting and not reporting implies that $\rho U_V[s(\theta, \Gamma) - pc + r(\theta, \Gamma, z)] + (1 - \rho)U_V[s, \theta, \Gamma) - pc] = \rho'U_V[s(0, \Gamma') + r(0, \Gamma', z')] + (1 - \rho')U_V[s(0, 0)]$, where the left side represents $U_V(\theta = 1)$, utility from reporting, and the right side represents $U_V(\theta = 0)$, utility from not reporting. In the indifference condition, Γ' represents the information revealed by others (witnesses) if the victim reveals none, and $z' \geq 0$ represents investigative activity undertaken by police and motivated by the information revelation of others. Exogenous variation in this indifference condition that renders $U_V(\theta = 1) \neq U_V(\theta = 0)$ either increases or decreases the victim's incentive to report, depending on the relative magnitude of any changes in $U_V(\theta = 1)$ and $U_V(\theta = 0)$. Study of such variation as comparative statics allows us to formulate testable hypotheses relating to the decision to report; below we derive results relating to the influence of witnesses and a crime's physical evidence. Further study of the victim and investigator payoffs over the various contingencies will reveal the economic implications of the reporting-investigation equilibria that may unfold as a consequence of the victim-investigator interaction implied by the model.

B. Comparative Statics and Equilibria

1. Witnesses In an aggregate sense, greater provision of information by witnesses clearly can benefit the investigation of crimes; investigators routinely and sometimes very publicly call for witnesses to come forward. But at a micro level, greater participation by witnesses may or may not encourage reporting by an individual victim. Suppose the presence of witnesses, denoted as w, directly impacts the information provided by nonvictims. Thus, $\Gamma(w>0) \geq \Gamma(w=0)$ and $\Gamma'(w>0) \geq \Gamma'(w=0)$, indicating that a greater presence of witnesses does not diminish and may enhance the provision of information by nonvictims, whether the victim herself reports or not. For conceptual purposes, I will define a witness as any person in a position to provide information to police about a crime against someone else. By this definition, some witnesses, but not all, will have directly observed that some or all of the incident occurs. If we differentiate both sides of the indifference condition introduced above with respect to w and simplify, the left side, representing $U_V(\theta=1)$, changes according to $\partial U_V(\theta=1)/\partial w = \partial\Gamma/\partial w$ $(\partial s/\partial\Gamma + \rho\partial r/\partial\Gamma)$, and the right side changes according to $\partial U_V(\theta=0)/\partial w = \partial\Gamma'/\partial w(\partial s/\partial\Gamma' + \rho'\partial r/\partial\Gamma')$. If $\partial U_V(\theta=1)/\partial w > \partial U_V(\theta=0)/\partial w$, then a greater presence of witnesses increases the victim's individual incentive to report; if $\partial U_V(\theta=1)/\partial w \leq \partial U_V(\theta=0)/\partial w$, then the victim's incentive to report remains the same or even declines given a greater presence of witnesses.

To see this further, we need to inspect the components inside the parentheses of the utility derivatives. If $\partial r/\partial\Gamma > \partial r/\partial\Gamma'$, $\rho>\rho'$, and $\partial s/\partial\Gamma > \partial s/\partial\Gamma'$, then corroboration by witnesses essentially does not matter; that is, no greater restitution, investigative pursuit likelihood, or social support would exist when witnesses provide information than when victims themselves provide information. This includes the simplest case in which no witnesses exist, wherein $\partial r/\partial\Gamma' = \partial s/\partial\Gamma' = 0$. By contrast, if $\partial r/\partial\Gamma \leq \partial r/\partial\Gamma'$, $\rho \leq \rho'$, and $\partial s/\partial\Gamma \leq \partial s/\partial\Gamma'$, then corroboration does matter in the creation of these victim goods. Outside the parentheses of the utility derivatives, we must compare $\partial\Gamma/\partial w$ and $\partial\Gamma'/\partial w$; respectively, these effects indicate the degree to which the presence of witnesses influences information provision when the victim herself reports and when she does not report. Similar to the above, corroboration implies that $\partial \Gamma'/\partial w \geq \partial \Gamma/\partial w$; that is, the effect on information provision of witnesses' presence will make at least as much of a contribution to restitution as a victim's information provision.

Overall, while a greater presence of witnesses potentially encourages an individual crime victim to report, effective corroboration introduces the possibility that a greater presence of witnesses may actually reduce the victim's personal incentive to report. The hypothetical investigator may receive essentially the same information about the incidence of the crime under either circumstance but, as illustrated later, he may respond in different ways depending on who provides that information.

2. *Physical Evidence*   Despite the investigative and restitutive value of witness information provision, police obtain some information about certain elements of crimes more compellingly from victims themselves. For example, a victim may have more accurate information about observable details of the offender and the specific physical circumstances of the incident. In addressing conceptually how the evidentiary circumstances of crimes influence the reporting decision, the intuition resembles what we see with respect to the role of witnesses, but the analytical mechanisms differ.

Suppose a crime's physical evidence, denoted as e, has a positive effect on ρ and ρ', implying that, regardless of the source of the information provision, better evidence associated with the crime increases the probability of investigative pursuit. Letting e vary, such that a higher value implies more valuable evidence, the left side of the reporting indifference condition changes according to $\partial U_V(\theta = 1)/\partial e = \partial \rho/\partial e U[r(\theta, \Gamma, z)]$ and the right side changes according to $\partial U_V(\theta = 0)/\partial e = \partial \rho'/\partial e U[r(0, \Gamma', z')]$, following simplification. As in the analysis of the influence of witnesses, comparison of the magnitudes of these two effects suggests how variation in evidentiary value might ultimately influence the victim's incentive to report. In r', by comparison to r, the victim substitutes the information provision of a witness for her own. This potentially makes no difference to the amount of restitution ultimately available to the victim, not unlike a possibility observed above in the context of witness variation. But consider

z and z'. If information provision by others creates corroboration, then $z' \geq z$, implying at least as much investigative activity when others provide information; otherwise, $z' < z$. Finally, compare the component effects $\partial p/\partial e$ and $\partial p'/\partial e$. If only the victim can attest compellingly to certain details of crimes (e.g., the suffering of injuries, thefts of property, or observable characteristics of offenders), then for at least some elements of the evidence, it would seem likely that $\partial p/\partial e > \partial p'/\partial e$, giving the victim a greater net incentive to report under evidentiary circumstances most compellingly known by the victim herself. Which actual circumstances influence matters in this exact way becomes an empirical question for later.

In general, the comparative statics developed here illustrate the potential importance of the role of witness corroboration. As part of the empirical analysis of reporting and investigation, univariate study of mean differences will give us an indication of whether observable investigative outcomes appear sensitive to the source of information provision, among other patterns. These observations will help motivate the specification and estimation of dichotomous logit models of the decision to report.

3. Reporting and Investigation Equilibria The present model supports five possible equilibrium outcomes, each describing a distinct sequence of victim (or witness) reporting and investigative pursuit. This aspect of the model resembles that of Cook (1986), whose similar analysis of possible equilibrium sequences of events related to victim resistance and offender attack we have discussed and extended previously. In the present setting, Equilibrium 1, victim reporting followed by pursuit, yields the following payoff set to the victim and investigator, respectively: $\{s(\theta, \Gamma) - pc + r(\theta, \Gamma, z), r(\theta, \Gamma, z) - kz\}$. Equilibrium 2, victim reporting followed by nonpursuit, yields victim and investigator payoffs of $\{s(\theta, \Gamma) - pc, 0\}$. Equilibrium 3, victim nonreporting but witness reporting followed by pursuit, yields victim and investigator payoffs of $\{s(0, \Gamma') + r(0, \Gamma', z), r(0, \Gamma', z) - kz\}$. Equilibrium 4, victim nonreporting and witness reporting followed by nonpursuit, yields victim and investigator payoffs of $\{s(0, \Gamma'), r(0, \Gamma', 0)\}$. In the default equilibrium, neither the victim nor any witness reports the crime, no investigative pursuit occurs, and the payoff set collapses to $\{0,0\}$. Analytical separation of these equilibria hinges on variation across victim and investigator payoffs; this same variation suggests the empirical factors that might support a given equilibrium outcome.

Comparative scrutiny of Equilibria 1 and 2 suggests what might make the difference between investigative pursuit and nonpursuit when the victim herself individually reports. Given that victim reporting occurs, the investigator will pursue the case if $r(\theta, \Gamma, z) - kz > 0$, which implies that $r(\theta, \Gamma, z) > kz$. In this situation, the investigator would gain enough information from the victim to justify incurring the costs of pursuit. As suggested above, the victim likely possesses the best information about certain physical details of the offender and the circumstances of the crime. Such information, whatever empirical form it ultimately takes, potentially reduces the investigation cost k, enhancing the investigator's incentive to pursue the case.

Scrutiny of Equilibria 1 and 3 gives an indication of what might motivate investigative pursuit when either the victim or alternatively a witness reports the crime. The victim will prefer Equilibrium 3 to Equilibrium 1 if $s(0, \Gamma') + r(0, \Gamma', z) > s(\theta, \Gamma) - pc + r(\theta, \Gamma, z)$. With either equilibrium, police learn of the incidence of the crime. But Equilibrium 3 affords the victim the opportunity for this information to flow without incurring an individual reporting cost, despite the possibility of receiving lesser social support. If the victim indeed gains less social support when others provide information about her victimization, then $s(0, \Gamma') \leq s(\theta, \Gamma)$. Other things being equal, given a relatively high expected reporting cost pc, the victim may prefer to have a witness report, if a witness exists. This observation illustrates one way that a victim of a particularly stigmatizing crime, such as rape, may individually exhibit a greater probability of reporting if she possesses a relatively more supportive social network. It also illustrates how a crime victim with relatively higher time costs of reporting, such as those associated with the demands of employment or child care, might report less readily than victims with lower opportunity costs.

From the investigator's perspective, little separates Equilibria 1 and 3. For the investigator to prefer Equilibrium 3, $r(0, \Gamma', z) - kz > r(\theta, \Gamma, z) - kz$ must hold; assuming equal investigative costs across information sources, this implies that $r(0, \Gamma', z) > r(\theta, \Gamma, z)$. As suggested within the comparative-static analysis, this may hold if reporting by witnesses has a demonstratively corroborative effect, whereby $r(\theta = 1, \Gamma' = 1, \cdot) \geq r(\theta = 1, \Gamma = 0, \cdot)$. Alternatively, however, an investigator may regard a *victim*'s information revelation as relatively more compelling from an evidentiary standpoint, in which case $r(\theta = 1, \cdot) < r(\theta = 0, \cdot)$. In this latter case, one might expect information about the incident uniquely conveyed by the victim to exert a greater marginal influence on Equilibrium 1 than on Equilibrium 3. As part of the empirical analysis, we will estimate multinomial logit (MNL) models of the four nontrivial equilibrium outcomes to examine how the variables that influence reporting in general influence specific *combinations* of reporting and investigation. These models will allow us to address, among other questions, whether certain incident-specific or even victim-specific factors lead to differential degrees of investigative pursuit.

When only a witness reports, the investigator must decide whether to pursue the case or not. Pursuit will occur if $r(0, \Gamma', z) - kz > r(0, \Gamma', 0)$, that is, if $r(0, \Gamma', z) - r(0, \Gamma', 0) > kz$. The investigator's restitutive gain to witness reporting would have to be sufficiently high to make pursuit worth the investigative cost kz. Because $kz > 0$ when pursuit occurs, $r(0, \Gamma', z)$ must exceed $r(0, \Gamma', 0)$ for this to hold. But the two restitutions differ only by the third term $z > 0$, indicating the degree to which pursuit actually contributes to restitution. It becomes entirely an empirical question as to what factors might make witness reporting more or less compelling to investigators.

III. EMPIRICAL ANALYSIS

A. Data and Methodology

Empirical analysis of the determinants of the reporting decision and the various reporting-investigation equilibria requires data on a sample of known crime victims. The data must also contain information on victims' decision to report the crime to police, the extent to which others (nonvictims serving as witnesses) informed police of the crime, and the extent of investigative pursuit of the crime. Data from the 2004 National Crime Victimization Survey (NCVS), introduced in Chapter 8, contain this information and other information useful for control purposes for more than 8,000 individuals who sustained victimizations during 2004. To ensure that sample subjects had reasonable degrees of autonomy in making their reporting decisions, I confine the sample to crime victims seventeen years of age or older at the time of the incident in question. To focus on cases in which victims had an actual opportunity to make a reporting decision, the sample used for statistical analysis excludes those for whom police already were present at the scene of the incident and cases in which the offender was a police officer. These criteria and the removal of unusable observations yield a sample of 6,667 victims. I will refer to this as the "full sample" for the remainder of this chapter.

As indicated earlier, Equilibria 3 and 4 could occur only if someone other than the victim provides information about the crime to police, whether investigative pursuit follows or not. Information about this circumstance emanates from an NCVS survey item that ascertains directly whether the respondent victim or someone other than the victim informed police about the crime. As a measure of investigative pursuit, I construct a variable called Police Actions based on information in the NCVS specifying the different types of investigative actions police may have taken in the aftermath of any reporting. The NCVS gave respondents the opportunity to cite several possible actions police might have taken: the taking of a report, questioning witnesses or suspects, the promise or conducting of surveillance or other physical investigation, the recovery of property, staying in touch with the victim or household, or other, unspecified actions. Police Actions excludes the actual making of an arrest because this outcome constitutes a form of restitution, the presumed immediate *objective* of the various investigative activities. Police Actions constitutes the sum of each of the investigative actions that victims indicated took place. Where respondents indicated that police took at least one action, this constitutes investigative pursuit having taken place; if a respondent indicated that none of these actions occurred, this constitutes investigative nonpursuit.

Among the full sample of 6,667 victims under analysis, 2,093 of whom (31.4%) indicated the presence of some investigative pursuit, the variable Police Actions ranged from 0 to 7 with mean 0.588 and standard deviation 1.04; among crimes reported by any person, Police Actions had mean 1.41 and standard deviation 1.20. Within the sample of 6,667, a total of 1,616 (24.2%) involved the victim (and no one else) reporting, followed by investigative pursuit; 523 (7.8%) involved victim reporting followed by nonpursuit. Among the remaining cases, 477 (7.2%) involved reporting only by a nonvictim, followed by pursuit, while 169 (2.5%) involved reporting only by a nonvictim followed by nonpursuit; 3,882 (58.2%) of the cases involved no reporting at all and, of course, nonpursuit.

The data set facilitates three primary statistical analyses. First, an analysis of means and mean differences will allow us to reveal regularities that exist within the sample, including indications of the extent to which the victims under analysis exhibited patterns consistent with the essential assumptions of the conceptual model. Second, we estimate a simple, dichotomous logit model of the decision to report, such as estimated in Allen (2007). This model will allow testing of hypotheses implied by the comparative statics seen earlier, particularly relating to the role of witnesses and evidentiary factors. Finally, a multinomial logit (MNL) model will reveal how the variables incorporated in the dichotomous logit model specifically impact the four primary equilibrium reporting-investigation outcomes highlighted in the previous section. The dichotomous logit model will incorporate the dependent variable Victim Reported, equal to 1 if indeed the victim provided information about the crime and 0 otherwise. For the MNL model, the unordered categorical dependent variable takes on values capturing Outcome 1 {victim report, pursue}, Outcome 2 {victim report, not pursue}, Outcome 3 {victim not report, nonvictim report, pursue}, and Outcome 4 {victim not report, nonvictim report, not pursue}. Cases involving no reporting at all and no pursuit will make up the reference category for the MNL model.

The dichotomous and multinomial logit models will incorporate regressors capturing characteristics of the victim and characteristics of the offender or incident. The victim characteristics include the victim's age at the time of the incident as well as dummy variables indicating whether the victim was female, nonwhite, educated beyond the attainment of an associate's degree, married, a home owner, employed at the time of the incident, and an urban dweller, as defined using U.S. Census classification criteria. These variables capture aspects of a respondent victim's social network, a potentially valuable source of social support, in the absence of NCVS variables that specifically ascertain this information. As suggested above, respondents employed at the time of their victimizations may also face a higher opportunity cost of reporting relative to jobless victims. We investigate the link between labor-market participation and the crime victimization experience more fully in Chapter 10.

The offender and incident characteristics capture whether all or most of the offenders were strangers to the victim, whether others (nonvictims) were present at the scene of the incident, and the total number of other *victims* at the scene. The presence of nonvictims at the incident represents the best available measure of the presence of potential witnesses at the incident, essential for Equilibria 3 and 4. Other variables capture the total number of injuries the victim sustained and the interaction of this variable with a dummy variable indicating whether the victim received medical care. The models will also incorporate variables indicating whether the offender acted alone, whether the offender was white, whether the lone or oldest offender was over thirty years of age (as judged by the victim), whether the incident occurred at or near the victim's home, whether the offender had a weapon, whether the offender physically attacked the victim, whether the victim resisted the offender, whether a theft of property occurred, and whether the incident constituted a personal crime. By NCVS definition, personal crimes include completed, attempted, and verbal threats of rape and sexual assault, completed and attempted robbery and aggravated assault, and completed and attempted purse-snatching and pickpocketing. Nonpersonal crimes generally constitute completed and attempted incidents involving little or no direct contact between victim and offender, such as personal larcenies, burglaries, forced entry into buildings owned by victims, and motor vehicle thefts.

B. An Analysis of Means

A key question raised in the conceptual model concerns witness corroboration: Does it matter? For the victims under analysis here, by several measures, it does appear to matter. Among the subjects for whom police became aware of the crime, an average of 1.68 Police Actions took place in cases where others reported, compared to 1.38 mean Police Actions when only the victims themselves reported, a statistically significant difference.

Within the same subsample, the dummy variable named Arrested/Charged, equal to 1 if victims indicated that police actually arrested or charged someone with the crime and 0 otherwise, has a mean of 0.246 when others reported and a mean of 0.094 when only victims reported, also a statistically significant difference. One can interpret the means of Arrested/Charged as conditional sample arrest rates. Respectively, these patterns suggest that $z' > z$ and $r' > r$ for these victims.

Arrested/Charged, which acts as an indicator of restitution, also appears positively related to investigative pursuit in a manner consistent with intuition and with an assumption of the model. For the full sample, Arrested/Charged has a mean of 0.138 when Police Actions > 0 and only 0.006 when Police Actions = 0, a statistically significant difference. Viewed from a different perspective, for the full sample, the cases under analysis exhibited mean Police Actions of 0.507 when police had arrested or charged no one but 2.21 when an arrest or charge had occurred, a statistically significant difference. These patterns provide univariate empirical evidence of a positive relationship between legal restitution and investigative pursuit, as implied by the conceptual formulation of r and r' as positive functions of z and z', respectively.

Regularities involving the type of crime give an indication of what sorts of crimes tend to occur in the presence of others, potentially making them more conducive to reporting by witnesses. For the full sample, over 80% of personal crimes occurred in the presence of nonvictims. Consistent with this, among those exhibiting any type of reporting, 35.1% of the incidents constituted a personal crime; in the absence of nonvictims, only 6.6% were personal crimes. Furthermore, among those not exhibiting the default equilibrium outcome, 34.9% of the incidents constituted a personal crime when a nonvictim reported, but only 17.9% constituted a personal crime when the *victim* reported. These patterns provide clear evidence that rapes, robberies, assaults, and other personal crimes represented in the NCVS data more frequently occurred in the presence of potential witnesses, leading to the greater tendency for witnesses to provide information about those crime types. Along similar lines, 54.5% of home owners in the sample, compared to 61.5% of home renters, suffered personal crimes. Because different types of crime may occur in different locations, this fact may reflect where home owners and home renters tend to live. Among the sample of 6,667, a significantly greater percentage of home renters live in urban areas, where we know crimes of all types occur more often (recall Glaeser and Sacerdote 1999). Logit analysis will reveal whether the type of crime and the other variables exert differential effects on the reporting and investigation outcomes.

That these univariate empirical patterns generally appear consistent with structural assumptions within the conceptual model suggests that the model may offer a reasonable approach to thinking about reporting and investigation, but of course the dichotomous and multinomial logit analysis will allow testing of the model's actual hypotheses.

IV. LOGIT ANALYSIS

A. The Decision to Report: Dichotomous Logit Results

An initial dichotomous logit model (results not shown) reveals essential determinants of the victim's decision to report. The conceptual model suggested the possibility that a greater presence of witnesses of the incident might reduce the likelihood that the victim would report, particularly if information provision by witnesses tended to corroborate that of victims. The univariate analysis revealed evidence of corroboration in this sample, and indeed the variable Others Present, capturing the presence of nonvictims (potential witnesses) at the incident, emerges as negative and statistically significant. Of course, in principle, the mere *presence* of potential witnesses guarantees neither witness reporting nor effective corroboration when they do report. Within a follow-up reporting logit model excluding the 228 cases in which someone else reported, Others Present loses statistical significance and the other significant variables exhibit qualitatively similar results. In light of the univariate evidence that witness corroboration exists, this provides evidence that corroborating witness reporting acts as a substitute for individual victim reporting, as suggested by the conceptual model. That is, when the presence of potential witnesses does not result in any witness reporting, the mere *presence* of others at the crime exerts no effect on reporting by victims themselves.

Returning to the main logit model, the presence of other *victims* at the incident also exerts no significant influence on reporting, suggesting that nonvictims may provide more effective corroboration than even that provided by other victims of the same crime.

The conceptual model suggested that certain incident-specific evidence of the crime—especially that most compellingly reported by victims themselves—would encourage reporting. Several offender incident characteristics appear influential along these lines. With respect to incident characteristics, the logit model indicates that victims more likely reported incidents occurring at or near the victim's home, when a theft occurred, when the victim offered resistance during the incident, in incidents involving multiple (rather than lone) offenders, and in personal rather than property crimes. Victims also more likely reported white offenders and offenders who had weapons. The further question becomes whether the evidentiary offender and incident characteristics that influence reporting influence specific investigative outcomes in systematic ways. We address this when we empirically disentangle the reporting and investigation equilibria in the next subsection.

Several of the victim characteristics appear to influence reporting as well. Older victims, nonwhite victims, home renters, victims residing outside urban areas, and victims who held jobs at the time of their victimization ($p = 0.07$) all show a significantly greater probability of reporting relative to their respective reference groups. From a conceptual perspective, these results essentially indicate, on balance, the set of demographic circumstances that present systematically greater benefits to reporting than costs of reporting. Victim demographics might conceivably explain differential investigative outcomes as well. If so, the question will become whether investigators favor certain demographic traits simply for their own sake or whether these demographic characteristics reflect interpersonal variation in the nature of crime victimization itself.

B. Empirically Disentangling the Equilibria: Multinomial Logit Results

Table 9.1 displays results from a multinomial logit model that casts the four reporting and investigation outcomes of interest as a categorical dependent variable; recall that the modal outcome, indicating no reporting at all and no investigative pursuit, acts as the reference category. As suggested within the conceptual discussion, the most economically meaningful empirical patterns emerge when we study comparable pairs among the equilibrium outcomes.

1. Outcomes 1 and 2 Consider Equilibrium 1 alongside Equilibrium 2. Examining the victim characteristics, Equilibrium 1—victim reporting followed by pursuit—occurs significantly more often, relative to the default

TABLE 9.1 *Multinomial Logit Results: Reporting and Investigation Outcomes*

	Outcome 1	Outcome 2	Outcome 3	Outcome 4
Intercept	−1.369[a]	−2.642[a]	−2.143[a]	−3.450[a]
	(0.180)	(0.296)	(0.289)	(0.469)
Offender and Incident Characteristics				
All or Most Strangers	−0.148	0.399[c]	0.173	−0.196
	(0.136)	(0.240)	(0.180)	(0.408)
Others Present	−0.066	−0.401	0.955[a]	0.143
	(0.132)	(0.251)	(0.199)	(0.436)
Other Victims	−0.046	−0.102	0.015	−0.205
	(0.105)	(0.249)	(0.115)	(0.369)
Total Injuries	0.050	−1.229	0.282	0.714
	(0.235)	(0.782)	(0.296)	(0.661)
Total Injuries × Received Medical Care	0.987[a]	0.996	1.177[a]	0.664
	(0.283)	(0.987)	(0.318)	(0.658)
Lone Offender	−0.481[a]	−0.487[c]	−0.943[a]	−0.791[c]
	(0.147)	(0.267)	(0.208)	(0.426)
White Offender	0.254[b]	0.162	0.019	0.451
	(0.136)	(0.243)	(0.180)	(0.399)
Offender over 30	0.332[a]	0.332	0.726[a]	−0.920[c]
	(0.136)	(0.262)	(0.189)	(0.530)
At or Near Home	0.303[a]	−0.099	−0.010	−0.502[a]
	(0.068)	(0.100)	(0.110)	(0.166)
Theft Occurred	0.097	0.312[c]	−0.538[a]	−0.483[c]
	(0.110)	(0.188)	(0.162)	(0.257)
Offender Had Weapon	0.770[a]	−0.039	1.014[a]	0.787
	(0.175)	(0.398)	(0.228)	(0.529)
Offender Attacked	−0.061	0.024	0.580[b]	0.007
	(0.198)	(0.393)	(0.268)	(0.665)

(continued)

TABLE 9.1   *(Continued)*

	Outcome 1	Outcome 2	Outcome 3	Outcome 4
Victim Resisted	0.354[a]	0.101	0.238	0.092
	(0.140)	(0.268)	(0.190)	(0.458)
Personal Crime	0.405[b]	0.167	−0.579[b]	−0.320
	(0.189)	(0.328)	(0.281)	(0.588)
Victim Characteristics				
Age	0.005[b]	0.004	−0.007[c]	0.007
	(0.002)	(0.003)	(0.004)	(0.006)
Female	0.137[b]	0.074	0.346[a]	0.153
	(0.061)	(0.095)	(0.104)	(0.162)
Nonwhite	0.222[a]	0.076	0.193	0.185
	(0.078)	(0.125)	(0.134)	(0.218)
Education	−0.208[a]	0.164	−0.198	0.271
	(0.076)	(0.108)	(0.128)	(0.175)
Married	0.025	0.020	0.427[a]	0.583[a]
	(0.065)	(0.100)	(0.109)	(0.174)
Home Owner	−0.118[c]	−0.035	0.081	0.417[b]
	(0.068)	(0.107)	(0.114)	(0.199)
Employed at	0.064	0.379[a]	0.270[b]	−0.143
Victimization	(0.069)	(0.116)	(0.120)	(0.181)
Urban Dweller	−0.176[b]	−0.093	−0.138	0.122
	(0.081)	(0.128)	(0.134)	(0.218)
Equation chi-square	167.92[a]	37.20[b]	271.42[a]	63.10[a]
Model chi-square		552.54[a]		
Sample size		6,667		

Notes: Outcome 1 describes victim reporting followed by investigative pursuit; Outcome 2 describes victim reporting followed by nonpursuit; Outcome 3 describes victim nonreporting, reporting by others, followed by pursuit; Outcome 4 describes victim nonreporting, reporting by others, followed by nonpursuit. Standard errors appear in parentheses. [a]Statistically significant at or better than 1% level; [b]Statistically significant at or better than 5% level; [c]Statistically significant at or better than 10% level.

category, for older victims, female victims, nonwhite victims, less-educated victims, home renters ($p = 0.08$), and non-urban dwellers. We see evidence, then, of a lesser probability of reporting among urban dwellers and that urban victims who do report tend to receive significantly less follow-up investigative pursuit than non-urban dwellers. This pattern resonates in light of the findings by Mathur (1978) and Glaeser and Sacerdote (1999) of lower arrest rates in cities. The present result raises the possibility that some urban victims simply refrain from reporting because they recognize the relatively low probability of receiving restitution. Among the offender and incident characteristics, Equilibrium 1 occurs significantly more often when victims received medical care for injuries, when the offenders were white, when the single or oldest offender was older than thirty, when the incident occurred at or near the victim's home, when the offender had a weapon, when the victim resisted, and for personal crimes.

Most of the variables noted here also emerged as statistically significant determinants of reporting in general, as discovered in the dichotomous logit model. Thus, most of the factors that influence the decision to report also appear to support the instance of follow-up investigative pursuit. But note two interesting exceptions. First, while a greater presence of others (nonvictims) at the incident significantly reduced the probability of *victim* reporting, this variable exerted no significant impact on Equilibrium 1 in the MNL setting, perhaps indicating that, in practice, witness corroboration becomes a particularly compelling motivator of follow-up pursuit. Second, the fact that victim injuries accompanied by medical care significantly increased the likelihood of victim reporting followed by pursuit (note the significant coefficient of +0.987 for Total Injuries interacted with Received Medical Care), despite exhibiting insignificance in the reporting logit model, suggests that this circumstance particularly motivates investigative pursuit. This pattern may reflect the fact that medical practitioners frequently have a professional or legal responsibility to notify police of injuries that appear related to crime victimization. It may otherwise reflect a greater degree of credibility among victims who report: victim injuries in essence may validate the severity of their crimes as perceived by investigators, implying greater restitutive gain to investigative activity and motivating more significant pursuit.

Three variables emerge as significant determinants of Equilibrium 2 and *not* Equilibrium 1, indicating circumstances under which investigative pursuit decidedly does not occur despite individual victim reporting. Victims employed at the time of the incident, those who sustained a theft, and those victimized by strangers more likely had their personal reporting met with nonpursuit—the latter two effects achieve significance only at $p = 0.10$. Readers scrutinizing the extent to which the significant determinants of reporting translate to significant "returns" to reporting might take some comfort from the fact that (1) very few factors overall significantly explain the outcome whereby victim reporting yields no investigative pursuit, that (2) these factors exhibit only marginal statistical significance, and that (3) most of the factors that explain victim reporting explain the instance of follow-up pursuit in the same direction. The victims under analysis largely received significant returns to reporting, at least as indicated by the investigative pursuit outcomes observable here.

Finally, only the variable Lone Offender emerged as significant for both Equilibria 1 *and* 2, its −0.481 and −0.487 coefficients indicating that each outcome was significantly less likely to occur, relative to the default category, when an offender acted alone. This result conforms to the dichotomous logit result indicating that lone offenders, relative to multiple offenders, tended to discourage victim reporting. However, we do see stronger statistical support (as indicated by significance levels) for the role of this variable as a determinant of Equilibrium 1 than of Equilibrium 2, suggesting that the presence of multiple offenders offers particularly influential evidentiary value to investigators. The relatively mild significance of the variable All or Most Strangers in Equilibrium 2, as noted above, gives some indication that the crime victims under analysis more likely had their reporting followed up with investigative pursuit when they could identify their offenders as known to them.

2. Outcomes 1 and 3   Equilibrium 3 captures the outcome whereby the victim does not report the crime to police, someone else does, and investigative pursuit occurs. In principle, regressors exhibiting the same sign and significance for Equilibria 1 and 3 would indicate that investigators regarded the associated factors as encouraging of pursuit regardless of whether the victim or witnesses provided the information. Among the victim characteristics, identical sign and significance emerge only for females, suggesting that women received a greater return to witness information provision than men received. The dichotomous logit model estimated earlier revealed no statistically significant difference in the probability of reporting between males and females. Does this result reflect an investigator bias toward the pursuit of crimes involving female victims, or merely fundamental differences between the nature of crime victimization between men and women? In Section V we probe the results relating to gender more closely.

An intriguing pattern of results in the transition from dichotomous to multinomial logit estimation also emerges in the context of some of the offender and incident characteristics. In the dichotomous logit model, injured victims who received medical care exhibited no significantly different likelihood of reporting than other victims. The MNL shows that these victims most prevalently exhibited Equilibria 1 and 3, suggesting that victim injuries accompanied by medical treatment significantly led to investigative pursuit whether the victim or someone else reported the crime. The same pattern holds for cases involving multiple offenders, relatively older offenders, and offenders who had weapons. For a given incident, simple visual observation of these circumstances by onlookers may have proved sufficiently compelling to motivate investigative pursuit, by contrast to a factor such as offender-victim familiarity.

Although the variables noted above appear compelling for investigative pursuit regardless of information source, other variables emerge as significant determinants of Equilibrium 1 but *not* Equilibrium 3, suggesting avenues by which information provision only by *victims* leads to investigative pursuit. Some of these variables pertain to characteristics of the offender or incident, which is reasonable given the assumed importance of a crime's evidentiary content. This pattern appears in cases involving nonwhite victims and in cases involving white offenders, suggesting that witness corroboration significantly compelled investigative pursuit particularly for white victims and that information about offender race compelled pursuit only when provided by victims themselves, not by witnesses. Among the empirical extensions analyzed in Section V, we will consider whether the white victims under analysis received greater "returns to corroboration" than nonwhite victims because of their race or because of correlative factors. The pattern also emerges for cases occurring at or near a victim's home, when victims resisted, and in personal rather than property crimes. Victims thus appear to convey more compelling information about these circumstances of crimes than witnesses convey. In practice, most onlookers or other witnesses (as broadly defined for this study) may have minimal compelling knowledge of the location of the victim's home or details about exactly what took place during an incident.

Variables that significantly explain Equilibrium 3 but not Equilibrium 1 indicate empirical circumstances that compel investigative pursuit only when *witnesses* convey the information. This pattern, comparatively rarer than the opposite pattern, predictably holds when others (nonvictims) were present at the incident. It also appears to hold when the offender physically attacked (note the +0.580 coefficient estimate for Offender Attacked within Outcome 3), suggesting that investigators did not respond to claims of a physical attack by an offender—clearly a very serious allegation—unless corroborated by a nonvictim third party.

Among the victim characteristics other than gender, we see intriguing patterns in relation to victim age and home ownership. The dichotomous logit model showed a greater probability of reporting among older victims at a strong level of significance. In the MNL, victim age emerges as significantly positive as a determinant of Equilibrium 1 and significantly negative as a determinant of Equilibrium 3, the latter at $p = 0.08$. Home owners exhibited a significantly lesser probability of reporting than home renters and exhibit the same sign pattern in the MNL model; note the -0.118 coefficient estimate for Owns Home (also $p = 0.08$) within Outcome 1. Older victims and home owners thus appear more likely to have received follow-up investigative pursuit when they reported and less likely to have received pursuit when others reported on their behalf. Meanwhile, echoing a pattern seen in relation to the presence of others at the crime and the incidence of an offender attack, Equilibrium 3 holds significantly for married victims and for those employed at the time of their victimizations. Further analysis of demographic variation, pursued below, may shed some light on these patterns.

3. Outcomes 2, 3, and 4 Multinomial logit results relevant to Equilibrium Outcomes 2, 3, and 4 reveal patterns that reinforce or lend perspective to results observed within the other equilibrium comparisons and raise new questions of their own. First, the variable All or Most Strangers, as noted earlier in the comparison of Outcomes 1 and 2, emerges as a positively, mildly significant determinant of victim reporting followed by nonpursuit and shows statistical significance in no other outcome. For the victims under analysis, this gives fairly definitive evidence that crimes committed by strangers likely yield investigative nonpursuit when reported by victims, other things being equal. From the perspective of the theoretical model, victim knowledge of the offender's identity appears to represent an important, albeit in this setting not a statistically overwhelming, contributor to the net legal restitution potentially available to victims and facilitated by investigative pursuit.

Elsewhere, the variable Theft Occurred emerges as a positive determinant of Equilibrium 2 and a negative determinant of Equilibria 3 and 4, illustrating that property thefts, other things being equal, discourage investigative pursuit—especially when *witnesses* report the crime in question. In the absence of more compelling evidentiary circumstances, investigators may perceive minimal restitutive gain to pursuing cases involving thefts. When thefts occur, victims also may receive as much or greater restitution through formal insurance than through police investigation, as we have intimated in our earlier discussions of self-protection. Among those in the sample who sustained a theft as part of their victimization, 7.7% reported their victimizations to an insurance company, and in only 2.8% of those cases had police arrested or charged someone for the crime, as compared to the overall sample arrest rate of 4.8%. By contrast, an arrest or formal charge occurred in 11.7% of the cases involving no property theft. Finally, we see evidence that individuals employed at the time of their victimizations exhibit a greater probability of Outcomes 2 and 3, suggesting that this victim characteristic discourages investigative pursuit whether the victim or someone else reports. This pattern, like others observed here, will further motivate a more careful probing of the results along demographic lines.

For this full-sample MNL model, Wald tests of the joint significance of the explanatory variables support rejection of the null hypothesis H_0: $\beta = 0$ for all four categorical equations, as indicated by statistically significant *equation* chi-square statistics. This provides evidence that the regressors, as a group, explain a significant degree of the variation in each of the equilibrium outcomes and that these outcomes constitute statistically distinct categories. Consistent with these diagnostics, the *model* chi-square statistic also emerges as strongly statistically significant.

V. EXTENSIONS

At one level, the dichotomous and multinomial logit results summarized above reveal victim-specific and incident-specific characteristics that influence the reporting decision and certain reporting-investigation outcomes. But they also hint at differences in the returns to reporting crime across victim gender, victim race, and other demographic lines. Do these demographic differences reflect investigative bias along these lines, or just fundamental demographic variation in crime victimization itself? In this section we study these results more carefully, focusing on the two demographic traits most immediately relevant to possible investigative bias: victim gender and victim race.

A. Victim Gender

Although the initial dichotomous logit analysis showed no significant gender difference in the probability of reporting, the main MNL model showed that female victims more likely report than male victims and that female victims more likely receive follow-up investigative pursuit, whether victims or witnesses provided information to police. Viewed another way, these results suggest that male crime victims who reported received systematically less pursuit than women who reported, even if witnesses reported for them. Do males and females exhibit differences in their victimizations that help to explain this pattern?

At the level of means, many presumably important characteristics related to victims and to the offender or incident actually show no significant variation by gender. Male and female victims in the sample do not differ significantly in their marital status, age, percentage nonwhite, or education level. They show no significant difference in the total number of injuries they sustained from their crimes, the frequency of victimization by multiple, white, or older offenders, or the frequency with which their offenders physically attacked them. But some significant differences do exist. Male victims more frequently than females were victims of only a *threat* of a crime, raising the possibility that investigators may have responded more vigorously to actual criminal behavior than to threats. Women in the sample also less frequently owned their homes, less frequently held jobs at the time of their incidents, more frequently knew their offenders, more frequently had other individuals present (both non-victims *and* other victims), less frequently encountered offenders with weapons, less frequently resisted, and less frequently sustained a personal crime (despite the categorization of rape and sexual assault among such crimes).

To probe whether these variables significantly influence the various logit outcomes in different ways for men and women, I divided the sample into the two groups of 3,629 female and 3,038 male victims and estimated for each group a dichotomous logit model of victim reporting, with each of the variables used earlier (other than the gender dummy) incorporated as regressors. I summarize the results in Table 9.2. Seven regressors emerged as statistically significant determinants of reporting for women but not men: Others Present (negative coefficient), Offender Had Weapon (positive), Victim Resisted (positive), Victim Nonwhite (positive), Education (negative), Home Owner (negative), and Urban Dweller (negative). Four variables uniquely explain male reporting: Offender White (positive), Theft Occurred (positive), Personal Crime (positive), and Victim Age (positive). Only one variable emerges as significant for both male and female victims: At or Near Home (positive for both). Male and female crime victims clearly report crimes for different reasons, but the deeper question becomes how these variables influence the various reporting-investigation outcomes. When we estimate gender-separated multinomial logit models (results not shown), several intriguing patterns do emerge.

For female victims, Others Present emerges with a negative coefficient for Equilibrium 2 ($p = 0.10$) and positive for Equilibrium 3; for males, it emerges as positive for Equilibrium 3. Thus, for both men and women, the presence of others at the incident led not to significant *victim* reporting followed by investigative nonpursuit but to *witness* reporting followed by pursuit. Males receive this benefit from the reporting of others despite the insignificance of Others Present as a determinant of male reporting, as indicated in the dichotomous logit model summarized in Table 9.2.

TABLE 9.2 *Dichotomous Logit Results for Reporting of Crime by Victim Gender and Race (Dependent Variable: Victim Reported)*

	Males	Females	Whites	Nonwhites
Intercept	−1.863[a]	−0.721[a]	−1.290[a]	−1.350[a]
	(0.247)	(0.204)	(0.178)	(0.393)
Offender and Incident Characteristics				
All or Most Strangers	−0.159	0.021	−0.068	−0.260
	(0.174)	(0.168)	(0.131)	(0.300)
Others Present	−0.294	−0.299[c]	−0.272[b]	−0.403
	(0.185)	(0.157)	(0.132)	(0.273)
Other Victims	−0.158	0.014	−0.157	0.141
	(0.141)	(0.128)	(0.114)	(0.199)
Total Injuries	−0.105	−0.230	−0.247	0.196
	(0.353)	(0.276)	(0.239)	(0.519)
Total Injuries × Received Medical Care	0.465	0.303	0.431[c]	−0.042
	(0.354)	(0.282)	(0.245)	(0.512)
Lone Offender	−0.320	−0.258	−0.336[b]	−0.045
	(0.192)	(0.178)	(0.146)	(0.281)
White Offender	0.384[b]	0.143	0.293[b]	−0.030
	(0.172)	(0.155)	(0.125)	(0.369)
Offender over 30	0.277	0.101	0.268[b]	0.002
	(0.185)	(0.162)	(0.136)	(0.271)
At or Near Home	0.299[a]	0.154[b]	0.239[a]	0.169
	(0.087)	(0.080)	(0.065)	(0.139)
Theft Occurred	0.561[a]	−0.026	0.256[b]	0.120
	(0.154)	(0.128)	(0.111)	(0.209)
Offender Had Weapon	0.352	0.556[a]	0.421[a]	0.327
	(0.214)	(0.226)	(0.172)	(0.339)
Offender Attacked	−0.317	0.034	−0.095	−0.165
	(0.270)	(0.241)	(0.197)	(0.407)
Victim Resisted	0.056	0.462[a]	0.174	0.596[b]
	(0.189)	(0.174)	(0.141)	(0.294)
Personal Crime	0.737[a]	0.230	0.503[a]	0.235
	(0.261)	(0.226)	(0.190)	(0.371)
Victim Characteristics				
Age	0.008[a]	0.003	0.006[a]	0.003
	(0.003)	(0.003)	(0.002)	(0.005)
Female	—	—	0.070	0.119
			(0.060)	(0.125)
Nonwhite	0.139	0.175[c]	—	—
	(0.105)	(0.093)		
Education	0.095	−0.253[a]	−0.099	−0.048
	(0.097)	(0.090)	(0.072)	(0.161)
Married	−0.033	−0.067	−0.043	−0.030
	(0.087)	(0.077)	(0.063)	(0.141)
Home Owner	−0.068	−0.140[c]	−0.115[c]	−0.116
	(0.089)	(0.082)	(0.067)	(0.134)

TABLE 9.2 *(Continued)*

	Males	Females	Whites	Nonwhites
Employed at Victimization	0.151 (0.102)	0.098 (0.078)	0.125[c] (0.069)	0.075 (0.139)
Urban Dweller	−0.082 (0.106)	−0.197[b] (0.097)	−0.184[a] (0.075)	0.310 (0.246)
Model chi-square (H_0: $\beta = 0$)	64.47[a]	68.09[a]	81.94[a]	17.65
Number of observations	3,038	3,629	5,453	1,214

Notes: Standard errors appear in parentheses. [a]Statistically significant at or better than 1% level; [b]Statistically significant at or better than 5% level; [c]Statistically significant at or better than 10% level.

Although female victims more frequently had others present at their crimes, they do not appear to have received particularly greater returns to witness reporting than males received.

The gender-separated dichotomous logit models showed that the presence of a weapon significantly motivated female victims to report; the gender-separated MNL shows that it tended to encourage pursuit regardless of the information source for female victims. The variable also takes on a positive coefficient for Equilibrium 4, indicating that weapon use tended to encourage witness information provision even when no pursuit occurred. Although weapon presence exerted no significant influence on reporting by males, it still led to significant pursuit regardless of information source. As with the presence of others at the crime, we see no compelling evidence that female victims received a reporting premium for the presence of a weapon.

In the gender-separated MNL model, victim resistance encourages pursuit for female victims only when they themselves, not witnesses, provide the information. Resistance, insignificant as a determinant of male reporting, encourages pursuit for males only when someone else attests to the crime. The performance of Victim Resisted in the initial results raises the possibility that investigators lend greater credence to alleged crimes involving victim resistance, if only because resistance can provide additional physical evidence that a crime took place. Consistent with this line of thinking, D'Alessio and Stolzenberg (1990) have observed that resistance can lead to physical altercations between offenders and victims (especially in the absence of firearms, which we know can *prevent* resistance) that of course can create visible evidence of the crime. Evidence of resistance may also aid the credibility of the victim. Ruback and Thompson (2001, p. 57) suggest that police, prosecutors, and the criminal justice system as a whole may be "less likely to blame the victim for the crime if he or she had resisted." Kleck and Sayles (1990) have also suggested that victim resistance can lengthen the duration of a criminal incident, thus increasing the likelihood of the incident attracting the attention of witnesses.

If such scenarios occurred within the present sample of victims, it did not appear to enhance the receipt of follow-up pursuit when others reported, as indicated by the insignificance of Victim Resisted for Equilibrium 3. If evidence of resistance encourages investigative pursuit, the standard appears higher for male victims, as investigators appear to require corroboration for male victims who resist. One might speculate that investigators may more likely suspect that male victims have simply engaged in a physical altercation for which both parties may share legal culpability. By contrast, investigators may be less likely to believe that a woman who resists would have been involved in a simple altercation, making corroboration less essential for female victims in the market for investigative pursuit.

Nonwhite female victims appear more likely to report than white female victims, and their reporting tends to yield investigative pursuit whether the victim or a witness provides the information. A positive result for Nonwhite emerges for Outcome 4, indicating that nonwhite victims tend to receive systematically more witness information provision resulting in nonpursuit. Victim race becomes insignificant for male victims in the gender-separated MNL, and it impacts none of the equilibrium outcomes significantly. Probing the racial variation more closely, an analysis of means reveals very few statistically significant differences by race in the victim and offender/incident characteristics that we have scrutinized in this section, but four variables do stand out. Relative to whites, nonwhites more frequently lived in urban areas, more frequently sustained their crimes at or near their homes, more frequently were victimized by individuals familiar to them, and more frequently suffered their crimes in the absence of others (nonvictims). These patterns raise the possibility that nonwhite victims may have sustained more crimes within the confines of residential urban neighborhoods, perhaps indicative of gang violence. We further investigate these possibilities, and variation by victim race generally, in the next subsection.

More-educated female victims appear less likely to report than less-educated females, indicated in the gender-separated dichotomous logit models. More-educated females who do report tend not to receive follow-up pursuit, even when others provide the information. Education level has no significant impact on males' decision to report, but more-educated males who do report appear to receive significant pursuit. The positive coefficient estimate for Equilibrium 4 but *not* Equilibrium 3, as emerges in the MNL, indicates that while more-educated male victims may systematically benefit from others' reporting, witness reporting yields no greater pursuit related to educational attainment. Overall, the results suggest investigative favoritism toward educated males and away from educated females. Either investigators have a systematic bias against certain crime victims or the victims themselves exhibit systematic differences in the victimization experience along socioeconomic lines.

Do individuals with different education levels (or, in essence, within different socioeconomic strata) exhibit different circumstances of crime victimization? Evidence at the level of means shows that more-educated individuals generally suffered somewhat more random and arguably less severe crimes than less-educated victims. Most notably, more-educated victims more frequently were victimized by weaponless offenders and, perhaps consistent with this, suffered significantly fewer injuries than less-educated victims. More-educated victims in the sample also more frequently live in urban areas and more frequently suffered their crimes away from home, circumstances relatively unfavorable to effective pursuit of offenders (recalling an earlier finding) or the presence of friendly witnesses; indeed, more-educated victims less frequently had others present at their crimes as well. That more-educated victims tended to suffer victimizations away from home seems consistent with their victimizations' occurring during their employment hours, a crime victimization syndrome studied seminally by Cohen and Felson (1979).

Overall, this set of victimization factors creates less compelling evidence for investigators, involves relatively lesser personal losses, or both, compared to circumstances suffered by lesser-educated individuals. Investigators then may have a relatively lesser incentive to pursue their cases, regardless of information source. Ironically, a factor that gives individuals a societal advantage in many tangible ways may place them at somewhat of a disadvantage in the acquisition of investigative pursuit and legal restitution when they report their crimes. Regarding differences in observable *restitution* by victim educational attainment, more-educated victims in the sample exhibited mean Arrested/Charged of 0.033 compared to 0.052 for less-educated victims—a statistically significant difference.

As seen in Table 9.2, female victims who own their homes do not report (individually) as prevalently as female victims who rent their homes, echoing the full-sample dichotomous logit result. In the gender-separated MNLs, the variable Home Owner exerts a positive impact on Outcome 4, suggesting at least that female home owner/victims have greater access to information provision by others; but its statistical insignificance in relation to Outcome 3 points to no particular investigative *gain* to this circumstance. At the same time, home ownership exerts no significant influence for male victims. This result pattern hints at the possibility that female victims may have more effective social networks (i.e., less social isolation) relative to male victims. As we shall see, social isolation may become particularly important in explaining *racial* differences in reporting-investigation outcomes.

Male victims who sustained thefts were more likely to report than males who did not. The MNL model estimated for males suggests that those who reported (themselves) were more likely to receive follow-up pursuit than those for whom others provided information. Apparently, information about thefts comes most compellingly from victims themselves, at least among males. The variable Theft Occurred achieves positive significance for Equilibria 1 and 2, indicating that theft victims tend to report in general and that a significant proportion of them received no follow-up pursuit, consistent with the main MNL results in Table 9.1. Females who sustained thefts appear comparable to males who sustained thefts only to the extent that others' reporting tends to yield nonpursuit. These results reinforce the conclusion that investigative pursuit in cases involving thefts happens most dependably when victims themselves provide information rather than when someone else does.

For male victims, sustaining the crime at or near home encourages pursuit regardless of information source. The variable At or Near Home achieves positive significance for Outcome 4 (among both males and females), indicating a greater availability of witnesses among those victimized in that circumstance. Female victims victimized at or near home do not appear to receive significant pursuit unless they themselves report. In the NCVS sample, individuals victimized at or near home differ along a number of potentially important dimensions relevant to crime reporting and investigation. Most notably, such victims more frequently sustained crimes committed by individuals familiar to them and by lone offenders, and they more frequently resisted. Moreover, such victims less frequently were employed at the time of the incident, raising the possibility that a large proportion of victims of this type were victimized at or near home because they did not work outside the home.

B. Victim Race

The initial dichotomous logit model showed a significantly greater probability of reporting by nonwhite victims relative to white victims. Probing deeper, the initial MNL model showed a significantly greater probability of victim reporting with follow-up pursuit among nonwhite victims; minority victims showed no significant tendency toward the other reporting and investigation outcomes. The gender-based extended analysis above reveals a tendency for nonwhite (female) victims to receive follow-up investigative pursuit regardless of information source. As part of a closer examination of the influence of victim race, we consider, first, whether different circumstances of crimes appear especially prevalent among nonwhite victims and, second, what those circumstances imply generally about the experience of crime victimization among minorities.

Dichotomous and multinomial logit models separated by victim race facilitate this analysis. Consider dichotomous reporting logit models for the 5,453 white and 1,214 nonwhite victims in the sample (Table 9.2). The logit model does quite well at explaining the reporting decision of white victims, indicated not only by the significant likelihood-ratio chi-square statistic ascertaining overall model performance but also by the fact that the determinants of reporting generally hold with the same signs and significance levels as seen in the primary logit model. A total of thirteen variables emerge as statistically significant in the logit reporting model estimated for white victims, and all explain reporting by whites uniquely. By contrast, only one variable emerges as significant in the model estimated for nonwhite victims: Victim Resisted is significantly positive and of course uniquely explains reporting by nonwhites. No explanatory variable achieves significance in both models. Note also that the logit model for nonwhites generates a model likelihood-ratio statistic of 17.65, significant only at $p = 0.67$, which inspires minimal confidence in the explanatory power of the econometric model as a whole. Evidently, we can learn very little from such a model about the reasons nonwhite crime victims report—even when using the same set of explanatory variables that, as a group, have proven illuminating and significant for white victims, male victims, and female victims separately. But despite the poor statistical performance of the logit model estimated for nonwhites, race-separated MNL results do provide a clue to at least one factor possibly relevant to the nonwhite victim experience: social isolation.

A number of patterns emerge from the MNL results. With respect to victim age, older white victims receive significant follow-up investigative pursuit, a pattern not seen for older nonwhites. Age takes on a negative coefficient for Outcome 3 among nonwhites, signifying that nonreporting/nonpursuit occurs more likely for older nonwhites than even witness *reporting* followed by pursuit. This raises the possibility not only that older minority victims disproportionately sustain unreported, uninvestigated crimes but also that older nonwhite victims may live more socially isolated lives than older whites. (It may also hint at one reason why government agencies such as the National Institute of Justice have in recent years increased their call for academic research on the crime victimization experience of older individuals.) Within the sample, 31.5% of the minority victims were married, compared to 47.1% of white victims, suggesting a greater possibility that nonwhite victims live alone. Moreover, within the five-year period immediately preceding the 2004 NCVS, nonwhite victims had changed residences an average of 1.53 times, compared to 1.38 moves for white victims, suggesting the possibility of less stable community relationships among minorities. We have already seen, in Chapter 7, how lesser social-network development among some minorities (namely, Hispanic university students) can influence their self-protection choices. Here we see how minority social isolation affects another important crime victim decision (and outcome).

In relation to the crimes themselves, similar analysis of means reveals that older victims in general showed a significantly higher frequency of victimization with no other individuals present, a pattern that holds for both white and nonwhite victims. Not only might older minority crime victims live more socially isolated lives; they also might have lesser association with or access to individuals who can potentially act as corroborating witnesses to their crimes when they happen. White home owner/victims exhibit witness reporting followed by investigative nonpursuit significantly more than any other reporting and investigation category, including the reference category. By contrast, nonwhite victims (who in this sample own homes at a rate of 45% compared to 64% for whites) show no particular tendency for any category on the basis of home ownership. Although white home owners show no greater returns to witness reporting, this additionally suggests a more relatively isolated social existence among nonwhite crime victims. Intriguingly, both reporting whites and reporting nonwhites who sustained injuries and received medical care received investigative pursuit, regardless of the source of information. The actions of medical professionals may well serve as a supplement for the relatively less effective social networks apparently possessed by nonwhite victims.

For the variable Urban, the initial full-sample MNL model (Table 9.1) showed a negative coefficient for Equilibrium 1 and statistical insignificance for all other outcomes. The pattern for white victims mirrors the full-sample result; more accurately, the pattern mirrors that for white *female* victims, recalling the earlier observation. White females who live in cities show a particular vulnerability to having their personal reporting met with investigative nonpursuit. A not dissimilar interpretation holds for nonwhites, though relevant to reporting by others. With respect to crimes occurring at or near the victim's home, the pattern for whites again mirrors the full-sample pattern. For whites (and overall), reported crimes occurring at or near home significantly receive follow-up pursuit when victims themselves report the crime. Nonwhites share the negative Equilibrium 4 result but without the pursuit benefit when reporting themselves.

Employed whites who report tend to receive investigative nonpursuit in return. Employed nonwhites who report exhibit the same result but do receive some benefit of others' reporting. Probing the victimization experience of employed victims more closely, three particularly striking univariate patterns emerge. Employed victims more frequently reside in urban areas, tend to have sustained their crimes away from home, and, not inconsistent with that pattern, less frequently have familiarity with their offenders. As with the effect of educational attainment, employment at the time of the incident may signify more advantageous socioeconomic circumstances and yet more random, anonymous crimes occurring in cities, a pattern not unique to a particular racial group.

The variable Lone Offender showed a mixture of signs and significance in the main MNL model, and a similar mixture emerges in the race-separated MNL. The pattern for whites indicates that white victims of lone offenders receive follow-up pursuit when they themselves report rather than when others report; evidently, white victims convey information about this circumstance to police more compellingly than do witnesses. Nonwhite victims appear altogether less likely even to report a crime committed by a lone offender, let alone to receive follow-up pursuit. At the level of means, one sees no significant difference in the frequency of victimization by lone offenders across racial groups (17.5% for whites, 18.5% for nonwhites). For that matter, nonwhite victims in the sample no more frequently than whites indicated a belief that their crimes were gang-related, and urban victims of all races did not indicate this belief any more frequently than nonurban victims. In fact, those who do invoke the possibility of gang involvement more frequently have others present at their crimes, raising the possibility that victims of gang-related crime may actually have more witnesses present than others, perhaps to the benefit of investigative pursuit of such crimes.

In summary, nonwhite victims show a greater probability of reporting compared to white victims, and nonwhites who do report tend to receive follow-up investigative pursuit. Although the empirical models do well, statistically, at explaining reporting by male, female, and white victims separately, they explain very little about the reporting of nonwhite victims. Taken as a whole, the models do suggest a greater degree of social isolation among nonwhite victims, a circumstance that may hamper their "returns to reporting" relative to white victims. Future theoretical and empirical research on reporting and investigation outcomes might work to address specific motivations for reporting by minority crime victims, possibly incorporating the influence of social-network structure and quality in a model of crime-victim information revelation.

For each set of gender-separated and race-separated MNL models estimated for this chapter, the model chi-square statistics emerge as strongly significant, indicating the essential validity of each MNL model as a whole. For both male and female victims, significant equation chi-square statistics emerge for categorical Outcomes 1, 3, and 4 but not Outcome 2, although, as noted above, several isolated variables do significantly explain Outcome 2. A comparable pattern emerges in the race-separated MNL models. Evidently, when we separate the sample by victim gender and victim race, we cannot statistically distinguish victim reporting followed by investigative nonpursuit from the reference category capturing *non*reporting and nonpursuit. Given that Equilibrium 3 remains statistically distinct, this development just gives further indication of the role of corroboration in determining investigative pursuit outcomes following the transmission of information about crimes to police.

VI. CONCLUSION

We do not have an especially vast literature devoted to the economics of crime victim reporting, but over the course of a few studies we have begun to see what essentially encourages and discourages the decision to report. The more we learn about these factors, the more we can take significant steps toward enhancing the benefits and reducing the costs of reporting, at least to the extent that it further solidifies the linkage between crime and punishment inherent in our basic models and fundamental to deterrence. For that matter, continuing research helps us define richer, more nuanced scholarly questions to pursue. In this chapter we work through another iteration of theoretical and empirical analysis of reporting and think carefully about one of the immediate consequences of reporting: investigative pursuit of crimes.

Most of all, and with some relief, we see that the majority of the factors that motivate victims to report also appear to yield significant pursuit by investigators. We get there by formulating a model of reporting that, first, recognizes that police may obtain information about crimes either from crime victims themselves or from witnesses and, second, demonstrates the role of corroboration (or its hypothetical absence) in shaping the individual victim reporting outcome. The empirical analysis yields results consistent with this model and furthermore shows how various reporting-investigation equilibrium outcomes become sensitive to the nature of the crime, the traits of offenders, and the demographic characteristics of victims. In this respect, the empirical models do well at explaining reporting by every victim demographic subsample of interest except minority victims, but extended results along the way point to social isolation as an underlying factor that may be shaping part of the minority crime victimization experience. Given the prevalence with which minorities become victims of crime, and the essential importance of reporting in the deterrence process, these observations indicate clear potential for expanded research on reporting by minority victims.

Once reporting and investigation have occurred (or not), most crime victims return to their lives, although their lives have certainly changed. Many people's lives revolve around the family and the home, and so we might wonder how, or if at all, crime affects that side of victims' lives—the nature of their relationships with their spouses, children, and friends, for example. A question like this remains open for economic research, formulated perhaps from intriguing blends of theory from crime economics and the economics of the family. Our lives also greatly reflect what we do *away* from home—at work—raising the question of whether, or to what extent, crime victimization alters a person's participation in the labor force. As noted in Chapter 6, studying the labor-market implications of crime or crime victimization, as a few have done, can yield insights beneficial to inquiry in not only crime economics but also labor economics. Perhaps we can learn something more about both, finally, in Chapter 10.

Labor-Market Consequences
of Crime Victimization

There is a point at which even justice does injury.

—SOPHOCLES

I. INTRODUCTION

We have seen how crime victimization—or the potential for becoming a crime victim—can motivate a wide range of victim behaviors and post-crime outcomes. People hedge against the possibility of victimization by engaging in self-protection. Victims of person-on-person crimes may offer resistance—physical or otherwise—that can impact outcomes related to injury or other loss. Victims may or may not report their victimizations to police, and those who do report receive varying degrees of investigative pursuit in the aftermath. All the while, the actions of offenders themselves, our emphasis in Part One but influential in all contexts, shape many of the circumstances of crimes and influence many of these victim behaviors and postvictimization outcomes. In this chapter, as a final exploration of the consequences of crime victimization, we investigate the manner by which crime affects the labor-market behavior of victims.

Economists have studied labor-market implications of crime victimization before, as we recall from the review of the crime victimization literature in Chapter 6. Most notably, Hamermesh (1999a) analyzed how the risk of crime victimization affects the individual timing of work, especially the desire to work nights in urban settings. Silverman and Mitchell (2004) analyzed how crime rates in a community influence the decision to opt for early retirement. Robst and Smith (2008) examined how early childhood sexual abuse victimization affected women's ability to earn income later in life. Powdthavee (2005) took a broader view, examining how crime in a community, one among many conceivably influential attributes of a community, affected not only familiar outcomes like individual psychological trauma and financial losses but also quality of life in general. This chapter contributes to this body of work by examining some of the specific mechanisms that connect aspects of crimes and offenders to the employment decision of victims, including the possibility that victims' involvement in the legal system itself (through reporting) can affect this outcome. The chapter reveals other mechanisms that shape a person's labor-supply behavior as well.

To investigate these issues, we first consider a simple economic model of labor-market behavior structured in the manner of time-allocation models commonly seen in the analysis of labor-supply decisions. The model presented here will allow for several circumstances uniquely relevant to the current problem: the fact that a crime victim may or may not have held a job at the time of victimization, the possibility that crime victimization impairs the individual's ability to work, the notion that a victim uniquely gains utility from legal restitution, and the fact that a victim can personally contribute to this restitution by reporting the crime to police—though not without cost. Although the theoretical and empirical analysis will focus on employment outcomes, the model still casts victim reporting, the central topic of Chapter 9, as a choice variable, which permits a slightly altered approach to conceptualizing the reporting decision. As we shall see, most of the empirical results conform to hypotheses derived from the model. Overall, the results of this chapter shed additional light on the connection between crime victimization and postvictimization employment outcomes and the factors that influence this connection.

II. CONCEPTUAL FOUNDATION

To set the stage analytically, suppose an individual gains utility from three commodities: labor income (W), leisure (L), and legal restitution (R). To obtain these commodities, as seen in a similar time-allocation model of crime victim behavior presented by Hamermesh (1999a), the individual must allocate time to work (h_W), leisure (h_L), and reporting (h_R), respectively. For present purposes the term *reporting* refers to time-allocation activity that facilitates the creation of legal restitution, including most directly the transmission of information about the crime to police, a crime victim's most immediate conduit to restitution. We can then express the individual's concave utility function in general form as $U = U[W(h_W), L(h_L), R(h_R)]$.

Prior to any crime victimization, the individual faces a time constraint $h_W + h_L + h_R = 1$, the available time normalized to 1; at this juncture, $h_R = 0$ under the assumption that the individual allocates no time to restitutive activity. Crime victimization alters the returns to restitution, and so the individual's use of time may change in accordance with this constraint. The incidence of injury due to the crime may impair the person's ability to work, such as due to physical or psychological impairment. Thus, if initially $h_W > 0$, h_W will fall by a factor θ, where $0 \le \theta \le 1$; someone who initially did not work already exhibits the lower bound of work time, $h_W = 0$. Define θ such that in functional terms $\theta = \theta(\rho; \alpha)$, where ρ captures the severity of the *crime* and α indexes the exogenous severity of any *injury*. In principle, a more severe violation of the law creates greater returns to restitution through a greater potential legal sanction and impairs the person's ability to work subject to the severity of any injury, as measurable by the extent of medical costs. In this formulation, a more severe *crime* by assumption impacts θ and R, acting through ρ in both functions as detailed further below. *Injury* severity affects only θ, such that $\partial\theta/\partial\alpha > 0$ and $\partial^2\theta/\partial\rho\partial\alpha > 0$: a more severe injury creates greater work impairment, and it reinforces the impairment caused by a more severe crime per se.

Following crime victimization, the individual faces an altered time constraint $h_W - \theta h_W + h_L + h_R = 1$. The person then selects levels of h_W, h_L, and h_R to maximize U subject to this postvictimization time constraint. Writing the postvictimization constraint as a function of h_W and imposing it directly into the utility function, we can express victim utility as

$$U = U\{W(h_W - \theta h_W; k), L[1 - h_R - (1 - \theta)h_W; \lambda],$$
$$R[1 - h_L - (1 - \theta)h_W; \rho]\}. \qquad (10.1)$$

In this objective function, comparable to Hamermesh's (1999a) treatment, the additional shift parameters k and λ capture exogenous returns to work time (e.g., human capital skills) and exogenous returns to leisure (e.g., the presence of a family), respectively. To emphasize the individual's work activity in this chapter, I will concentrate on the victim's selection of utility-maximizing h_W and develop comparative statics that illustrate the impact of exogenous factors on work time. One might also use the basic structure of this model to study the utility-maximizing selection of restitution time and derive comparative statics illustrating how various exogenous factors affect a victim's optimal interaction with police, such as reporting.

The first-order condition for maximization of U with respect to h_W requires that

$$\frac{\partial U}{\partial h_W} = (1-\theta)\left(\frac{\partial U}{\partial W}\frac{\partial W}{\partial h_W} - \frac{\partial U}{\partial L}\frac{\partial L}{\partial h_W} - \frac{\partial U}{\partial R}\frac{\partial R}{\partial h_W}\right) = 0, \qquad (10.2)$$

from which we can derive comparative statics of variation in h_W^* with respect to the returns to restitution, the decision to report, the severity of any injury, the returns to work, and the returns to leisure.

A. Returns to Restitution

Variation in the returns to restitution affects utility-maximizing work time according to the derivative $\partial h_W^*/\partial \rho = -(\partial^2 U/\partial h_W \partial \rho)/(\partial^2 U/\partial h_W^2)$. Given concavity in U, the sign of $\partial h_W^*/\partial \rho$ will mirror that of $\partial^2 U/\partial h_W \partial \rho$. Realizing that $\theta = \theta(\rho; \alpha)$, we know that

$$\frac{\partial^2 U}{\partial h_W \partial \rho} = \left(-\frac{\partial \theta}{\partial \rho}\right)\left(\frac{\partial U}{\partial W}\frac{\partial W}{\partial h_W} - \frac{\partial U}{\partial L}\frac{\partial L}{\partial h_W} - \frac{\partial U}{\partial R}\frac{\partial R}{\partial h_W}\right) - (1-\theta)\frac{\partial U}{\partial R}\frac{\partial^2 R}{\partial h_W \partial \rho}.$$

$$(10.3)$$

The sign of $\partial h_W^*/\partial \rho$ depends on two important factors: the severity of any injury resulting from the crime and the nature of the crime or its evidence. In the most severe case, the victim sustains an injury that completely impairs the victim's ability to work, so that $\theta = 1$. In this case, the second term above vanishes, leaving only the negative first term. In this complete-impairment case, we would predict that the individual would work less given greater returns to restitution, such as is implied by a more severe crime.

But a more severe *crime* does not necessarily imply a more severe *injury* or any injury at all, and so we must consider the possibility that $\theta < 1$. In this case, the work-reduction effect of greater returns to restitution may occur less dramatically or not at all. The most obvious intuition along these lines simply indicates that a less than completely impaired crime victim need not lose work if he or she remains physically able to work. In this way, $\theta < 1$ and $(1 - \theta) > 0$ in the second term of Equation (10.3). Within that same term, $\partial U / \partial R > 0$ unambiguously (legal restitution creates utility), but $\partial^2 R / \partial h_W \partial \rho$ has no unambiguous sign ex ante. If we deconstruct this component, we can first note that $\partial R / \partial h_W$ (<0) captures the inverse relationship between work time and restitution R in the presence of a binding time constraint. The second-order effect $\partial^2 R / \partial h_W \partial \rho$ then captures how marginally greater returns to restitution (as indicated, for example, by a greater codified sanction for the crime) affects the restitution loss associated with greater work time. Perhaps most intuitively $\partial^2 R / \partial h_W \partial \rho < 0$, as this would imply that greater such restitutive returns *reduce* this loss. For example, if authorities have more physical evidence of the crime, or have captured the offender, the loss of restitution associated with one unit more of work time decreases, perhaps to zero. Such possibilities would reinforce the relationship whereby higher returns to restitution reduce employment, to the extent that these returns function through the degree of injury. By contrast, $\partial^2 R / \partial h_W \partial \rho > 0$ seems less intuitive, as this would mean that similarly greater exogenous returns to restitution would exert *more* of a penalty to the victim. Data on crime type (and thus its implied severity), the severity of any injury, and the individual's postvictimization employment decision will allow empirical investigation of this comparative static. The conditional nature of these effects also suggests the incorporation of interactions between measures of restitution and of crime and injury severity in the empirical analysis of the postvictimization employment outcome.

B. Reporting

The derivative $\partial h_W{}^*/\partial h_R$ captures how the allocation of time to the acquisition of legal restitution—such as in the form of reporting—affects employment. The sign of the derivative will reflect that of $\partial^2 U/\partial h_W \partial h_R = -(1-\theta)$ $(\partial R/\partial h_W)(\partial^2 U/\partial R \partial h_R) \leq 0$. To see that this expression has a nonpositive sign, observe that $-(1-\theta) \leq 0$, that $\partial R/\partial h_W < 0$ given a binding time constraint, and that $\partial^2 U/\partial R \partial h_R < 0$ given the concavity of U—altogether indicating that $\partial h_W{}^*/\partial h_R \leq 0$. That $\partial h_W{}^*/\partial h_R \leq 0$ suggests that reporting, potentially the most obvious way that a person allocates scarce time to legal restitution, can lead to a reduction in work time. Because h_R represents a victim choice variable that affects another choice (the decision to work) in this model, empirical investigation of the hypotheses emanating from this theoretical framework must allow for the possible endogeneity of reporting.

C. Injury Severity

The derivative $\partial h_W{}^*/\partial \alpha$ captures the effect of injury severity on employment. The sign of $\partial h_W{}^*/\partial \alpha$ will reflect that of

$$\frac{\partial^2 U}{\partial h_W \partial \alpha} = -\frac{\partial \theta}{\partial \alpha}\left(\frac{\partial U}{\partial W}\frac{\partial W}{\partial h_W} - \frac{\partial U}{\partial L}\frac{\partial L}{\partial h_W} - \frac{\partial U}{\partial R}\frac{\partial R}{\partial h_W}\right). \quad (10.4)$$

Because $-\partial \theta/\partial \alpha < 0$ and the parenthesized term is nonnegative, $\partial h_W{}^*/\partial \alpha \leq 0$, formalizing the very intuitive prediction that equilibrium work time decreases with greater injury severity, other things being equal.

D. Returns to Work

Exogenous variation in the returns to work affects equilibrium work time according to $\partial h_W{}^*/\partial k$, the sign of which reflects that of $\partial^2 U/\partial h_W \partial k = (1-\theta)$ $[(\partial U/\partial W)(\partial^2 W/\partial h_W \partial k)]$. This expression will be positive if $\theta < 1$; it will equal zero if $\theta = 1$. For someone less than completely impaired by injury resulting from the crime ($\theta < 1$), the effect is positive because, in the second term, $\partial U/\partial W > 0$ (work income creates utility) and $\partial^2 W/\partial h_W \partial k > 0$ (the returns to work enhance the degree to which work time contributes to earnings). This would indicate that greater returns to work encourage employment following crime victimization, other things being equal. But given complete impairment, $\theta = 1$ and $\partial h_W{}^*/\partial k = \partial^2 U/\partial h_W \partial k = 0$. The impairment would prevent the individual from taking advantage of these greater returns. Empirically, this comparative static motivates the hypothesis that crime victims with greater degrees of human capital or who exhibited previctimization labor-force participation (indicative of nontrivial returns to work prior to victimization) would exhibit greater postvictimization work activity than others.

E. Returns to Leisure

Exogenous variation in the returns to leisure affects equilibrium work time according to $\partial h_W{}^*/\partial \lambda$, the sign of which reflects that of $\partial^2 U/\partial h_W$ $\partial \lambda = -(1-\theta)(\partial U/\partial L)(\partial^2 L/\partial h_W /\partial \lambda) \leq 0$. This formalizes the prediction that exogenous factors that make nonwork time more valuable, such as the presence of children or a large network of friends, discourage work time, other things being equal.

III. EMPIRICAL ANALYSIS

A. Data and Methodology

Empirical analysis of the determinants of postvictimization employment, in the context of the time-allocation model developed above, requires data on a sample of known crime victims that contains information on victims' employment status before and after their crime victimization, information about their decision to report the crime to police, and other information pertinent to victims and their crimes for control purposes. As in Chapters 8 and 9, I make use of data from the 2004 National Crime Victimization Survey (NCVS). As in Chapter 9, I confine the sample to crime victims seventeen years of age or older at the time of the incident in question to ensure that sample subjects had reasonable degrees of autonomy in making their reporting decisions. I have also included victims no older than sixty years of age to minimize the possibility that the sample contains retired individuals, who do not make a traditional labor-supply choice. These criteria and the removal of unusable observations yield a sample of 6,344 victims.

As in Chapter 9, a short analysis of means and mean differences, appearing in the next subsection, will allow us to see regularities that exist within the sample, including indications of the extent to which the victims under analysis exhibit patterns consistent with the essential assumptions of the conceptual model. The primary empirical analysis will take the form of probit models estimating determinants of postvictimization employment, measured using a dichotomous variable equal to 1 if the individual was employed after victimization and 0 otherwise.

The probit models estimated for this chapter will incorporate familiar regressors capturing characteristics of the victim and characteristics of the offender or incident. The primary dependent variable of interest for this study, Employed, captures whether the individual was employed after the episode of crime victimization detailed within the data set. The dummy variable Victim Reported captures whether indeed the victim reported the crime to police. The dummy variable Arrested/Charged, capturing whether police had arrested or charged someone for the crime by the time of sampling, again serves as an indicator of legal restitution. Relevant to this study, 73% of the sample of victims were employed after victimization, 43% reported their crimes, and in 5% of the cases the assailants had been arrested or charged at the time of sampling.

The victim characteristics include the victim's age (and its square) at the time of the incident, the number of children in the household, and dummy variables indicating whether the victim was female, nonwhite, educated beyond high school, married, a home owner, a resident of a central or a noncentral metropolitan statistical area (MSA), and a resident of the Midwest, Northeast, or West (the omitted region is the South). These variables capture exogenous indicators of a victim's returns to leisure and returns to work and control for a victim's demographic traits.

On the subject of victim gender in this context, Hamermesh (1999a) documented a stronger tendency among women to avoid night work in association with higher homicide rates in cities, and female respondents in Powdthavee's (2005) study similarly showed a significantly lesser personal quality of life due to crime. These patterns suggest that female victims, who make up 55% of the sample analyzed for this chapter, may suffer greater psychological losses from crime than males suffer, possibly leading to more significant postvictimization nonparticipation in the labor force. Very important for the research question at hand, the victim characteristics also include dummies indicating whether the victim was employed or unemployed at the time of the incident, the omitted category capturing previctimization labor force *non*participation. These variables and the variable College, a measure of human capital attainment, capture previctimization returns to work. Prior to victimization, 76% of this sample held jobs and about 2% were jobless and searching for work; after victimization, the sample rate of employment was 73%, suggestive of some degree of labor-market attrition attributable to the crime.

The probit models will also incorporate a set of offender and incident characteristics that capture whether others (victims and nonvictims) were present at the scene of the incident, the type of crime (rape/sexual assault, robbery, purse-snatching/pickpocketing, and simple and aggravated assault, mere threats acting as the omitted category), and the total number of injuries and the actual medical costs (in thousands of dollars) incurred by the victim. Variables indicating the type of crime and the extent of victim injury act as measurements of the severity of the crime and the severity of any bodily impairment to victims, as discussed within the theory section. We have seen in previous chapters and in previous research how the type of crime can influence many of the economic choices crime victims make, typically by way of the degree of *loss* sustained by a crime victim; the magnitude of this loss has direct implications for individual labor-market outcomes.

B. An Analysis of Means

Let us first consider the essential empirical environment in which the victims under analysis made their employment decisions, particularly relating to univariate patterns of variation among legal restitution, returns to leisure (or nonwork) time, and previctimization employment.

A key assumption of the model holds that legal restitution increases in the restitutive activity by an individual—the reporting of the crime. Using Arrested/Charged as a measure of restitution, we see clear evidence of such a relationship. For these victims, those who reported the crime exhibit a 12% sample arrest rate, while those who did not report exhibit a 0% arrest rate, a statistically significant difference wholly consistent with observations from Chapter 9 on reporting and follow-up investigation. While not a surprising pattern, it does support the modeling specification of legal restitution as a positive function of restitutive activity by a hypothetical victim. Restitution also appears to increase with the severity of the crime. More severe crimes, as indicated by the type of crime, may create victim injuries that require medical care. The ninety victims in this sample who received postcrime medical care exhibit an offender arrest rate of 28.9% compared to the 4.8% rate for those who received no medical care for injuries. One might similarly view personal crimes—incidents involving direct contact between offender and victim (e.g., rape, robbery, or assault)—as more severe than other crimes, such as due to their greater potential for injury or for stronger sanctions. Those who sustained personal crimes exhibit a sample arrest rate of 15%, while other victims exhibit only a 3% arrest rate, additional evidence of a positive relationship between a crime's severity and the acquisition of legal restitution. Either pattern may well reflect greater investigative attention afforded to victims of more violent crimes.

To probe the role of returns to nonwork time, consider connections between the presence of children (under age twelve) and victims' previctimization employment status. An initial *t*-test shows that those employed at the time of their victimizations had 0.2 fewer children on average than jobless victims. A similar *t*-test further indicates a lower rate of previctimization employment among those with at least one child (77.6%) compared to childless victims (72.7%). These patterns suggest the presence of a time constraint that impacts victims' work time and nonwork time allocations, the latter conceptually including time allocated to child care. Given that women historically allocate more time to child care relative to men, might we see different previctimization time-allocation patterns along gender lines?

Probing this, among female victims one does find a more pronounced difference in previctimization employment by children's presence compared to the full sample: 64% of women with at least one child had worked at the time of their victimization, compared to a 73% rate among childless women. Men show the opposite pattern: male victims with children exhibited a greater tendency to work (at a rate of 87.8%) than males without children, possibly reflective of greater labor force participation by *married* men. (For illuminating discussions of this topic, see Lundberg 1988 and Lundberg and Rose 2002.) So, although we generally see univariate empirical evidence of an inverse relationship between the presence of children (incorporated as a measure of the returns to leisure, or nonwork time) and the previctimization tendency to work, we also see that the overall pattern may especially reflect the circumstances and choices of female crime victims. Male-female differences along these lines may carry implications for gender differences in the employment effects of crime victimization, as we study more carefully below.

IV. EMPIRICAL RESULTS

A pair of probit models explore the instance of postvictimization employment, as summarized in Table 10.1. Model 1 incorporates no interaction variables; Model 2 incorporates a set of interactions that enables investigation of the extent to which injury severity influences the impact of returns to restitution on employment, as discussed further below. The results of these probit models conform to predictions emanating from the theoretical model.

Among the broadly defined returns to work, those employed or searching for work at the time of the victimization incident show a significantly greater likelihood of employment afterward, consistent with the theoretical prediction $\partial h_W{}^* / \partial k > 0$. Numerically, the large coefficient estimates of +2.437 for Employed at Victimization and +0.725 for Unemployed at Victimization translate to a 0.76 higher postvictimization probability for those already employed and a 0.15 higher employment probability for those looking for work at the time of the crime. The variable College also emerges as positive and significant, further support for the hypothesis. The probability of employment appears to increase at a decreasing rate with victim age, as indicated by a significantly positive coefficient for Age and a significantly negative coefficient for Age Squared. Making use of the marginal probabilities associated with these variables, the estimated maximum probability of postvictimization employment

TABLE 10.1 *Probit Analysis of Postvictimization Employment*
(Dependent Variable: Employed)

	Model 1		Model 2	
	$\hat{\beta}$ (SE)	p	$\hat{\beta}$ (SE)	p
Intercept	−1.541 (0.227)	0.00	−1.534 (0.227)	0.00
Offender and Incident Characteristics				
Victim Reported	−0.022 (0.047)	0.63	−0.019 (0.047)	0.69
Others Present	0.101 (0.071)	0.15	0.100 (0.071)	0.15
Other Victims	0.007 (0.065)	0.92	0.004 (0.065)	0.95
Rape/Sexual Assault	−0.047 (0.295)	0.87	−0.014 (0.297)	0.96
Robbery	−0.260 (0.157)	0.10	−0.300 (0.157)	0.07
Purse-Snatching/Pickpocketing	0.220 (0.333)	0.51	0.218 (0.333)	0.51
Total Injuries	0.023 (0.113)	0.84	0.053 (0.116)	0.65
Medical Costs	−0.141 (0.065)	0.03	−0.466 (0.235)	0.05
Arrested/Charged	−0.189 (0.104)	0.07	−0.221 (0.107)	0.05
Medical Costs × Arrested/Charged	—	—	0.398 (0.236)	0.09
Robbery × Arrested/Charged	—	—	0.305 (0.482)	0.53
Victim Characteristics				
Employed at Victimization	2.437 (0.051)	0.00	2.437 (0.051)	0.00
Unemployed at Victimization	0.725 (0.127)	0.00	0.723 (0.127)	0.00
Age	0.035 (0.013)	0.01	0.034 (0.013)	0.01
Age Squared	−0.0005 (0.000)	0.01	−0.0005 (0.0002)	0.01
College	0.093 (0.046)	0.04	0.095 (0.046)	0.04
Female	−0.222 (0.046)	0.00	−0.224 (0.046)	0.00
Married	0.063 (0.052)	0.23	0.063 (0.052)	0.22

(*continued*)

TABLE 10.1 *(Continued)*

	Model 1		Model 2	
Children	−0.058 (0.024)	0.02	−0.058 (0.024)	0.02
Home Owner	0.116 (0.049)	0.02	0.120 (0.049)	0.02
MSA Central	0.060 (0.074)	0.42	0.061 (0.074)	0.41
MSA Noncentral	0.110 (0.073)	0.13	0.109 (0.073)	0.14
Midwest	−0.255 (0.058)	0.00	−0.256 (0.059)	0.00
Northeast	−0.260 (0.072)	0.00	−0.260 (0.072)	0.00
West	−0.142 (0.057)	0.01	−0.143 (0.057)	0.01
Nonwhite	0.047 (0.058)	0.43	0.049 (0.058)	0.40
Chi-square (H$_0$: $\beta = 0$)	3430.50	0.00	3434.66	0.00
Sample size	6,344		6,344	

Note: SE = Standard Error.

occurs at approximately 35.8 years of age; based on this calculation, one might expect the probability of employment to dissipate for victims in their late thirties and beyond. Model 1 also suggests that southern dwellers exhibit a significantly higher probability of employment than victims in other areas, as indicated by significantly negative coefficients for the Midwest, Northeast, and West region dummy variables.

The theoretical model suggested an inverse relationship between postvictimization employment and returns to legal restitution. Among the crime-type dummy variables incorporated to address this factor, only Robbery emerges as significantly negative, consistent with the prediction that relatively more severe crimes discourage employment. Statistically, neither Rape/Sexual Assault nor Purse-Snatching/Pickpocketing appears influential in this regard. As an alternative, and arguably more direct, measure of the returns to restitution, the probit models also incorporate the dummy variable Arrested/Charged. In Model 1, the significant coefficient estimate of −0.189 for this variable provides further support for the returns-to-restitution hypothesis; those for whom the assailant had been arrested or charged exhibit a 0.057 lower probability of employment, other things being equal. The theoretical model also suggested that greater injury severity would discourage employment. Although the variable Total Injuries emerges as statistically insignificant in the probit model, the variable Medical Costs emerges as significantly negative, consistent with the injury-severity prediction; for every $1,000 in medical costs, the probability of employment falls by about 0.14.

As a further probe of the role of returns to restitution and injury severity, Model 2 incorporates the uninteracted variables Robbery, Medical Costs, and Arrested/Charged as well as interactions of Medical Costs and Robbery with Arrested/Charged. (Because of the statistical insignificance of Total Injuries and the other crime-type measures in Model 1, I do not incorporate them in interactions.) In Model 2, these focus variables retain their signs and significance levels from the initial model. The interaction of Medical Costs with Arrested/Charged emerges as significantly positive, but the Robbery interaction proves statistically insignificant. In the context of the theoretical model, the pattern of results relating to Medical Costs (ultimately the most robust measure of injury severity) and Arrested/Charged provides empirical evidence that the basic negative impact of restitution on postvictimization employment may dissipate given greater injury severity.

Recall that, conceptually, this possibility, which we observed in the signing of the comparative static $\partial h_w^*/\partial \rho$, meant that a hypothetical victim in general would incur a greater rather than a lesser penalty (in the form of lost restitution due to work time) from additional restitution—the less intuitive possibility. However, when we study the coefficients more closely, the more intuitive interpretation dominates. Using the coefficient estimates from Model 2, we can calculate the marginal effect of variation in Arrested/Charged as $-0.221 + 0.398M$, where M represents Medical Costs. At the mean level of Medical Costs ($= 0.026$, about $26), this marginal effect calculates to -0.211, only slightly higher than the basic negative effect. Moreover, we might consider when this marginal effect actually becomes positive, that is, when $-0.221 + 0.398M > 0$. Solving this inequality yields $M > 0.555$, indicating a medical-cost tipping point above which greater legal restitution (as measured by the arrest of charging of an offender) encourages postvictimization employment. But in the present sample, only 24 of 6,344 victims (less than 0.5%) exhibit $M > 0.555$. Ultimately, the findings relating to the role of legal restitution and injury severity support the most intuitive prediction of the time-allocation model for the overwhelming majority of sample victims.

Among the remaining regressor variables, home owners exhibit a greater probability of postvictimization employment compared to their reference group, other things being equal; viewed in terms of the marginal probability, the probit models reveal that home owners have essentially a 0.03 greater probability of employment compared to home renters. Neither marital status nor location in a relatively urban or rural setting appears influential. Meanwhile, female victims and victims with more children under age twelve in the household show significantly lower probabilities of postvictimization employment, findings consistent with observations made earlier in the analysis of means that suggested an inverse relationship between previctimization employment and the presence of children. Numerically, the probit result for female victims implies a 0.06 lower probability of postvictimization employment compared to that of men, and the result for children under twelve implies that this probability declines by about 0.017 for each child present, other things being equal. While one can capture individual returns to leisure (nonwork time) only with caution empirically, these results may reflect the presence of comparatively more valuable nonwork time, at the margin, for crime victims with household situations that exert greater time demands.

A Wald test reveals no statistically significant evidence of endogeneity of victim reporting in association with these models; that is, reporting appears predetermined in this empirical setting. Most likely, by the time the victims under analysis made their postvictimization labor-supply decisions, they had already made their reporting decisions; indeed, as observed earlier, some had even begun to *benefit* from this reporting in the form of restitution via an arrest or charging of an offender. To illustrate the formation of this diagnostic test, which has the potential to become relevant in any study where crime victim choices may unfold simultaneously, we can first write the reduced-form probit equation for employment (y_{1i}) as $y_{1i} = \alpha x_i + v_i$, where the error term $v_i = \varphi_i \beta + u_i$. Then, the probit log-likelihood equation would have the general form $l(y_{1i}, \alpha x_i + \varphi_i \lambda)$. The Wald test of H_0: $\lambda = 0$ essentially ascertains whether the suspicious regressor with parameter β (victim reporting in the present setting) contains systematic error in its contribution to explaining variation in employment, y_{1i}.

For this study, using additional measures of the characteristics of the crimes and offenders as instruments for reporting (e.g., the familiarity of the offender to the victim, the race of the offender), this Wald test yielded chi-square statistics that did not support rejection of the null hypothesis. If the test had revealed evidence of significant endogeneity, indicated by rejection of H_0, we would have investigated instrumental-variables probit models that correct for endogeneity, as described by Amemiya (1978), Smith and Blundell (1986), Newey (1987), and Rivers and Vuong (1988). Although other measures of legal restitution emerged as statistically significant in explaining postvictimization employment, as summarized above, victim reporting ultimately did not.

V. CONCLUSION

Analysis of the labor-supply implications of crime victimization has resonance for economists and other social scientists because it carries direct implications for how crime impacts an integral part of people's daily lives and by extension how it impacts society's overall productivity. This chapter applies a fairly traditional time-allocation modeling approach to illustrate important connections between the postvictimization labor-supply choice and aspects of crime victimization. We modify the traditional model by imagining that a crime victim gains utility from the usual commodities—income from labor (or the access it allows to consumption goods) and leisure (time spent away from work for pay)—as well as from legal restitution. As with the more traditional commodities, an economic agent cannot obtain this restitution without cost.

We already know that crime frequently imposes costs on victims in the form of physical injury; we have even seen some evidence, in this book and elsewhere, that injured victims more prevalently report their crimes, to varying investigative effects. In this chapter we find, among other empirical results, that more significant postcrime medical costs, indicative of more serious physical impairment to the ability to work, reduce the probability of postvictimization job-holding. Other results show that the acquisition of restitution itself, as indicated empirically by the formal arrest or charging of an offender in a victim's case, also reduces labor supply. Legal restitution indeed does not appear to be costless in practice, nor would we predict otherwise given the presence of constrained societal and individual restitutive resources, most notably time itself. In principle, if results like these held widely, we might like employers to assist in the societal creation of legal restitution by easing time burdens required of workers who sustain crimes, and we might like the legal system to ease burdens associated with the individual time costs incurred by worker/victims in the acquisition of that restitution. Cohen (2005) and Meadows (2007) extensively describe many "reactive responses" to crime victimization that exist in the United States, including some that involve paid leave and monetary compensation for victims. Future research might investigate the extent to which these sorts of efforts at assistance already occur, implications of their potential expansion, and what it all costs.

If the analysis in Part Two of this book reveals nothing else, it should demonstrate the central, if sometimes overlooked, role of victim behavior as it pertains to the wider desire to deter crime or reduce its consequences. Victims reap clear, understandable benefits from legal restitution, and so they have an inherent incentive to make choices that serve the creation of that restitution; fortunately, those choices generally accord with *society's* desire to deter crime as well. But, as we see in this chapter and others, victims make these choices with nontrivial costs that exert influences all along the victimization time line, logically implying an internal limit to the restitutive actions victims willingly take in the aftermath of crime. At some point, even victims of the most violent crimes have to get on with their lives, and that includes their work lives one way or another. Ultimately, all research on the economic behavior of crime victims seeks clarity on how we might enhance the benefits and lessen the costs of the many victim behaviors that help us achieve socially favorable outcomes regarding crime.

Epilogue

WE HAVE LEARNED a great deal about the actions of criminals and victims, and the consequences of those actions, over the decades in which
economists have studied them. The reviews of literature contained in
Chapters 1 and 6 document contributions made in major areas of inquiry
that serve as the primary infrastructure for the study of the economics of
crime and victimization that continues today—especially in research
aimed at explaining the behavior of individuals, the orientation of this
book. The remaining eight analytical chapters take great motivation
from the recognition, along the way, that many important research questions in this area remain unaddressed or underdeveloped. For that matter, as emphasized throughout, many of these open topics suggest a natural life cycle or time line over which certain criminal actions and victim
actions unfold. Certain behaviors and considerations sensibly follow others. So, what have we learned from this exercise? What is the story that
our analyses reveal and that we might easily share with others?

As pertains to offenders and their time line, we have examined as a
matter of concentration the notion, broached in criminology but not as
well developed in economics, that criminals engage in planning behavior,
an action that naturally precedes the actual commission of a crime. And
we have wrestled carefully with the possible connection between criminal planning and criminal injury outcomes—perhaps the first serious in-
kling in our narrative of the inevitable intertwining that occurs between
offenders and victims. Potential targets of crime can, through their actions, make criminal planning more costly and reduce the possibility of
injury, although targets remain somewhat vulnerable to the pure viciousness of certain criminals, the tendency for which victims do not always
easily discern. To discover more in this area, future researchers should
consider taking an even broader-based view of crime planning, examining the entirety of a planning exercise, from an offender's planning to his

entry into a crime scene to his exit from it; we also should probe further how offenders engage in planning alongside other activities, legal and otherwise.

We have investigated an important decision that a criminal offender faces once he or she has completed the primary crime: whether or not to destroy evidence. Curtailing evidence destruction certainly has the potential to deter crime itself, a fact that makes spoliation behavior centrally relevant to what we are studying in these pages, but the connection is complicated by the reality of scarce enforcement resources. Society can adopt procedures or enact formal law meant to deter evidence destruction by individuals and by conspirators, but the effectiveness of these measures depends, not without some difficulty, on consistency of application, as elucidated in Chapter 4. The model can serve as a foundation for many types of empirical studies going forward, such as on the economic environment of political and corporate cover-ups and unethical or illegal purges of electronic data (e.g., accounting or financial information) in white-collar crimes.

Whether an offender destroys evidence or not, the offender might have a chance to commit crime again, which motivates the scholarly investigation of recidivism, including our exploration in Chapter 5. We observe that we can use the basic but powerful Beckerian economic model of crime to study a single crime or even (with minor modifications) the re-commission of crime, and we learn that some white-collar criminals exhibit tendencies similar to those of street criminals when it comes to how their criminal careers unfold. This analysis reveals the potential for conducting truly dynamic (as opposed to static) theoretical and empirical analyses of recidivism that directly incorporate the role of time; if criminal careers represent *paths* of illegality, then the policy challenge becomes moving offenders or would-be offenders off those paths, for good.

The comparable time line for victims arguably starts before any crime victimization ever takes place, at the self-protection stage—planning that parallels criminals' precrime plotting. Ultimately, we all have to find the right balance between living well and living cautiously, and of course the equilibria vary from person to person; the eternal coexistence of the benefits of fun activities and the risk of victimization makes self-protection an ideal topic for economic analysis. Future researchers might use the essential model structure applied in Chapter 7 to investigate self-protection in other empirical environments, perhaps comparing experiences across urban and rural neighborhoods or even across specific approaches to law enforcement, such as between nations. How people simultaneously determine the right blend of fun activity and self-protection also remains a fertile research question for economists or other analysts.

Individuals who sustain person-on-person crimes, regardless of their self-protection behavior, may find themselves in a position to offer resistance—physical or otherwise—to their offenders, and we have studied the conditions under which this might occur and its consequences. Physical resistance does not appear to provoke violence, and nonphysical forms of resistance can become quite effective, when feasible. That said, we could still use more extensive data that track the history of violence among criminal offenders, as a way of gaining a better idea of their taste for violence and how this factor influences the dynamics of assault and resistance inside actual crimes. The theoretical model developed in Chapter 8 gives us a reasonable idea of what to expect. It also remains unclear to what extent nonphysical forms of resistance—yelling and running away—either prevent or provoke criminal offenders, and we should work to find that out.

In the aftermath of a crime, a victim may have an opportunity to report the crime to police; we have seen not only what influences reporting generally but also that investigative outcomes favorable to victims may ultimately depend on *who* reports exactly *what*. Individuals who lead relatively isolated lives may receive somewhat lesser "returns to reporting" because of a reduced ability to tap into social resources that aid restitution, in particular the corroboration or reporting of other people around them. The study of the antecedents and consequences of social-network formation has become one of the hottest areas in economic research. One could imagine that the application of analytical tools from this subfield could shed a great deal of light on the issue of crime reporting, especially as it pertains to vulnerable groups like the elderly, immigrants, and minorities.

Finally, we have learned that crime victimization can impact a person's labor-supply behavior, whether caused by bodily injury sustained as a consequence of the crime or caused by a victim's involvement in the criminal justice process itself. To the extent that society values restitution for victims, we can make it easier for them to achieve it by recognizing the labor-market implications of victimization and its aftermath. Researchers, however, should aggressively examine the efficiency of the various reactive responses to crime victimization intended to ameliorate some of the time costs of obtaining restitution.

As discussed in Chapters 1 and 6, many of our existing insights on crime and victimization emanate from scholarship outside economics, such as in criminology or psychology. The two halves of this book demonstrate the potential for applying rigorous economic models to various research questions relevant to the experiences of criminals and victims, allowing us to take best advantage of the assumption of rational decision making while at the same time incorporating insights gained from throughout the social sciences. As a central part of the analytical journey we take, our examination of the life cycles or time lines of criminality and victimization helps us see not only how different acts within a crime or within the victim's experience inexorably connect to one another but also that, as a society, we can address individual elements of crime and victimization to achieve favorable outcomes. Scholars and policy makers need not take a broad-brush approach to the deterrence of crime or the reduction of its consequences, at least not all the time; good ideas and effective policy also can come from finer, more surgical strokes, homing in on a seemingly minor, component aspect of crime or victimization, as emphasized from chapter to chapter in this book.

In the end, an economic approach to the analysis of crime is empowering. It empowers our scholarship by lending sharp clarity to the motivations, constraining factors, and implications of decisions made by those who would commit crime and those who suffer from it. This facilitates sound inferential judgments, procedure, and public policy. But it also empowers crime victims themselves, by directly recognizing that they have critical decisions to make that bear as much on society as criminal decisions do; as crime researchers, we miss a lot of the story if we pay attention *only* to the actions of criminals, or when we focus solely on the 10,000-foot view of the landscape of crime. I hope that this book not only informs readers interested in the scholarly analysis of these matters but also sparks the development of new ideas, new research, and new solutions to the problem of crime and victimization.

References

Allen, W. David. 2002. "Crime, Punishment, and Recidivism: Lessons from the National Hockey League." *Journal of Sports Economics* 3 (February): 39–60.

Allen, W. David. 2005. "Cultures of Illegality in the National Hockey League." *Southern Economic Journal* 71 (January): 494–513.

Allen, W. David. 2007. "The Reporting and Underreporting of Rape." *Southern Economic Journal* 73 (January): 623–641.

Allen, W. David. 2009. "Interview Effects in the Reporting of Domestic Violence." *Journal of Socio-Economics* (March): 288–300.

Amemiya, Takeshi. 1978. "The Estimation of a Simultaneous Equation Generalized Probit Model." *Econometrica* 46 (September): 1193–1205.

Arrow, Kenneth J. 1963. "Uncertainty and the Welfare Economics of Medical Care." *American Economic Review* 53 (December): 941–973.

Arrow, Kenneth J. 1964. "The Role of Securities in the Optimal Allocation of Risk-Bearing." *Review of Economic Studies* 31 (April): 91–96.

Baik, Kyung Hwan, and In-Gyu Kim. 2001. "Optimal Punishment when Individuals May Learn Deviant Values." *International Review of Law and Economics* 21 (September): 271–285.

Bar-Gill, Oren, and Alon Harel. 2001. "Crime Rates and Expected Sanctions: The Economics of Deterrence Revisited." *Journal of Legal Studies* 30 (June): 485–501.

Bartel, Ann P. 1975. "An Analysis of Firm Demand for Protection Against Crime." *Journal of Legal Studies* 4 (June): 443–478.

Barton, Russell R., and Bruce W. Turnbull. 1981. "A Failure Rate Regression Model for the Study of Recidivism." In *Models in Quantitative Criminology*, edited by James Alan Fox. New York: Academic Press.

Becker, Gary S. 1965. "A Theory of the Allocation of Time." *Economic Journal* 75 (September): 493–517.

Becker, Gary S. 1968. "Crime and Punishment: An Economic Approach." *Journal of Political Economy* 76 (March–April): 169–217.

Becker, Gary S. 1974. "A Theory of Social Interactions." *Journal of Political Economy* 82 (November–December): 1063–1093.

Benoît, Jean-Pierre, and Juan Dubra. 2004. "Why Do Good Cops Defend Bad Cops?" *International Economic Review* 45 (August): 787–809.

Benson, Bruce L., Iljoong Kim, and David W. Rasmussen. 1994. "Estimating Deterrence Effects: A Public Choice Perspective on the Economics of Crime Literature." *Southern Economic Journal* 61 (July): 161–168.

Benson, Bruce L., David W. Rasmussen, and Iljoong Kim. 1998. "Deterrence and Public Policy: Trade-Offs in the Allocation of Police Resources." *International Review of Law and Economics* 18 (March): 77–100.

Block, M. K., and J. M. Heineke. 1975. "A Labor Theoretic Analysis of the Criminal Choice." *American Economic Review* 65 (June): 314–325.

Borland, Jeff, and Boyd Hunter. 2000. "Does Crime Affect Employment Status? The Case of Indigenous Australians." *Economica* 67 (February): 123–144.

Bowlus, Audra J., and Shannon Seitz. 2006. "Domestic Violence, Employment, and Divorce." *International Economic Review* 47 (November): 1113–1149.

Bureau of Alcohol, Tobacco and Firearms (ATF). 2000. *State Laws and Published Ordinances—Firearms.* Washington, DC: U.S. Department of the Treasury.

Burnovski, Moshe, and Zvi Safra. 1994. "Deterrence Effects of Sequential Punishment Policies: Should Repeat Offenders Be More Severely Punished?" *International Review of Law and Economics* 14 (September): 341–350.

Calvó-Armengol, Antoni, Thierry Verdier, and Yves Zenou. 2007. "Strong and Weak Ties in Employment and Crime." *Journal of Public Economics* 91 (February): 203–233.

Calvó-Armengol, Antoni, and Yves Zenou. 2004. "Social Networks and Crime Decisions: The Role of Social Structure in Facilitating Delinquent Behavior." *International Economic Review* 45 (August): 939–958.

Cappellari, Lorenzo, and Stephen P. Jenkins. 2003. "Multivariate Probit Regression Using Simulated Maximum Likelihood." Paper presented at the United Kingdom Stata Users' Group Meetings 2003 10, Stata Users Group.

Case, Anne C., and Lawrence F. Katz. 1991. "The Company You Keep: The Effects of Family and Neighborhood on Disadvantaged Youths." NBER Working Paper 3705, May.

Cazenave, Noel A., and Murray A. Straus. 1990. "Race, Class, Network Embeddedness, and Family Violence: A Search for Potent Support Systems." In *Physical Violence in American Families,* edited by Murray A. Straus and Richard J. Gelles. New Brunswick, NJ: Transaction Publishers.

Chang, Juin-Jen, Heui-Chung Lu, and Mingshen Chen. 2005. "Organized Crime or Individual Crime? Endogenous Size of a Criminal Organization and the Optimal Law Enforcement." *Economic Inquiry* 43 (July): 661–675.

Chiang, Alpha C. 1984. *Fundamental Methods of Mathematical Economics.* New York: McGraw-Hill.

Chiu, W. Henry, and Paul Madden. 1998. "Burglary and Income Inequality." *Journal of Public Economics* 69 (July): 123–141.

Clotfelter, Charles T. 1977a. "Public Services, Private Substitutes, and the Demand for Protection Against Crime." *American Economic Review* 67 (December): 867–877.

Clotfelter, Charles T. 1977b. "Urban Crime and Household Protective Measures." *Review of Economics and Statistics* 59 (November): 499–503.

Coase, R. H. 1960. "The Problem of Social Cost." *Journal of Law and Economics* 3 (October): 1–44.

Cohen, Lawrence E., and Marcus Felson. 1979. "Social Change and Crime Rate Trends: A Routine Activity Approach." *American Sociological Review* 44 (August): 588–608.

Cohen, Mark A. 2005. *The Costs of Crime and Justice.* New York: Routledge.

Coleman, James William. 1998. *The Criminal Elite: Understanding White-Collar Crime.* New York: St. Martin's Press.

Cook, Philip J. 1986. "The Relationship between Victim Resistance and Injury in Noncommercial Robbery." *Journal of Legal Studies* 15 (June): 405–416.

Cook, Philip J., and Jens Ludwig. 2000. *Gun Violence.* Oxford: Oxford University Press.

Cornwell, Christopher, and William N. Trumbull. 1994. "Estimating the Economic Model of Crime with Panel Data." *Review of Economics and Statistics* 76 (May): 360–366.

Cox, D. R. 1972. "Regression Models and Life Tables." *Journal of the Royal Statistical Society, Series B* 34: 187–200.

Crocker, Keith J., and Joel Slemrod. 2005. "Corporate Tax Evasion with Agency Costs." *Journal of Public Economics* 89 (September): 1593–1610.

Cullen, Julie Berry, and Steven D. Levitt. 1999. "Crime, Urban Flight, and the Consequences for Cities." *Review of Economics and Statistics* 81 (May): 159–169.

Curry, Philip A., and Tilman Klumpp. 2009. "Crime, Punishment, and Prejudice." *Journal of Public Economics* 93 (February): 73–84.

D'Alessio, Stewart, and Lisa Stolzenberg. 1990. "A Crime of Convenience: The Environment and Convenience Store Robbery." *Environment and Behavior* 22 (March): 255–271.

Danziger, Sheldon, and David Wheeler. 1975. "The Economics of Crime: Punishment or Income Redistribution." *Review of Social Economy* 33 (October): 113–131.

Demombynes, Gabriel, and Berk Özler. 2005. "Crime and Local Inequality in South Africa." *Journal of Development Economics* 76 (April): 265–292.

Demougin, Dominique, and Claude Fluet. 2006. "Preponderance of Evidence." *European Economic Review* 10 (May): 963–976.

Doyle, Joanne M., Ehsan Ahmed, and Robert N. Horn. 1999. "The Effects of Labor Markets and Income Inequality on Crime: Evidence from Panel Data." *Southern Economic Journal* 65 (April): 717–738.

Ehrlich, Isaac. 1972. "The Deterrent Effect of Criminal Law Enforcement." *Journal of Legal Studies* 1 (June): 259–276.

Ehrlich, Isaac. 1973. "Participation in Illegitimate Activities: A Theoretical and Empirical Investigation." *Journal of Political Economy* 81 (May–June): 521–565.

Ehrlich, Isaac. 1981. "On the Usefulness of Controlling Individuals: An Economic Analysis of Rehabilitation, Incapacitation, and Deterrence." *American Economic Review* 71 (June): 307–322.

Ehrlich, Isaac. 1996. "Crime, Punishment, and the Market for Offenses." *Journal of Economic Perspectives* 10 (Winter): 43–67.

Ehrlich, Isaac, and Gary S. Becker. 1972. "Market Insurance, Self-Insurance, and Self-Protection." *Journal of Political Economy* 80 (July–August): 623–648.

Emons, Winand. 2003. "A Note on the Optimal Punishment for Repeat Offenders." *International Review of Law and Economics* 23 (September): 253–259.

Eng, Kevin. 1999. "Spoliation of Electronic Evidence." *Boston University Journal of Science & Technology Law* 13 (June): 1–9.

Evans, William N., and Emily G. Owens. 2007. "COPS and Crime." *Journal of Public Economics* 91 (February): 181–201.

Fajnzylber, Pablo, Daniel Lederman, and Norman Loayza. 2002. "What Causes Violent Crime?" *European Economic Review* 46 (July): 1323–1357.

Farmer, Amy, and Jill Tiefenthaler. 1996. "Domestic Violence: The Value of Services as Signals." *American Economic Review* 86 (May): 274–279.

Farmer, Amy, and Jill Tiefenthaler. 1997. "An Economic Analysis of Domestic Violence." *Review of Social Economy* 55 (Fall): 337–358.

Farmer, Amy, and Jill Tiefenthaler. 2003. "Explaining the Recent Decline in Domestic Violence." *Contemporary Economic Policy* 21 (April): 158–172.

Federal Bureau of Investigation (FBI). 1995. *Crime in the United States 1995: Uniform Crime Reports.* Washington, DC: U.S. Department of Justice.

Federal Bureau of Investigation (FBI). 2008. *Crime in the United States 2008: Uniform Crime Reports.* Washington, DC: U.S. Department of Justice.

Feess, Eberhard, and Markus Walzl. 2004. "Self-Reporting in Optimal Law Enforcement When There Are Criminal Teams." *Economica* 71 (August): 333–348.

Fisher, Bonnie S., John J. Sloan III, and Francis T. Cullen. 2001. *Understanding Crime Victimization among College Students in the United States, 1993–1994* [computer file]. ICPSR version. Cincinnati, OH: University of Cincinnati [producer], 2000. Ann Arbor, MI: Inter-university Consortium for Political and Social Research [distributor].

Foreman-Peck, James, and Simon C. Moore. 2010. "Gratuitous Violence and the Rational Offender Model." *International Review of Law and Economics* 30 (June): 160–172.

Frank, Robert H. 1988. *Passions within Reason.* New York: Norton.

Freeborn, Beth A. 2009. "Arrest Avoidance: Law Enforcement and the Price of Cocaine." *Journal of Law and Economics* 52 (February): 19–40.

Freeman, Richard B. 1996. "Why Do So Many Young American Men Commit Crimes and What Might We Do About It?" *Journal of Economic Perspectives* 10 (Winter): 25–42.

Friehe, Tim. 2008. "Optimal Sanctions and Endogeneity of Differences in Detection Probabilities." *International Review of Law and Economics* 28 (June): 150–155.

Funk, Patricia, and Peter Kugler. 2003. "Dynamic Interactions between Crimes." *Economics Letters* 79 (June): 291–298.

Garoupa, Nuno. 2001. "Optimal Magnitude and Probability of Fines." *European Economic Review* 45 (October): 1765–1771.

Gelles, Richard J. 1976. "Abused Wives: Why Do They Stay?" *Journal of Marriage and the Family* 38 (November): 659–668.

Geweke, John. 1989. "Bayesian Inference in Econometric Models Using Monte Carlo Integration." *Econometrica* 57 (November): 1317–1340.

Giles-Sims, Jean. 1998. "The Aftermath of Partner Violence." In *Partner Violence*, edited by Jana L. Jasinski and Linda M. Williams. Thousand Oaks, CA: Sage Publications.

Glaeser, Edward L., and Bruce Sacerdote. 1999. "Why Is There More Crime in Cities?" *Journal of Political Economy* 107 (December): S225–S258.

Glaeser, Edward L., Bruce Sacerdote, and José A. Scheinkman. 1996. "Crime and Social Interactions." *Quarterly Journal of Economics* 111 (May): 507–548.

Goldberg, Itzhak, and Frederick C. Nold. 1980. "Does Reporting Deter Burglars? An Empirical Analysis of Risk and Return in Crime." *Review of Economics and Statistics* 62 (August): 424–431.

Golob, Thomas F., and Amelia C. Regan. 2002. "Trucking Industry Adoption of Information Technology: A Structural Multivariate Probit Model." *Transportation Research Part C: Emerging Technologies* 10 (June): 205–228.

Gordon, James P. F. 1989. "Individual Morality and Reputation Costs as Deterrents to Tax Evasion." *European Economic Review* 33 (April): 797–805.

Gorelick, Jamie S., Stephen Marzen, and Lawrence B. Solum. 2002. *Destruction of Evidence.* New York: Aspen.

Gould, Eric D., Bruce A. Weinberg, and David B. Mustard. 2002. "Crime Rates and Local Labor Market Opportunities in the United States: 1979–1997." *Review of Economics and Statistics* 84 (February): 45–61.

Grambsch, Patricia M., and Terry M. Therneau. 1994. "Proportional Hazards Tests and Diagnostics Based on Weighted Residuals." *Biometrika* 81 (August): 515–526.

Green, Diane L., and Elizabeth Pomeroy. 2007. "Crime Victimization: Assessing Differences between Violent and Nonviolent Experiences." *Victims and Offenders* 2 (January): 63–76.

Greenberg, David F., and Ronald C. Kessler. 1981. "Panel Models in Criminology." In *Methods in Quantitative Criminology*, ed. James Alan Fox. New York: Academic Press.

Greene, William H. 2008. *Econometric Analysis.* Upper Saddle River, NJ: Pearson Prentice Hall.

Grogger, Jeff. 1998. "Market Wages and Youth Crime." *Journal of Labor Economics* 16 (October): 756–791.

Grogger, Jeff, and Michael Willis. 2000. "The Emergence of Crack Cocaine and the Rise in Urban Crime Rates." *Review of Economics and Statistics* 82 (November): 519–529.

Grogger, Jeffrey. 1991. "Certainty vs. Severity of Punishment." *Economic Inquiry* 29 (April): 297–309.

Gronau, Reuben. 1977. "Leisure, Home Production, and Work: The Theory of the Allocation of Time Revisited." *Journal of Political Economy* 85 (December): 1099–1123.

Guttel, Ehud, and Michael T. Novick. 2004. "A New Approach to Old Cases: Reconsidering Statutes of Limitation." *University of Toronto Law Journal* 54 (Spring): 129–183.

Hajivassiliou, V. 1990. "Smooth Simulation Estimation of Panel Data LDV Models." Unpublished working paper, Yale University.

Hamermesh, Daniel S. 1999a. "Crime and the Timing of Work." *Journal of Urban Economics* 45 (March): 311–330.

Hamermesh, Daniel S. 1999b. "The Timing of Work over Time." *Economic Journal* 109 (January): 1–30.

Hazelwood, Robert R., Roland Reboussin, and Janet I. Warren. 1989. "Serial Rape: Correlates of Increased Aggression and the Relationship of Offender Pleasure to Victim Resistance." *Journal of Interpersonal Violence* 4 (March): 65–78.

Hobfoll, Stevan E., John Freedy, Carol Lane, and Pamela Geller. 1990. "Conservation of Social Resources: Social Support Resource Theory." *Journal of Social and Personal Relationships* 7 (November): 465–478.

Ihlanfeldt, Keith. 2002. "Spatial Mismatch in the Labor Market and Racial Differences in Neighborhood Crime." *Economics Letters* 76 (June): 73–76.

Ihlanfeldt, Keith R. 2003. "Rail Transit and Neighborhood Crime: The Case of Atlanta, Georgia." *Southern Economic Journal* 70 (October): 273–294.

Innes, Robert. 1999. "Self-Policing and Optimal Law Enforcement When Violator Remediation Is Valuable." *Journal of Political Economy* 107 (December, part 1): 1305–1325.

Innes, Robert. 2001. "Violator Avoidance Activities and Self-Reporting in Optimal Law Enforcement." *Journal of Law, Economics, and Organization* 17 (April): 239–256.

Iyengar, Radha. 2009. "Does the Certainty of Arrest Reduce Domestic Violence? Evidence from Mandatory and Recommended Arrest Laws." *Journal of Public Economics* 93 (February): 85–98.

Jost, Peter-J. 2001. "Crime, Coordination, and Punishment: An Economic Analysis." *International Review of Law and Economics* 21 (March): 23–46.

Kalbfleisch, John D., and Ross L. Prentice. 1980. *The Statistical Analysis of Failure Time Data.* New York: Wiley.

Keane, Michael, and Robert Moffitt. 1998. "A Structural Model of Multiple Welfare Program Participation and Labor Supply." *International Economic Review* 39 (August): 553–589.

Keane, Michael P. 1994. "A Computationally Practical Simulation Estimator for Panel Data." *Econometrica* 62 (January): 95–116.

Kim, Iljoong, Bruce L. Benson, David W. Rasmussen, and Thomas W. Zuehlke. 1993. "An Economic Analysis of Recidivism among Drug Offenders." *Southern Economic Journal* 60 (July): 169–183.

Kleck, Gary, and Miriam A. DeLone. 1993. "Victim Resistance and Offender Weapon Effects in Robbery." *Journal of Quantitative Criminology* 9 (March): 55–81.

Kleck, Gary, and Marc Gertz. 1995. "Armed Resistance to Crime: The Prevalence and Nature of Self-Defense with a Gun." *Journal of Criminal Law & Criminology* 86 (Fall): 150–187.

Kleck, Gary, and Susan Sayles. 1990. "Rape and Resistance." *Social Problems* 37 (May): 149–162.

Komesar, Neil K. 1973. "A Theoretical and Empirical Study of Victims of Crime." *Journal of Legal Studies* 2 (June): 301–321.

Kowal, Steven M. 1999. "When Unexpected Government Agents Drop In: Responding to Requests for Immediate Interviews." *Food and Drug Law Journal* 54 (Issue 1): 93–110.

Kreimer, Seth F., and David Rudovsky. 2002. "Double Helix, Double Bind: Factual Innocence and Postconviction DNA Testing." *University of Pennsylvania Law Review* 151 (December): 547–617.

Lakdawalla, Darius, and George Zanjani. 2005. "Insurance, Self-Protection, and the Economics of Terrorism." *Journal of Public Economics* 89 (September): 1891–1905.

Landes, William M., and Richard A. Posner. 1975. "The Private Enforcement of Law." *Journal of Legal Studies* 4 (January): 1–46.

Langan, Patrick A., and David J. Levin. 2002. "Recidivism of Prisoners Released in 1994." Bureau of Justice Statistics Special Report, NCJ 193427, June, pp. 1–16.

Lerman, Steven R., and Charles F. Manski. 1981. "On the Use of Simulated Frequencies to Approximate Choice Probabilities." In *Structural Analysis of Discrete Data with Econometric Applications*, edited by Charles F. Manski and Daniel McFadden. Cambridge, MA: MIT Press.

Leung, Ambrose, Frances Woolley, Richard E. Tremblay, and Frank Vitaro. 2005. "Who Gets Caught? Statistical Discrimination in Law Enforcement." *Journal of Socio-Economics* 34 (May): 289–309.

Levitt, Steven D. 1997. "Using Electoral Cycles in Police Hiring to Estimate the Effect of Police on Crime." *American Economic Review* 87 (June): 270–290.

Levitt, Steven D. 1998. "Why Do Increased Arrest Rates Appear to Reduce Crime: Deterrence, Incapacitation, or Measurement Error?" *Economic Inquiry* 36 (July): 353–372.

Levitt, Steven D., and Stephen J. Dubner. 2005. *Freakonomics*. New York: Morrow.

Lin, Ming-Jen. 2008. "Does Unemployment Increase Crime? Evidence from U.S. Data 1974–2000." *Journal of Human Resources* 43 (Spring): 413–436.

Lin, Ming-Jen. 2009. "More Police, Less Crime: Evidence from US State Data." *International Review of Law and Economics* 29 (June): 73–80.

Lott, John R., Jr. 1992. "Do We Punish High Income Criminals Too Heavily?" *Economic Inquiry* 30 (October): 583–605.

Loureiro, Paulo R. A., Mário Jorge Cardoso de Mendonça, Tito Belchior Silva Moreira, and Adolfo Sachsida. 2009. "Crime, Economic Conditions, Social Interactions and Family Heritage." *International Review of Law and Economics* 29 (September): 202–209.

Lundberg, Shelly. 1988. "Labor Supply of Husbands and Wives: A Simultaneous Equations Approach." *Review of Economics and Statistics* 70 (May): 224–235.

Lundberg, Shelly, and Elaina Rose. 2002. "The Effects of Sons and Daughters on Men's Labor Supply and Wages." *Review of Economics and Statistics* 84 (May): 251–268.

Maddala, G. S. 1983. *Limited-Dependent and Qualitative Variables in Econometrics*. Cambridge: Cambridge University Press.

Malik, Arun S. 1990. "Avoidance, Screening, and Optimum Enforcement." *RAND Journal of Economics* 21 (Autumn): 341–353.

Manser, Marilyn, and Murray Brown. 1980. "Marriage and Household Decision-Making: A Bargaining Analysis." *International Economic Review* 21 (February): 31–44.

Markowitz, Sara. 2005. "Alcohol, Drugs, and Violent Crime." *International Review of Law and Economics* 25 (March): 20–44.

Mathieson, Donald, and Peter Passell. 1976. "Homicide and Robbery in New York City: An Economic Model." *Journal of Legal Studies* 5 (January): 83–98.

Mathur, Vijay K. 1978. "Economics of Crime: An Investigation of the Deterrent Hypothesis for Urban Areas." *Review of Economics and Statistics* 60 (August): 459–466.

Mauser, Gary A., and Dennis Maki. 2003. "An Evaluation of the 1977 Canadian Firearm Legislation: Robbery Involving a Firearm." *Applied Economics* 35 (March): 423–436.

McCormick, Robert E., and Robert D. Tollison. 1984. "Crime on the Court." *Journal of Political Economy* 92 (April): 223–235.

McDonald, John F., and Steven Balkin. 1983. "Citizen Demand for Exposure to Street Crime." *Urban Studies* 4 (November): 419–429.

McElroy, Marjorie B., and Mary Jean Horney. 1981. "Nash-Bargained Household Decisions: Toward a Generalization of the Theory of Demand." *International Economic Review* 22 (June): 333–349.

Meadows, Robert J. 2007. *Understanding Violence and Victimization*. Upper Saddle River, NJ: Pearson Prentice Hall.

Mehlum, Halvor, Karl Moene, and Ragnar Torvik. 2005. "Crime Induced Poverty Traps." *Journal of Development Economics* 77 (August): 325–340.

Mialon, Hugo M., and Thomas Wiseman. 2005. "The Impact of Gun Laws: A Model of Crime and Self-Defense." *Economics Letters* 88 (August): 170–175.

Mookherjee, Dilip, and I. P. L. Png. 1992. "Monitoring vis-à-vis Investigation in Enforcement of Law." *American Economic Review* 82 (June): 556–565.

Myers, Samuel L., Jr., and Chanjin Chung. 1998. "Criminal Perceptions and Violent Criminal Victimization." *Contemporary Economic Policy* 16 (July): 321–333.

Neumayer, Eric. 2005. "Inequality and Violent Crime: Evidence from Data on Robbery and Violent Theft." *Journal of Peace Research* 42 (January): 101–112.

Newey, Whitney K. 1987. "Efficient Estimation of Limited Dependent Variable Models with Endogenous Explanatory Variables." *Journal of Econometrics* 39 (November): 231–250.

Nussim, Jacob, and Avraham D. Tabbach. 2009. "Deterrence and Avoidance." *International Review of Law and Economics* 29 (December): 314–323.

Ognedal, Tone. 2005. "Should the Standard of Proof Be Lowered to Reduce Crime?" *International Review of Law and Economics* 25 (March): 45–61.

Owens, Emily G. 2009. "More Time, Less Crime? Estimating the Incapacitative Effect of Sentence Enhancements." *Journal of Law and Economics* 52 (August): 551–579.

Owens, Emily G., and Jordan Matsudaira. 2010. "The Economics of Rape Reporting: Will Victims Pay for Police Involvement?" Working paper, Cornell University, January: 1–43.

Paul, Chris, and Al Wilhite. 1994. "Illegal Markets and the Social Costs of Rent-Seeking." *Public Choice* 79 (April): 105–115.

Pettiway, Leon E. 1982. "Mobility of Robbery and Burglary Offenders: Ghetto and Nonghetto Spaces." *Urban Affairs Quarterly* 18 (December): 255–270.

Philipson, Tomas J., and Richard A. Posner. 1996. "The Economic Epidemiology of Crime." *Journal of Law and Economics* 39 (October): 405–433.

Polinsky, A. Mitchell. 2006. "The Optimal Use of Fines and Imprisonment When Wealth Is Unobservable." *Journal of Public Economics* 90 (May): 823–835.

Polinsky, A. Mitchell, and Daniel L. Rubinfeld. 1991. "A Model of Fines for Repeat Offenders." *Journal of Public Economics* 46 (December): 291–306.

Polinsky, A. Mitchell, and Steven Shavell. 1991. "A Note on Optimal Fines When Wealth Varies among Individuals." *American Economic Review* 81: 618–621.

Polinsky, A. Mitchell, and Steven Shavell. 1998. "On Offense History and the Theory of Deterrence." *International Review of Law and Economics* 18 (September): 305–324.

Polinsky, A. Mitchell, and Steven Shavell. 2000. "The Economic Theory of Public Enforcement of Law." *Journal of Economic Literature* 38 (March): 45–76.

Pollak, Robert A. 1994. "For Better or Worse: The Roles of Power in Models of Distribution within Marriage." *American Economic Review* 84 (May): 148–152.

Pollak, Robert A. 2004. "An Intergenerational Model of Domestic Violence." *Journal of Population Economics* 17 (June): 311–329.

Porat, Ariel, and Alex Stein. 1997. "Liability for Uncertainty: Making Evidential Damage Actionable." *Cardozo Law Review* 18 (April): 1891–1960.

Powdthavee, Nattavudh. 2005. "Unhappiness and Crime: Evidence from South Africa." *Economica* 72 (August): 531–547.

Pyne, Derek. 2004. "Can Making It Harder to Convict Criminals Ever Reduce Crime?" *European Journal of Law and Economics* 18 (September): 191–201.

Ralston, Roy W. 1999. "Economy and Race: Interactive Determinants of Property Crime in the United States, 1958–1995." *American Journal of Economics and Sociology* 58 (July): 405–434.

Rasmusen, Eric. 1996. "Stigma and Self-Fulfilling Expectations of Criminality." *Journal of Law and Economics* 39 (October): 519–543.

Rennison, Callie Marie. 2001. "Criminal Victimization 2000, Changes 1993–2001." Washington, DC: U.S. Department of Justice, NCJ-187007, 1–16.

Risinger, D. Michael, Michael J. Saks, William C. Thompson, and Robert Rosenthal. 2002. "The *Daubert/Kumho* Implications of Observer Effects in Forensic Science: Hidden Problems of Expectation and Suggestion." *California Law Review* 90 (January): 3–56.

Rivers, Douglas, and Quang H. Vuong. 1988. "Limited Information Estimators and Exogeneity Tests for Simultaneous Probit Models." *Journal of Econometrics* 39 (November): 347–366.

Robst, John, and Stacy Smith. 2008. "The Effect of Childhood Sexual Victimization on Women's Income." *Eastern Economic Journal* 34 (Winter): 27–40.

Ruback, R. Barry, and Martie P. Thompson. 2001. *Social and Psychological Consequences of Violent Victimization.* Thousand Oaks, CA: Sage.

Sanchirico, Chris William. 2004. "Evidence Tampering." Mimeograph. University of Pennsylvania, June.

Schmidt, Peter D., and Ann D. Witte. 1984. *An Economic Analysis of Crime and Justice: Theory, Methods, and Applications*. Orlando, FL: Academic Press.

Shavell, Steven. 1991. "Individual Precautions to Prevent Theft: Private versus Socially Optimal Behavior." *International Review of Law and Economics* 11 (September): 123–132.

Silberberg, Eugene. 1990. *The Structure of Economics: A Mathematical Analysis*. New York: McGraw-Hill.

Silverman, Dan. 2004. "Street Crime and Street Culture." *International Economic Review* 45 (August): 761–786.

Silverman, Dan, and Olivia S. Mitchell. 2004. "Crime and Early Retirement among Older Americans." Boettner Working Paper No. 2004-1. Available at SSRN: http://ssrn.com/abstract=556610.

Sjoquist, David Lawrence. 1973. "Property Crime and Economic Behavior: Some Empirical Results." *American Economic Review* 63 (June): 439–446.

Smith, Richard J., and Richard W. Blundell. 1986. "An Exogeneity Test for the Simultaneous Equation Tobit Model with an Application to Labor Supply." *Econometrica* 54 (May): 679–685.

Soares, Rodrigo R. 2004. "Development, Crime and Punishment: Accounting for the International Differences in Crime Rates." *Journal of Development Economics* 73 (February): 155–184.

Solum, Lawrence, and Stephen Marzen. 1987. "Truth and Uncertainty: Legal Control of the Destruction of Evidence" (mimeograph, pp. 1–99) *Emory Law Journal* 36 (Fall): 1085–1194.

Sommers, Richard J., and Andreas G. Seibert. 1999. "Intentional Destruction of Evidence: Why Procedural Remedies Are Insufficient." *Canadian Bar Review* 78 (March): 38–62.

Strube, Michael J., and Linda S. Barbour. 1983. "The Decision to Leave an Abusive Relationship: Economic Dependence and Psychological Commitment." *Journal of Marriage and the Family* 45 (November): 785–793.

Tark, Jongyeon, and Gary Kleck. 2004. "Resisting Crime: The Effects of Victim Action on the Outcomes of Crimes." *Criminology* 42 (November): 861–909.

Tauchen, Helen, Ann Dryden Witte, and Harriet Griesinger. 1994. "Criminal Deterrence: Revisiting the Issue with a Birth Cohort." *Review of Economics and Statistics* 76 (August): 399–412.

Tauchen, Helen V., Ann Dryden Witte, and Sharon K. Long. 1991. "Domestic Violence: A Nonrandom Affair." *International Economic Review* 32 (May): 491–511.

Trumbull, William N. 1989. "Estimations of the Economic Model of Crime Using Aggregate and Individual Level Data." *Southern Economic Journal* 56 (October): 423–439.

Ullman, Sarah E. 1998. "Does Offender Violence Escalate When Rape Victims Fight Back?" *Journal of Interpersonal Violence* 13 (April): 179–192.

Ullman, Sarah E., and Raymond A. Knight. 1992. "Fighting Back: Women's Resistance to Rape." *Journal of Interpersonal Violence* 7 (March): 31–43.

Van Koppen, Peter J., and Robert W. J. Jansen. 1998. "The Road to the Robbery: Travel Patterns in Commercial Robberies." *British Journal of Criminology* 38 (Spring): 230–246.

Vollaard, Ben, and Pierre Koning. 2009. "The Effect of Police on Crime, Disorder and Victim Precaution: Evidence from a Dutch Victimization Survey." *International Review of Law and Economics* 29 (December): 336–348.

Weisburd, David, Elin Waring, and Ellen Chayet. 1995. "Specific Deterrence in a Sample of Offenders Convicted of White-Collar Crimes." *Criminology* 33 (November): 587–607.

Weisburd, David, Elin Waring, and Ellen Chayet. 2000. *White-Collar Criminal Careers, 1976–1978: Federal Judicial Districts* [computer file]. ICPSR version. Newark, NJ: Rutgers University [producer], 1995. Ann Arbor, MI: Inter-university Consortium for Political and Social Research [distributor].

Wellford, Charles F. 2000. *Convenience Store Crime in Georgia, Massachusetts, Maryland, Michigan, and South Carolina, 1991–1995.* Ann Arbor, MI: Inter-university Consortium for Political and Social Research.

Western, Bruce. 2006. *Punishment and Inequality in America.* New York: Sage.

Wilhite, Allen. 2006. "Protection and Social Order." *Journal of Economic Behavior and Organization* 61 (December): 691–709.

Wilhite, Allen, and W. David Allen. 2008. "Crime, Protection, and Incarceration." *Journal of Economic Behavior and Organization* 67 (August): 481–494.

Williams, Jenny, and Robin C. Sickles. 2002. "An Analysis of the Crime as Work Model: Evidence from the 1958 Philadelphia Birth Cohort Study." *Journal of Human Resources* 37 (Summer): 479–509.

Witte, Ann Dryden. 1980. "Estimating the Economic Model of Crime with Individual Data." *Quarterly Journal of Economics* 94 (February): 57–84.

Wolpin, Kenneth I. 1978. "An Economic Analysis of Crime and Punishment in England and Wales, 1894–1967." *Journal of Political Economy* 86 (October): 815–840.

Wolpin, Kenneth I. 1980. "A Time Series-Cross Section Analysis of International Variation in Crime and Punishment." *Review of Economics and Statistics* 62 (August): 417–423.

Zavoina, William, and Richard D. McKelvey. 1975. "A Statistical Model for the Analysis of Ordinal Level Dependent Variables." *Journal of Mathematical Sociology* 4 (Summer): 103–120.

Zenou, Yves. 2003. "The Spatial Aspects of Crime." *Journal of the European Economic Association* 1 (April): 459–467.

Zimring, Franklin E. 2007. *The Great American Crime Decline.* Oxford: Oxford University Press.

Zimring, Franklin E., and James Zuehl. 1986. "Victim Injury and Death in Urban Robbery: A Chicago Study." *Journal of Legal Studies* 15 (January): 1–40.

Index